Women OF THE BIBLE

LARGE PRINT WORD SEARCH

WHITAKER HOUSE

Women of the Bible Large Print Word Search
150 Puzzles to Inspire Your Faith

ISBN: 979-8-88769-018-6

Printed in Colombia

Whitaker House
1030 Hunt Valley Circle
New Kensington, PA 15068
www.whitakerhouse.com

1 2 3 4 5 6 7 8 9 10 11 30 29 28 27 26 25 24 23

1. THE GENEALOGY OF JESUS CHRIST: MATTHEW 1:1–17

It may seem counterintuitive to start this word search book with a genealogy that features mostly men. However, the women included are remarkable for their stories, and it is important to remember that although much of the Bible was written during patriarchal times, women contributed to our shared history and ultimately the birth of our Savior Himself. We are here to celebrate their faith and the understanding of God we glean from their stories.

The book of the generation of Jesus Christ, the son of David, the son of Abraham. Abraham fathered Isaac; and Isaac fathered Jacob; and Jacob fathered Judas and his brethren; and Judas fathered Phares and Zara of Thamar; and Phares fathered Esrom; and Esrom fathered Aram; and Aram fathered Aminadab; and Aminadab fathered Naasson; and Naasson fathered Salmon; and Salmon fathered Booz of Rachab; and Booz fathered Obed of Ruth; and Obed fathered Jesse; and Jesse fathered David the king; and David the king fathered Solomon of her that had been the wife of Urias; and Solomon fathered Roboam; and Roboam fathered Abia; and Abia fathered Asa; and Asa fathered Josaphat; and Josaphat fathered Joram; and Joram fathered Ozias; and Ozias fathered Joatham; and Joatham fathered Achaz; and Achaz fathered Ezekias; and Ezekias fathered Manasses; and Manasses fathered Amon; and Amon father Josias; and Josias fathered Jechonias and his brethren, about the time they were carried away to Babylon: and after they were brought to Babylon, Jechonias fathered Salathiel; and Salathiel fathered Zorobabel; and Zorobabel fathered Abiud; and Abiud fathered Eliakim; and Eliakim fathered Azor; and Azor fathered Sadoc; and Sadoc fathered Achim; and Achim fathered Eliud; and Eliud fathered Eleazar; and Eleazar fathered Matthan; and Matthan fathered Jacob; and Jacob fathered Joseph the husband of Mary, of whom was born Jesus, who is called Christ. So all the generations from Abraham to David are fourteen generations; and from David until the carrying away into Babylon are fourteen generations; and from the carrying away into Babylon to Christ are fourteen generations.

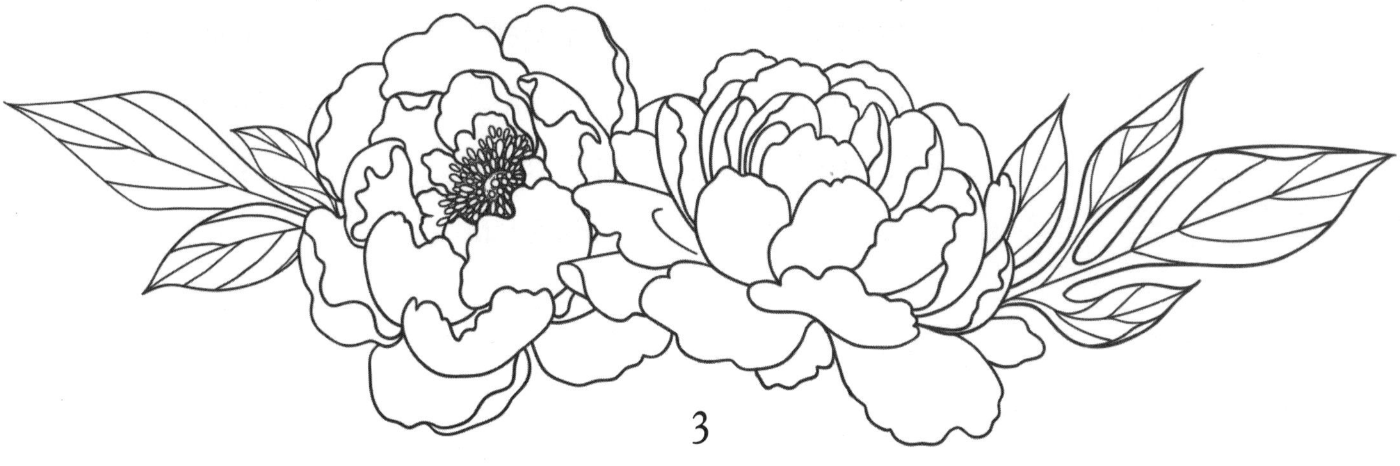

F	Z	B	K	L	Z	L	R	P	I	E	B	D	O	R	S	K	M	Q	L
C	K	Y	O	C	E	Z	G	X	M	Y	A	J	D	N	Z	O	O	O	S
F	O	E	T	A	R	Y	U	O	Q	B	T	B	W	O	Y	R	T	Z	U
V	K	V	F	V	Z	E	Q	K	W	H	H	Z	F	H	I	H	H	C	Z
Y	V	V	T	O	L	R	T	J	E	O	S	F	A	Y	H	V	E	G	W
Q	T	C	I	A	U	R	I	C	J	B	H	C	T	S	R	F	R	E	O
O	X	I	U	P	M	R	A	J	J	M	E	D	H	V	P	Z	Y	N	K
Y	M	J	A	R	W	A	T	J	R	F	B	X	E	J	D	G	I	E	S
U	V	E	C	G	Y	W	R	E	B	Q	A	X	R	G	I	R	R	A	Z
D	X	S	N	C	R	J	B	J	E	S	B	W	E	O	C	Y	U	L	N
L	O	U	W	Y	J	J	G	H	R	N	E	B	D	T	O	E	T	O	Y
D	Q	S	L	N	Y	G	E	N	E	R	A	T	I	O	N	S	H	G	E
I	I	C	B	Z	A	J	P	N	J	Q	I	L	A	K	J	O	G	Y	Q
K	W	H	Z	B	R	A	H	A	B	O	C	X	E	O	A	Z	D	G	Z
R	S	R	O	O	M	S	B	R	Z	L	S	O	I	N	C	Z	A	A	K
G	X	I	J	O	B	A	H	N	J	U	I	E	N	M	O	H	V	T	W
F	D	S	G	O	C	E	R	Y	P	D	I	G	P	Y	B	A	I	Z	H
Z	Q	T	T	L	W	D	D	Y	W	B	X	V	H	H	P	A	D	S	N
	J	E	S	S	E	S	O	L	O	M	O	N	G	Y	J	I	L	N	O
	W	T	W	Y	N	A	B	R	A	H	A	M	I	S	A	A	C	B	W

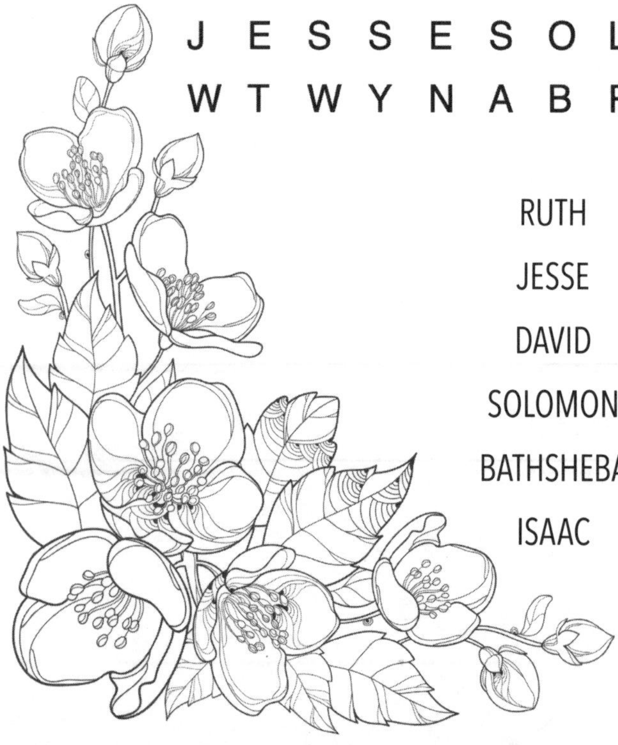

RUTH	JOSEPH	FATHERED
JESSE	MARY	MOTHER
DAVID	TAMAR	GENEALOGY
SOLOMON	RAHAB	GENERATIONS
BATHSHEBA	GENERATIONS	JESUS CHRIST
ISAAC	ABRAHAM	JACOB
	BOAZ	OBED

2. JUDAH AND TAMAR: GENESIS 38:6–30

Here's a story from Jesus's genealogy. Though Tamar suffered, her experiences became part of a larger plan and led to the birth of Jesus!

And Judah took a wife for Er his firstborn, whose name was Tamar. And Er, Judah's firstborn, was wicked in the sight of the Lord; and the Lord slew him. And Judah said to Onan, Go in to your brother's wife, and marry her, and raise up seed to your brother. And Onan knew that the seed should not be his; and it came to pass, when he went in to his brother's wife, that he spilled it on the ground, lest that he should give seed to his brother. And the thing which he did displeased the Lord: wherefore He slew him also. Then said Judah to Tamar his daughter in law, Remain a widow at your father's house, till Shelah my son be grown: for he said, Lest perhaps he die also, as his brethren did. And Tamar went and dwelt in her father's house.

And it was told Tamar, saying, Behold your father in law goes up to Timnath to shear his sheep. And she put her widow's garments off from her, and covered her with a veil, and wrapped herself, and sat in an open place, which is by the way to Timnath; for she saw that Shelah was grown, and she was not given to him as a wife. When Judah saw her, he thought her to be a harlot; because she had covered her face.

And he turned to her by the way, and said, Go to, I pray you, let me come in to you; (for he knew not that she was his daughter in law.) And she said, What will you give me, that you may come in to me? And he said, I will send you a kid from the flock. And she said, Will you give me a pledge, till you send it? And he said, What pledge shall I give you? And she said, your signet, and your bracelets, and your staff that is in your hand. And he gave it her, and came in to her, and she conceived by him. And she arose, and went away, and laid by her veil from her, and put on the garments of her widowhood. And Judah sent the kid by the hand of his friend the Adullamite, to receive his pledge from the woman's hand: but he found her not. Then he asked the men of that place, saying, Where is the harlot, that was openly by the way side? And they said, There was no harlot in this place. And he returned to Judah, and said, I cannot find her; and also the men of the place said, that there was no harlot in this place.

And it came to pass about three months after, that it was told Judah, saying, Tamar your daughter in law has played the harlot; and also, behold, she is with child by whoredom. And Judah said, Bring her forth, and let her be burned. When she was brought forth, she sent to her father in law, saying, By the man, whose these are, am I with child: and she said, Discern, I pray you, whose are these, the signet, and bracelets, and staff. And Judah acknowledged them, and said, She has been more righteous than I; because that I gave her not to Shelah my son.

And it came to pass in the time of her travail, that, behold, twins were in her womb. And it came to pass, when she travailed, that the one put out his hand: and the midwife took and bound upon his hand a scarlet thread, saying, This came out first. And it came to pass, as he drew back his hand, that, behold, his brother came out: and she said, How have you broken forth? this breach be upon you: therefore his name was called Pharez. And afterward came out his brother, that had the scarlet thread upon his hand: and his name was called Zarah.

V	E	R	T	H	I	C	Y	X	C	R	Q	M	Q	X	W	C	Q	H	L
W	O	B	R	A	C	E	L	E	T	Z	L	D	V	G	I	H	S	X	S
J	A	P	D	J	P	H	A	R	E	Z	A	S	Y	E	D	W	V	M	I
A	H	M	J	W	X	M	A	K	B	W	A	R	G	W	O	J	E	N	U
Y	O	B	T	L	W	Y	Q	D	R	F	B	I	A	D	W	S	I	P	J
Y	M	J	W	V	M	L	J	P	O	L	F	D	P	H	H	S	L	L	W
B	K	E	I	K	L	P	O	C	K	O	Y	S	A	G	O	H	I	E	Y
R	F	Y	N	W	A	M	K	X	E	C	F	S	U	H	O	E	J	D	O
A	L	Y	S	E	K	X	H	J	N	K	V	E	U	C	D	L	U	G	Q
L	O	W	O	A	Q	S	E	R	F	U	U	V	C	B	R	A	D	E	T
M	T	Z	N	T	O	T	Y	Y	O	R	Q	H	D	C	Y	H	A	R	I
H	O	F	V	Q	Y	C	G	D	R	S	Y	I	N	B	S	H	H	B	Z
A	P	B	S	C	O	L	D	S	T	A	F	F	X	Y	Z	P	Z	Q	O
R	N	I	E	Q	F	I	Z	U	H	L	S	H	U	A	H	P	Y	Y	Z
E	Q	Z	A	J	L	W	I	C	K	E	D	O	L	O	G	C	C	Y	S
R	I	G	H	T	E	O	U	S	L	N	S	V	Z	I	D	N	L	O	K
R	T	I	M	N	A	T	H	I	X	B	M	R	S	I	G	N	E	T	R
Y	O	U	N	G	K	I	D	D	U	X	F	D	T	Z	W	U	C	A	I
E	O	N	A	N	J	I	O	X	W	N	W	B	P	E	P	O	Y	K	O
X	C	R	G	T	G	Q	O	P	Z	F	T	X	S	H	L	X	Y	W	T

JUDAH	RIGHTEOUS	TIMNATH	PLEDGE	PHAREZ
SHUAH	FLOCK	SHELAH	WICKED	TWINS
ER	WIDOWHOOD	SIGNET	ZARAH	YOUNG KID
ONAN	VEIL	BRACELET	BROKEN FORTH	STAFF

3. THE FAITH OF RAHAB: JOSHUA 2:1–22

Rahab is an example of a gentile who was grafted into Israel because of her faith. Not only is she included in the genealogy of Jesus Christ, but she is listed in the "faith chapter," Hebrews 11. "By faith the harlot Rahab perished not with them that believed not, when she had received the spies with peace" (Hebrews 11:31).

And Joshua the son of Nun sent out of Shittim two men to spy secretly, saying, Go view the land, even Jericho. And they went, and came into a harlot's house, named Rahab, and lodged there. And it was told the king of Jericho, saying, Behold, there came men in here to night of the children of Israel to search out the country. And the king of Jericho sent to Rahab, saying, Bring forth the men that are come to you, which are entered into your house: for they be come to search out all the country.

And the woman took the two men, and hid them, and said thus, There came men to me, but I knew not where they were: and it came to pass about the time of shutting of the gate, when it was dark, that the men went out: where the men went I know not: pursue after them quickly; for you shall overtake them. But she had brought them up to the roof of the house, and hid them with the stalks of flax, which she had laid in order upon the roof.... And as soon as they which pursued after them were gone out, they shut the gate....

She came up to them upon the roof; and she said to the men, I know that the Lord has given you the land, and that your terror is fallen upon us, and that all the inhabitants of the land faint because of you.... For the Lord your God He is God in heaven above, and in earth beneath. Now therefore, I pray you, swear to me by the Lord, since I have showed you kindness, that you will also show kindness to my father's house, and give me a true token: and that you will save alive my father, and my mother, and my brethren, and my sisters, and all that they have, and deliver our lives from death.

And the men answered her, Our life for yours, if you utter not this our business. And it shall be, when the Lord has given us the land, that we will deal kindly and truly with you. Then she let them down by a cord through the window: for her house was upon the town wall, and she dwelled upon the wall. And she said to them, Get you to the mountain, lest the pursuers meet you; and hide yourselves there three days, until the pursuers be returned: and afterward may you go your way. And the men said to her, We will be blameless of this your oath which you have made us swear. Behold, when we come into the land, you shall bind this line of scarlet thread in the window which you did let us down by: and you shall bring your father, and your mother, and your brethren, and all your father's household, home to you. And it shall be, that whosoever shall go out of the doors of your house into the street, his blood shall be upon his head, and we will be guiltless and whosoever shall be with you in the house, his blood shall be on our head if any hand be upon him. And if you utter this our business, then we will be quit of your oath which you have made us to swear.

And she said, According to your words, so be it. And she sent them away, and they departed: and she bound the scarlet line in the window. And they went, and came to the mountain, and abode there three days, until the pursuers were returned: and the pursuers sought them throughout all the way, but found them not.

M	C	F	Y	P	K	O	S	H	H	R	W	D	Q	W	P	G	J	E	M
D	R	S	Y	U	B	I	F	A	Y	Q	A	P	U	K	J	U	V	D	O
N	U	U	N	P	Q	H	N	V	V	F	L	P	A	G	O	I	T	G	U
T	R	X	W	Y	S	M	E	D	I	E	L	L	Z	O	W	L	E	K	N
M	E	O	D	H	P	F	S	X	N	B	A	Z	E	X	K	T	P	R	T
W	L	R	A	S	P	O	H	R	K	E	G	L	Z	U	G	L	U	F	A
I	L	Y	R	T	S	P	I	E	S	M	S	R	I	D	Z	E	R	H	I
N	V	C	F	O	H	E	T	L	S	A	C	S	V	V	U	S	S	L	N
N	G	T	G	X	R	V	T	X	S	P	J	N	C	N	E	S	U	A	D
F	Z	G	O	U	U	G	I	T	H	C	P	O	R	A	N	R	E	X	A
K	U	Z	V	K	T	I	M	T	G	O	T	V	F	M	R	C	R	A	A
W	M	H	E	E	E	Z	J	T	Z	B	U	X	V	Z	C	L	S	V	J
W	I	N	D	O	W	N	Y	H	Q	H	F	S	T	F	X	L	E	M	E
I	N	Z	B	F	U	A	E	F	V	V	E	J	E	B	Q	A	S	T	R
K	Q	L	Q	S	E	A	H	N	R	B	L	F	O	H	F	I	D	A	I
Y	Z	X	Y	T	T	V	L	H	I	D	D	E	N	R	O	Z	O	V	C
P	P	Y	O	R	I	R	F	M	U	P	E	Q	K	U	O	L	R	W	H
X	X	X	A	N	F	L	A	X	H	Q	U	F	T	S	R	O	D	N	O
Y	N	S	B	E	L	I	E	V	E	D	A	H	I	A	S	K	F	A	V
K	E	R	N	M	E	D	W	L	E	F	T	H	R	E	A	D	F	H	Y

SHITTIM
JERICHO
HIDDEN
KINDNESS
SCARLET
THREAD
FLAX
WINDOW
MOUNTAIN
PURSUERS
SPIES
BELIEVED
SAVE ALIVE
ROOF
WALL
HOUSEHOLD
OATH
GUILTLESS
TERROR
TOKEN

4. RUTH AND NAOMI: THE POWER OF FRIENDSHIP RUTH 1:1–22

Like Rahab, Ruth was not an Israelite, but from the country of Moab. Because of her devotion to her mother-in-law, she became an ancestor of King David and ultimately Jesus Christ.

Now it came to pass...that there was a famine in the land. And a certain man of Bethlehemjudah went to sojourn in the country of Moab, he, and his wife, and his two sons....And Elimelech Naomi's husband died; and she was left, and her two sons. And they took them wives of the women of Moab; the name of the one was Orpah, and the name of the other Ruth: and they dwelled there about ten years. And Mahlon and Chilion died also both of them; and the woman was left of her two sons and her husband.

Then she arose with her daughters in law, that she might return from the country of Moab: for she had heard in the country of Moab how that the LORD had visited His people in giving them bread. Wherefore she went forth out of the place where she was, and her two daughters in law with her; and they went on the way to return to the land of Judah. And Naomi said to her two daughters in law, Go, return each to her mother's house: the LORD deal kindly with you, as you have dealt with the dead, and with me. The LORD grant you that you may find rest, each of you in the house of her husband. Then she kissed them; and they lifted up their voice, and wept. And they said to her, Surely we will return with you to your people.

And Naomi said, Turn again, my daughters: why will you go with me? are there yet any more sons in my womb, that they may be your husbands? Turn again, my daughters, go your way; for I am too old to have a husband. If I should say, I have hope, if I should have a husband also to night, and should also bear sons; would you tarry for them till they were grown? would you stay for them from having husbands? nay, my daughters; for it grieves me much for your sakes that the hand of the LORD is gone out against me. And they lifted up their voice, and wept again: and Orpah kissed her mother in law; but Ruth clung to her. And she said, Behold, your sister in law is gone back to her people, and to her gods: return you after your sister in law.

And Ruth said, Entreat me not to leave you, or to return from following after you: for where you go, I will go; and where you lodge, I will lodge: your people shall be my people, and your God my God: Where you die, will I die, and there will I be buried: the LORD do so to me, and more also, if anything but death part you and me. When she saw that she was steadfastly minded to go with her, then she left speaking to her. So they two went until they came to Bethlehem....

When they were come to Bethlehem, that all the city was moved about them, and they said, Is this Naomi? And she said to them, Call me not Naomi, call me Mara: for the Almighty has dealt very bitterly with me. I went out full, and the Lord has brought me home again empty: why then call you me Naomi, seeing the Lord has testified against me, and the Almighty has afflicted me? So Naomi returned, and Ruth the Moabitess, her daughter in law, with her, which returned out of the country of Moab: and they came to Bethlehem in the beginning of barley harvest.

G	F	H	P	B	V	M	A	H	L	O	N	K	E	M	P	T	Y	N	H
D	N	A	E	E	V	G	H	A	R	V	E	S	T	R	M	U	Z	A	B
K	O	D	M	N	O	I	G	X	R	F	I	D	B	R	R	R	N	O	E
S	M	W	Q	I	T	P	H	O	K	T	F	A	O	W	E	G	B	M	T
L	E	A	V	E	N	R	L	J	B	G	F	U	Y	Y	T	F	D	I	H
E	E	A	X	M	V	E	E	E	R	R	L	G	P	A	U	Q	V	D	L
T	X	V	H	H	P	M	L	A	C	N	G	H	M	N	R	K	O	T	E
Q	C	F	C	L	V	X	L	R	T	C	B	T	A	F	N	D	A	C	H
N	S	T	E	A	D	F	A	S	T	L	Y	E	R	J	T	D	Y	A	E
P	R	J	T	S	M	M	S	I	R	D	J	R	A	L	V	X	O	P	M
P	M	K	L	G	E	C	Q	K	O	U	Z	I	I	O	P	I	L	P	A
E	B	F	G	E	Y	L	L	H	M	Q	G	N	Y	D	B	U	U	S	Q
F	O	L	L	O	W	I	N	G	Y	A	X	L	V	G	A	D	Q	O	G
P	F	L	D	F	P	X	O	W	P	H	S	A	K	E	R	O	T	C	B
N	B	K	L	V	B	S	Y	M	W	G	G	W	B	A	L	J	M	E	Q
Q	Q	H	Z	O	I	V	V	I	J	N	M	O	A	B	E	H	V	C	X
U	Q	R	M	S	G	E	U	O	R	P	A	H	R	R	Y	B	B	R	A
I	S	L	H	M	U	R	X	J	A	O	F	F	L	G	J	T	X	W	U
S	K	R	M	R	Q	V	B	I	T	T	E	R	Z	Z	M	L	J	N	D
D	V	C	H	I	L	I	O	N	G	E	S	S	O	P	X	S	N	I	Z

FAMINE	NAOMI	MAHLON	RETURN	LEAVE
ORPAH	DAUGHTER IN LAW	ENTREAT	MARA	BITTER
FOLLOWING	STEADFASTLY	BETHLEHEM	PEOPLE	EMPTY
BARLEY	HARVEST	CHILION	MOAB	LODGE

5. RUTH MEETS BOAZ: RUTH 2:1–23

And Naomi had a kinsman of her husband's, a mighty man of wealth, of the family of Elimelech; and his name was Boaz. And Ruth the Moabitess said to Naomi, Let me now go to the field, and glean ears of corn after him in whose sight I shall find grace. And she said to her, Go, my daughter. And she went, and came, and gleaned in the field after the reapers: and her hap was to light on a part of the field belonging to Boaz, who was of the kindred of Elimelech....

Then said Boaz to his servant that was set over the reapers, Whose damsel is this? And the servant that was set over the reapers answered and said, It is the Moabitish damsel that came back with Naomi out of the country of Moab: and she said, I pray you, let me glean and gather after the reapers among the sheaves: so she came, and has continued even from the morning until now, that she tarried a little in the house. T

hen said Boaz to Ruth, Hear you not, my daughter? Go not to glean in another field, neither go from here, but abide here fast by my maidens: let your eyes be on the field that they do reap, and go you after them: have I not charged the young men that they shall not touch you? and when you are thirsty, go to the vessels, and drink of that which the young men have drawn.

Then she fell on her face, and bowed herself to the ground, and said to him, Why have I found grace in your eyes, that you should take knowledge of me, seeing I am a stranger?

And Boaz answered and said to her, It has fully been showed me, all that you have done to your mother in law since the death of your husband: and how you have left your father and your mother, and the land of your nativity, and are come to a people which you knew not before. The Lord recompense your work, and a full reward be given you of the Lord God of Israel, under whose wings you are come to trust.

Then she said, Let me find favor in your sight, my lord; for that you have comforted me, and for that you have spoken friendly to your handmaid, though I be not like to one of your handmaidens. And Boaz said to her, At mealtime come you here, and eat of the bread, and dip your morsel in the vinegar. And she sat beside the reapers: and he reached her parched corn, and she did eat, and was sufficed, and left. And when she was risen up to glean, Boaz commanded his young men, saying, Let her glean even among the sheaves, and reproach her not: and let fall also some of the handfuls of purpose for her, and leave them, that she may glean them, and rebuke her not. So she gleaned in the field until evening, and beat out that she had gleaned: and it was about an ephah of barley. And she took it up, and went into the city: and her mother in law saw what she had gleaned: and she brought forth, and gave to her that she had reserved after she was sufficed. And her mother in law said to her, Where have you gleaned to day? and where worked you? blessed be he that did take knowledge of you. And she showed her mother in law with whom she had worked, and said, The man's name with whom I worked to day is Boaz. And Naomi said to her daughter in law, Blessed be he of the Lord, who has not left off His kindness to the living and to the dead. And Naomi said to her, The man is near of kin to us, one of our next kinsmen.

P	J	A	R	J	R	C	L	G	X	C	U	C	P	Q	W	K	A	E	X
K	C	C	M	X	X	E	J	U	L	Q	Y	R	X	E	Q	C	T	M	K
A	B	K	N	Q	Q	R	A	E	W	E	I	H	A	R	V	E	S	T	K
P	P	D	A	M	S	E	L	P	N	W	A	R	F	O	J	P	G	P	F
R	N	W	W	W	A	C	T	Y	E	K	C	N	X	P	P	P	P	W	I
V	J	P	Z	L	E	K	I	J	K	R	M	H	W	H	E	A	T	E	E
L	V	D	A	J	Q	A	R	O	O	N	S	A	Q	E	U	R	M	P	L
Q	X	K	T	K	H	N	L	Y	K	J	Z	N	F	C	Q	D	E	H	D
S	H	E	A	V	E	S	R	T	F	U	B	D	O	P	K	S	A	A	U
T	K	F	U	N	W	W	A	X	H	C	U	F	V	A	I	C	L	H	C
M	I	I	S	V	I	H	N	E	I	K	T	U	Q	C	N	V	T	T	S
B	N	A	B	D	F	I	X	H	C	V	R	L	I	J	D	G	I	A	F
T	S	N	M	K	P	O	O	M	D	F	S	S	S	Z	N	R	M	R	X
W	M	G	A	M	E	L	I	M	E	L	E	C	H	R	E	R	E	R	U
H	A	V	I	N	E	G	A	R	Y	O	P	F	I	H	S	T	Z	I	R
O	N	C	D	A	M	R	P	F	M	Y	T	F	I	E	S	T	Q	E	H
K	J	X	E	E	X	G	D	J	E	A	R	O	F	C	O	R	N	D	S
S	D	W	N	V	X	Y	H	Q	X	Y	M	R	A	Z	D	W	C	D	H
V	V	C	S	P	S	E	I	Y	Y	E	Z	M	P	Q	D	Z	B	L	H
M	O	R	S	E	L	Q	N	C	L	G	A	T	H	E	R	F	G	G	X

KINSMAN	GLEAN	MAIDENS	TARRIED	FIELD
WEALTH	GATHER	WHEAT	HANDFULS	MEALTIME
ELIMELECH	REAPERS	DAMSEL	EPHAH	MORSEL
EAR OF CORN	HARVEST	SHEAVES	KINDNESS	VINEGAR

6. RUTH'S REDEMPTION ASSURED: RUTH 3:1–18

Then Naomi her mother in law said to her, My daughter, shall I not seek rest for you, that it may be well with you? And now is not Boaz of our kindred, with whose maidens you were? Behold, he winnows barley tonight in the threshingfloor. Wash yourself therefore, and anoint you, and put your raiment upon you, and get you down to the floor: but make not yourself known to the man, until he shall have done eating and drinking. And it shall be, when he lies down, that you shall mark the place where he shall lie, and you shall go in, and uncover his feet, and lay you down; and he will tell you what you shall do. And she said to her, All that you say to me I will do. And she went down to the floor, and did according to all that her mother in law bid her.

And when Boaz had eaten and drunk, and his heart was merry, he went to lie down at the end of the heap of corn: and she came softly, and uncovered his feet, and laid her down. And it came to pass at midnight, that the man was afraid, and turned himself: and, behold, a woman lay at his feet. And he said, Who are you? And she answered, I am Ruth your handmaid: spread therefore your skirt over your handmaid; for you are a near kinsman. And he said, Blessed be you of the Lord, my daughter: for you have showed more kindness in the latter end than at the beginning, inasmuch as you followed not young men, whether poor or rich. And now, my daughter, fear not; I will do to you all that you require: for all the city of my people does know that you are a virtuous woman. And now it is true that I am your near kinsman: however there is a kinsman nearer than I. Tarry this night, and it shall be in the morning, that if he will perform to you the part of a kinsman, well; let him do the kinsman's part: but if he will not do the part of a kinsman to you, then will I do the part of a kinsman to you, as the Lord lives: lie down until the morning.

And she lay at his feet until the morning: and she rose up before one could know another. And he said, Let it not be known that a woman came into the floor. Also he said, Bring the veil that you have upon you, and hold it. And when she held it, he measured six measures of barley, and laid it on her: and she went into the city. And when she came to her mother in law, she said, Who are you, my daughter? And she told her all that the man had done to her. And she said, These six measures of barley gave he me; for he said to me, Go not empty to your mother in law.

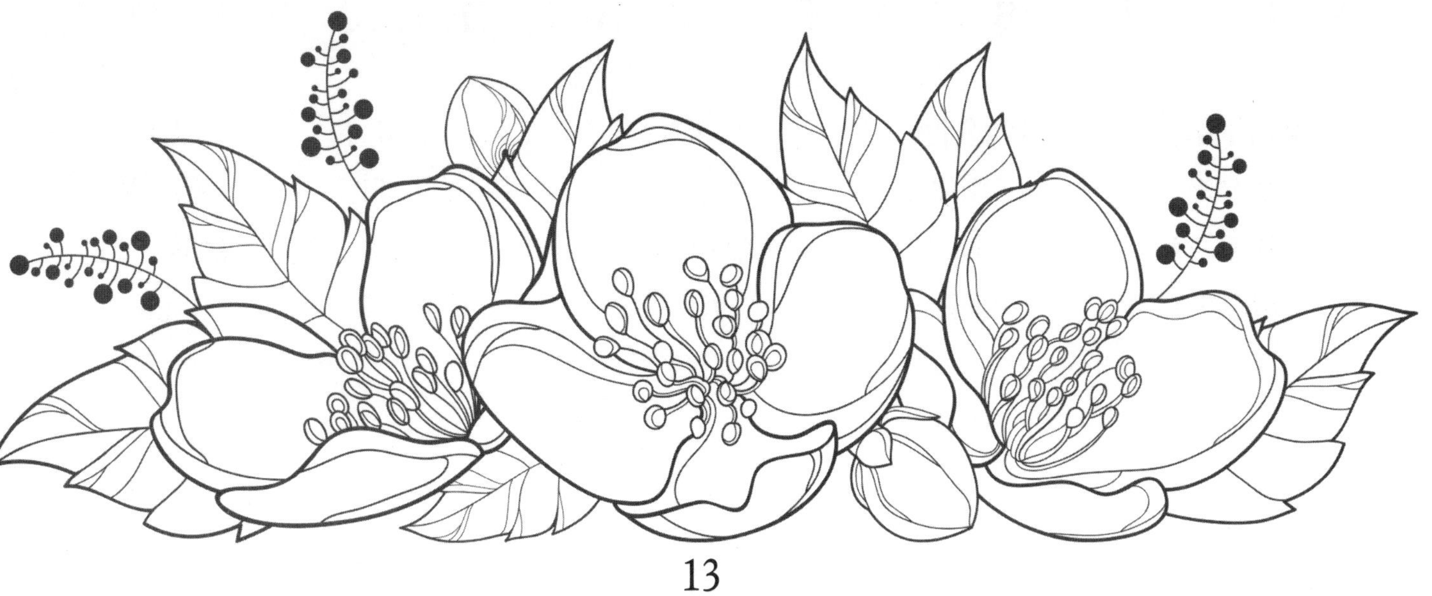

E	D	N	D	I	C	T	M	A	T	I	Y	N	H	J	F	B	O	V	Y
D	F	O	Z	R	E	S	N	I	P	D	T	M	W	A	R	M	X	E	O
A	X	Y	U	M	U	Z	I	K	D	R	R	S	J	K	H	K	C	P	X
U	R	I	N	R	O	N	V	X	V	N	X	M	T	U	F	F	E	I	T
G	G	G	C	O	P	R	K	R	M	F	I	A	K	L	L	Y	V	P	D
H	B	H	O	E	N	B	N	N	I	E	V	G	Q	T	A	R	R	Y	Q
T	J	C	V	O	M	Z	M	I	F	K	A	E	H	L	E	M	M	R	A
E	A	T	E	N	F	W	D	P	N	K	S	S	M	T	C	Q	R	F	E
R	W	Y	R	Y	M	A	Q	H	B	G	K	C	U	P	Y	C	G	O	W
L	P	P	F	V	Z	A	V	N	G	G	O	P	O	R	T	P	O	P	I
P	S	D	A	V	E	R	R	A	I	M	E	N	T	E	E	Y	N	K	N
Q	C	J	C	Y	Y	I	C	G	R	H	O	W	J	P	W	S	A	V	N
F	W	W	Y	B	V	G	L	C	F	S	Y	O	O	Q	E	W	O	I	O
P	L	F	K	U	G	T	G	B	W	N	L	X	N	O	I	V	V	R	W
K	X	O	L	M	X	U	Y	V	Z	V	X	U	T	W	I	E	A	T	S
C	Z	B	O	B	R	H	N	I	H	K	R	E	S	T	M	M	U	U	A
F	V	V	W	R	H	A	N	D	M	A	I	D	M	E	R	R	Y	O	P
V	P	T	H	R	E	S	H	I	N	G	L	I	K	X	Q	K	V	U	G
D	M	P	M	F	Z	I	F	Z	G	F	I	N	I	S	H	E	D	S	H
P	A	T	H	I	S	F	E	E	T	K	R	G	Q	K	J	R	P	Q	J

WINNOWS	THRESHING	FLOOR	RAIMENT	EATEN
MERRY	VIRTUOUS	TARRY	SIX MEASURES	EMPTY
UNCOVER	MIDNIGHT	HANDMAID	DAUGHTER	MORNING
FINISHED	REST	VEIL	AT HIS FEET	DRUNK

7. BOAZ AND RUTH: A LOVE STORY: RUTH 4:1–5:22

Then went Boaz up to the gate, and sat him down there: and, behold, the kinsman of whom Boaz spoke came by.... And he took ten men of the elders of the city, and said, Sit you down here. And they sat down. And he said to the kinsman, Naomi, that is come again out of the country of Moab, sells a parcel of land, which was our brother Elimelech's: and I thought to advertise you, saying, Buy it before the inhabitants, and before the elders of my people. If you will redeem it, redeem it: but if you will not redeem it, then tell me, that I may know: for there is none to redeem it beside you; and I am after you. And he said, I will redeem it.

Then said Boaz, What day you buy the field of the hand of Naomi, you must buy it also of Ruth the Moabitess, the wife of the dead, to raise up the name of the dead upon his inheritance. And the kinsman said, I cannot redeem it for myself, lest I mar my own inheritance: redeem you my right to yourself; for I cannot redeem it. Now this was the manner in former time in Israel concerning redeeming and concerning changing, for to confirm all things; a man plucked off his shoe, and gave it to his neighbor: and this was a testimony in Israel. Therefore the kinsman said to Boaz, Buy it for you. So he drew off his shoe.

And Boaz said to the elders, and to all the people, You are witnesses this day, that I have bought all that was Elimelech's, and all that was Chilion's and Mahlon's, of the hand of Naomi. Moreover Ruth the Moabitess, the wife of Mahlon, have I purchased to be my wife, to raise up the name of the dead upon his inheritance, that the name of the dead be not cut off from among his brethren, and from the gate of his place: you are witnesses this day.

And all the people that were in the gate, and the elders, said, We are witnesses. The Lord make the woman that is come into your house like Rachel and like Leah, which two did build the house of Israel: and do you worthily in Ephratah, and be famous in Bethlehem: And let your house be like the house of Pharez, whom Tamar bore to Judah, of the seed which the Lord shall give you of this young woman. So Boaz took Ruth, and she was his wife: and when he went in to her, the Lord gave her conception, and she bore a son....

And Naomi took the child, and laid it in her bosom, and became nurse to it. And the women her neighbors gave it a name, saying, There is a son born to Naomi; and they called his name Obed: he is the father of Jesse, the father of David.

C	B	W	T	G	P	A	R	C	E	L	P	L	U	K	E	D	Y	U	Y
O	O	Z	M	E	O	J	D	V	S	W	R	M	T	R	V	O	X	Y	R
H	S	G	G	O	S	E	I	A	T	G	N	J	C	E	O	V	P	V	E
F	O	T	L	A	L	T	Y	N	G	X	B	E	X	S	F	L	S	L	D
T	M	Q	I	O	T	D	I	S	K	Y	H	L	Y	T	W	J	Y	B	E
Y	P	A	H	I	E	E	A	M	P	U	R	H	N	O	H	Z	B	I	E
N	L	Y	V	N	B	J	L	G	O	A	R	A	E	R	K	O	N	N	M
Q	C	Y	Q	U	U	W	B	T	E	N	Y	K	I	E	Y	T	Y	H	T
C	U	P	C	F	O	R	S	H	K	L	Y	D	G	R	P	H	F	E	I
W	T	Z	X	P	L	M	S	X	C	R	F	M	H	D	U	T	I	R	X
O	O	X	C	F	V	C	K	E	B	H	P	Q	B	N	R	N	I	I	V
V	F	W	J	L	U	U	W	F	R	G	M	X	O	R	C	U	K	T	D
S	F	N	O	U	R	I	S	H	E	R	N	R	R	O	H	K	J	A	P
	W	O	R	T	H	I	L	Y	N	V	P	A	S	Q	A	O	E	N	R
			G	H	N	J	R	T	G	B	P	S	C	B	S	A	F	C	F
			G	Q	F	A	M	O	U	S	C	D	B	J	E	I	N	E	N
			A	S	E	V	E	N	S	O	N	S	B	F	D	S	B	T	J
			E	F	O	N	U	C	H	I	L	D	E	L	D	E	R	S	O
			C	Q	I	X	M	K	S	H	O	E	A	K	E	F	G	X	B
			L	I	J	P	K	K	L	L	B	C	S	L	S	X	L	N	I

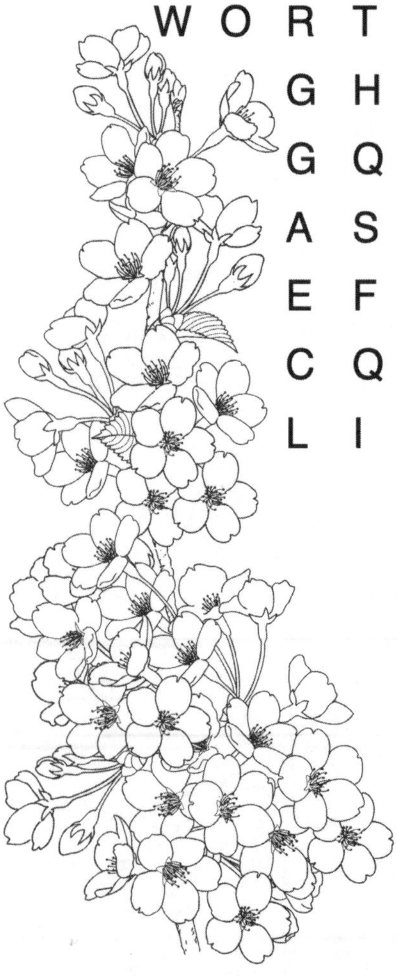

ELDERS	PARCEL	REDEEM	PLUCKED
TESTIMONY	CUT OFF	PURCHASED	INHERITANCE
FAMOUS	RESTORER	NOURISHER	OLD AGE
NURSE	BOSOM	NEIGHBORS	SEVEN SONS
GATE	SHOE	WORTHILY	CHILD

8. BATHSHEBA: 2 SAMUEL 11:1–27

At the time when kings go forth to battle, that David...tarried still at Jerusalem. And it came to pass in the evening, that David arose from off his bed, and walked upon the roof of the king's house: and from the roof he saw a woman washing herself; and the woman was very beautiful to look upon. And David sent and inquired after the woman. And one said, Is not this Bathsheba, the daughter of Eliam, the wife of Uriah the Hittite?

And David sent messengers, and took her; and she came in to him, and he lay with her; for she was purified from her uncleanness: and she returned to her house. And the woman conceived, and sent and told David, and said, I am with child. And David sent to Joab, saying, Send me Uriah the Hittite. And Joab sent Uriah to David. And when Uriah was come to him, David...said to Uriah, Go down to your house, and wash your feet. And Uriah departed out of the king's house, and there followed him a mess of meat from the king. But Uriah slept at the door of the king's house with all the servants of his lord, and went not down to his house.

And when they had told David, saying, Uriah went not down to his house, David said to Uriah, Came you not from your journey? why then did you not go down to your house? And Uriah said to David, The ark, and Israel, and Judah, abide in tents; and my lord Joab, and the servants of my lord, are encamped in the open fields; shall I then go into my house, to eat and to drink, and to lie with my wife? as you live, and as your soul lives I will not do this thing....

And it came to pass in the morning, that David wrote a letter to Joab, and sent it by the hand of Uriah. And he wrote in the letter, saying, Set you Uriah in the forefront of the hottest battle, and retire you from him, that he may be smitten, and die. And it came to pass, when Joab observed the city, that he assigned Uriah to a place where he knew that valiant men were. And the men of the city went out, and fought with Joab: and there fell some of the people of the servants of David; and Uriah the Hittite died also....

And when the wife of Uriah heard that Uriah her husband was dead, she mourned for her husband. And when the mourning was past, David sent and brought her to his house, and she became his wife, and bore him a son. But the thing that David had done displeased the LORD.

H	Z	F	U	O	S	D	C	E	V	F	Y	Q	F	S	B	M	X	S	J
P	A	I	Q	R	P	X	B	A	Q	H	H	X	J	I	T	D	P	K	O
H	I	T	T	I	T	E	L	G	R	S	U	M	L	D	I	X	I	P	U
I	Z	Y	E	G	B	T	I	O	M	Y	T	O	P	I	P	G	H	L	R
T	G	U	O	X	B	R	X	Z	B	Q	T	U	V	S	R	G	C	B	N
M	O	Y	M	E	S	S	E	N	G	E	R	R	L	P	E	F	X	E	E
I	W	A	S	H	I	N	G	R	D	N	N	N	C	L	V	C	O	A	Y
L	U	A	P	K	G	I	F	Q	M	M	U	E	F	E	A	W	A	U	D
L	V	E	T	O	Z	F	C	S	L	M	I	D	X	A	I	C	A	T	E
S	A	N	Y	T	C	Q	Z	E	A	I	T	W	U	S	L	N	L	I	V
T	L	T	H	C	H	F	G	V	S	J	H	Z	W	E	E	B	D	F	O
O	I	E	L	S	I	E	S	H	J	B	E	Q	Y	D	D	E	P	U	U
N	A	R	A	G	N	T	T	W	H	M	B	M	J	T	H	R	W	L	R
E	N	I	U	A	M	T	Y	I	O	T	E	J	E	U	R	O	O	F	S
B	T	N	P	K	F	V	O	G	M	R	Z	Y	E	Q	K	K	J	Y	W
P	C	G	P	L	C	F	V	A	A	E	D	G	X	R	Y	W	N	U	U
F	F	P	U	H	G	B	Y	K	S	T	U	G	O	D	J	E	P	E	N
K	L	M	P	J	K	I	G	Q	Y	I	E	H	A	U	R	I	A	H	I
M	J	I	D	N	Z	A	T	T	H	E	D	O	O	R	A	G	Q	M	V
B	A	T	T	L	E	T	N	W	T	R	U	P	H	E	R	H	S	E	K

AT THE TIME	BEAUTIFUL	JOURNEY	MOURNED	DEVOURS
BATTLE	URIAH	VALIANT	DISPLEASED	THEBEZ
ROOF	HITTITE	MILLSTONE	MESSENGER	CITY GATE
WASHING	AT THE DOOR	PREVAILED	SWORD	ENTERING

9. THE DEATH OF BATHSHEBA'S SON: 2 SAMUEL 12:15–25

The Lord struck the child that Uriah's wife bore to David, and it was very sick. David therefore besought God for the child; and David fasted, and went in, and lay all night upon the earth. And the elders of his house arose, and went to him, to raise him up from the earth: but he would not, neither did he eat bread with them. And it came to pass on the seventh day, that the child died. And the servants of David feared to tell him that the child was dead.... And he said, While the child was yet alive, I fasted and wept: for I said, Who can tell whether God will be gracious to me, that the child may live? But now he is dead, why should I fast? can I bring him back again? I shall go to him, but he shall not return to me. And David comforted Bathsheba his wife, and went in to her, and lay with her: and she bore a son, and he called his name Solomon: and the Lord loved him. And he sent by the hand of Nathan the prophet; and he called his name Jedidiah, because of the Lord.

F	V	I	X	R	O	R	R	Z	W	N	E	F	W	Y	J	I	A	W	M
P	I	A	N	O	I	N	T	E	D	B	U	A	A	L	I	M	L	L	R
M	T	G	D	Q	X	P	F	U	Z	D	W	S	M	Y	P	P	I	K	I
J	E	R	I	N	A	T	H	A	N	I	K	T	F	K	H	E	V	G	S
W	V	A	C	O	M	F	O	R	T	E	D	A	B	J	B	R	E	W	E
H	J	C	J	R	E	T	U	R	N	J	L	N	R	S	F	C	Y	B	A
I	N	I	A	P	P	A	R	E	L	C	P	D	E	I	A	E	S	B	N
S	Q	O	U	U	Z	C	F	A	I	H	A	W	A	C	S	I	P	N	D
P	N	U	U	V	L	M	Y	G	W	I	J	E	D	K	T	V	Q	E	E
E	P	S	R	P	F	W	W	J	O	L	W	E	I	E	E	E	F	A	A
R	B	E	S	O	U	G	H	T	D	D	H	P	W	N	D	D	D	R	T
E	C	V	H	J	E	D	I	D	I	A	H	M	S	I	O	B	N	T	H
D	K	E	L	D	E	R	S	F	F	S	T	C	P	L	T	O	T	H	W
H	E	A	R	K	E	N	P	K	G	T	V	V	V	Q	H	S	A	Y	T

NATHAN	CHILD	APPAREL	GRACIOUS	EAT
BESOUGHT	FASTED	BREAD	HEARKEN	ELDERS
PERCEIVED	ALIVE	RISE AND COMFORTED	RETURN	ANOINTED
WHISPERED	EARTH	JEDIDIAH	SICK	FAST AND WEEP

10. SOLOMON PROCLAIMED KING: 1 KINGS 1:28–39

[Bathsheba] came into the king's presence, and stood before the king. And the king swore, and said, As the LORD lives, that has redeemed my soul out of all distress, even as I swore to you by the LORD God of Israel, saying, Assuredly Solomon your son shall reign after me, and he shall sit upon my throne in my stead; even so will I certainly do this day.... And king David said, Call me Zadok the priest, and Nathan the prophet, and Benaiah the son of Jehoiada. And they came before the king. The king also said to them, Take with you the servants of your lord, and cause Solomon my son to ride upon my own mule, and bring him down to Gihon: and let Zadok the priest and Nathan the prophet anoint him there king over Israel: and blow you with the trumpet, and say, God save king Solomon. Then you shall come up after him, that he may come and sit upon my throne; for he shall be king in my stead: and I have appointed him to be ruler over Israel and over Judah....And Zadok the priest took a horn of oil out of the tabernacle, and anointed Solomon. And they blew the trumpet; and all the people said, God save king Solomon.

G	T	W	X	I	R	A	P	H	O	R	N	O	F	O	I	L	A	I	L
T	B	H	T	R	B	A	Z	Z	Z	Z	I	T	R	U	M	P	E	T	Q
C	L	O	R	O	M	R	E	V	E	R	E	N	C	E	I	P	G	W	H
Z	I	U	W	O	V	H	N	S	O	I	Q	J	W	W	Z	R	O	Y	T
Z	A	X	K	E	N	O	T	A	B	E	R	N	A	C	L	E	D	T	W
E	T	D	I	O	D	E	C	A	A	W	C	H	H	I	F	S	S	D	R
I	Y	O	O	A	T	L	T	R	E	I	G	N	N	I	V	E	A	I	E
S	Y	F	L	K	U	P	O	Q	I	D	L	A	L	N	C	N	V	S	P
L	O	A	S	S	U	R	E	D	L	Y	A	W	D	R	J	C	E	T	E
N	K	J	X	B	M	U	L	E	X	W	G	R	E	A	T	E	R	R	N
P	S	X	G	M	H	Q	A	P	P	O	I	N	T	E	D	T	K	E	W
R	U	L	E	R	N	B	G	S	Z	N	K	S	O	U	L	C	Z	S	J
S	W	O	R	E	E	Z	E	J	Z	T	S	T	E	A	D	K	C	S	S
V	G	G	I	H	J	S	A	K	I	N	G	S	O	L	O	M	O	N	E

PRESENCE	SOUL	RULER	GOD SAVE	HORN OF OIL
DISTRESS	SWORE	APPOINTED	REVERENCE	ZADOK
ASSUREDLY	REIGN	KING SOLOMON	BOWED	TRUMPET
THRONE	STEAD	TABERNACLE	MULE	GREATER

11. MARY, THE MOTHER OF JESUS: LUKE 1:26–35

The angel came in to [Mary], and said, Hail, you that are highly favored, the Lord is with you: blessed are you among women. And when she saw him, she was troubled at his saying, and cast in her mind what manner of salutation this should be. And the angel said to her, Fear not, Mary: for you have found favor with God. And, behold, you shall conceive in your womb, and bring forth a son, and shall call His name JESUS. He shall be great, and shall be called the Son of the Highest: and the Lord God shall give to Him the throne of His father David: and He shall reign over the house of Jacob for ever; and of His kingdom there shall be no end.

Then said Mary to the angel, How shall this be, seeing I know not a man? And the angel answered and said to her, The Holy Ghost shall come upon you, and the power of the Highest shall overshadow you: therefore also that holy thing which shall be born of you shall be called the Son of God....For with God nothing shall be impossible. And Mary said, Behold the handmaid of the Lord; be it to me according to your word.

Q	I	V	B	S	O	D	A	K	A	M	F	K	W	A	T
A	A	M	U	K	C	M	V	D	C	S	A	I	G	N	T
C	J	G	P	H	S	O	O	D	H	A	V	N	N	G	H
C	K	H	L	O	H	K	N	T	P	C	O	G	N	E	R
O	G	W	O	N	S	H	T	C	Q	V	R	D	L	L	O
R	T	A	R	U	O	S	I	X	E	K	E	O	N	O	N
D	B	B	B	O	S	T	I	G	P	I	D	M	E	V	E
I	L	Z	A	R	U	E	H	B	H	A	V	P	S	E	M
N	E	K	M	R	I	U	O	I	L	E	P	E	P	R	O
G	S	W	A	C	R	E	L	F	N	E	S	D	O	S	E
R	S	L	J	K	X	E	L	C	J	G	E	T	U	H	N
K	E	V	I	R	G	I	N	K	U	A	U	M	S	A	B
C	D	M	S	I	X	T	H	L	L	J	C	I	E	D	T
W	C	V	G	G	A	L	I	L	E	E	O	O	D	O	D
H	K	S	O	N	O	F	G	O	D	C	M	M	B	W	B
S	N	A	Z	A	R	E	T	H	L	L	C	G	E	G	T

SIXTH
GALILEE
VIRGIN
ANGEL
BLESSED
HIGHEST
OVERSHADOW
KINGDOM
BARREN
IMPOSSIBLE
GABRIEL
ESPOUSED
FAVORED
CONCEIVE
THRONE
HOUSE OF JACOB
SON OF GOD
NOTHING
ACCORDING
NAZARETH

12. CHRIST IS BORN OF MARY: MATTHEW 1:18–25

Now the birth of Jesus Christ was on this wise: When as His mother Mary was engaged to Joseph, before they came together, she was found with child of the Holy Ghost. Then Joseph her husband, being a just man, and not willing to make her a public example, was minded to put her away privily. But while he thought on these things, behold, the angel of the Lord appeared to him in a dream, saying, Joseph, you son of David, fear not to take to you Mary your wife: for that which is conceived in her is of the Holy Ghost. And she shall bring forth a son, and you shall call His name JESUS: for He shall save His people from their sins. Now all this was done, that it might be fulfilled which was spoken of the Lord by the prophet, saying, Behold, a virgin shall be with child, and shall bring forth a Son, and they shall call His name Immanuel, which being interpreted is, God with us.

H	M	G	O	D	W	I	T	H	U	S	H	P	A	X
Z	U	F	S	J	U	S	T	M	A	N	W	A	F	O
P	B	S	Q	G	M	Y	Q	P	D	Z	M	O	T	X
D	O	W	B	W	R	P	H	R	Z	V	P	B	X	E
I	Z	W	Z	A	I	G	G	I	G	P	T	K	J	N
K	A	G	Q	I	N	F	D	V	G	C	H	N	U	G
F	Z	R	H	R	N	D	E	A	K	T	W	B	F	A
I	N	T	E	R	P	R	E	T	E	D	I	I	B	G
J	U	H	V	S	T	B	O	E	F	H	T	D	H	E
N	Z	X	A	P	E	X	Y	L	F	A	H	D	O	D
V	B	A	I	R	S	S	O	Y	I	L	C	E	L	O
P	U	B	L	I	C	J	E	W	R	F	H	N	Y	X
R	A	W	P	J	O	F	B	H	S	H	I	Y	G	D
O	I	M	M	A	N	U	E	L	T	S	L	R	H	J
P	H	Z	N	E	J	S	W	L	B	Q	D	N	O	S
H	D	M	W	D	X	N	Y	E	O	E	K	V	S	G
E	L	P	J	W	P	A	L	Y	R	K	S	T	T	K
T	J	E	S	U	S	U	M	K	N	V	J	I	G	Z
P	U	T	A	W	A	Y	X	P	I	T	J	Q	P	G
G	O	H	M	S	O	N	Z	M	L	J	V	O	D	H
A	A	E	L	J	A	J	H	D	R	E	A	M	S	C
M	O	T	H	E	R	D	E	Y	R	Z	J	M	X	M

MOTHER
ENGAGED
WITH CHILD
HUSBAND
WIFE
JUST MAN
PUBLIC
EXAMPLE
PUT AWAY
PRIVATELY
DREAM
HOLY GHOST
JESUS
IMMANUEL
INTERPRETED
GOD WITH US
PROPHET
BIDDEN
FIRSTBORN SON

13. MARY'S COUSIN ELIZABETH: LUKE 1:5–25

There was in the days of Herod, the king of Judaea, a certain priest named Zechariah,...his wife was of the daughters of Aaron, and her name was Elisabeth. And they were both righteous before God, walking in all the commandments and ordinances of the Lord blameless. And they had no child, because that Elisabeth was barren, and they both were now well stricken in years.

And it came to pass, that while he executed the priest's office before God in the order of his course.... And there appeared to him an angel of the Lord standing on the right side of the altar of incense. And when Zechariah saw him, he was troubled, and fear fell upon him. But the angel said to him, Fear not, Zechariah: for your prayer is heard; and your wife Elisabeth shall bear you a son, and you shall call his name John. And you shall have joy and gladness; and many shall rejoice at his birth. For he shall be great in the sight of the Lord, and shall drink neither wine nor strong drink; and he shall be filled with the Holy Ghost, even from his mother's womb. And many of the children of Israel shall he turn to the Lord their God. And he shall go before Him in the spirit and power of Elijah, to turn the hearts of the fathers to the children, and the disobedient to the wisdom of the just; to make ready a people prepared for the Lord.

And Zechariah said to the angel, Whereby shall I know this? for I am an old man, and my wife well stricken in years. And the angel answering said to him, I am Gabriel, that stand in the presence of God; and am sent to speak to you, and to show you these glad tidings. And, behold, you shall be dumb, and not able to speak, until the day that these things shall be performed, because you believe not my words, which shall be fulfilled in their season. And the people waited for Zechariah, and marveled that he tarried so long in the temple. And when he came out, he could not speak to them: and they perceived that he had seen a vision in the temple: for he beckoned to them, and remained speechless. And it came to pass, that, as soon as the days of his ministration were accomplished, he departed to his own house.

And after those days his wife Elisabeth conceived, and hid herself five months, saying, Thus has the Lord dealt with me in the days wherein He looked on me, to take away my reproach among men.

Q	Z	X	S	S	Z	U	A	X	N	A	J	U	D	A	E	A	C	O	P
W	Y	S	O	R	D	I	N	A	N	C	E	S	P	F	J	X	H	T	E
N	E	B	U	F	F	V	Q	L	N	T	Z	L	R	E	K	M	Y	E	O
G	E	L	I	J	A	H	B	F	V	S	M	X	I	A	N	U	D	M	M
W	B	L	A	M	E	L	E	S	S	T	D	E	E	R	O	L	B	P	E
T	G	L	A	D	N	E	S	S	H	R	A	V	S	N	J	T	I	L	G
J	M	G	H	W	C	Z	V	E	I	O	C	N	T	O	J	I	X	E	B
Y	U	M	F	L	I	K	Y	Y	I	N	T	L	S	T	O	T	V	D	V
O	R	N	L	K	B	N	K	M	B	G	N	V	O	B	H	U	Y	H	L
J	O	Y	G	Q	N	X	E	K	P	D	P	S	F	C	N	D	W	M	O
Z	T	T	F	A	C	X	N	H	J	R	L	P	F	Y	K	E	V	J	F
M	T	R	O	U	B	L	E	D	F	I	U	X	I	Q	X	R	G	L	K
J	S	A	A	R	O	N	N	X	A	N	W	D	C	H	A	V	G	N	Y
Y	H	S	K	H	T	P	T	Q	F	K	T	M	E	E	A	S	M	A	V
L	Z	E	C	H	A	R	I	A	H	F	H	Z	P	J	X	I	R	Q	A
S	W	J	G	P	V	H	E	R	O	D	K	N	P	F	R	F	J	V	T
X	N	Z	N	S	E	G	F	C	L	J	I	Y	R	P	F	N	P	F	C
V	P	B	V	W	F	L	P	M	C	C	P	Q	K	P	H	D	F	R	Y
M	W	V	A	H	U	O	C	O	M	M	A	N	D	M	E	N	T	S	P
K	N	S	P	E	E	C	H	L	E	S	S	I	N	C	E	N	S	E	P

HEROD	JUDAEA	ZECHARIAH	AARON	COMMANDMENTS
ORDINANCES	BLAMELESS	PRIEST'S OFFICE	INCENSE	TEMPLE
MULTITUDE	TROUBLED	FEAR NOT	JOHN	JOY
GLADNESS	WINE	STRONG DRINK	ELIJAH	SPEECHLESS

14. THE SONG OF MARY: LUKE 1:39–56

And Mary…entered into the house of Zechariah, and saluted Elisabeth….When Elisabeth heard the salutation of Mary, the babe leaped in her womb; and Elisabeth was filled with the Holy Ghost: and…said, Blessed are you among women, and blessed is the fruit of your womb. And what is this to me, that the mother of my Lord should come to me? For, lo, as soon as the voice of your salutation sounded in my ears, the babe leaped in my womb for joy. And blessed is she that believed: for there shall be a performance of those things which were told her from the Lord.

And Mary said, My soul does magnify the Lord. And my spirit has rejoiced in God my Savior. For He has regarded the low estate of His handmaiden: for, behold, from hereafter all generations shall call me blessed. For He that is mighty has done to me great things; and holy is His name. And His mercy is on them that fear Him from generation to generation. He has showed strength with His arm; He has scattered the proud in the imagination of their hearts. He has put down the mighty from their seats, and exalted them of low degree. He has filled the hungry with good things; and the rich He has sent empty away. He has helped His servant Israel, in remembrance of His mercy; as He spoke to our fathers, to Abraham, and to His seed for ever.

R	F	X	W	C	I	Z	P	I	B	C	J	Q	Z	E	V	P	Y	T	D
X	E	I	M	P	N	P	S	N	N	A	C	F	F	X	Z	J	A	F	L
X	Y	J	L	P	D	W	B	Q	H	F	B	W	U	A	C	P	X	Z	W
S	H	W	O	L	R	U	K	U	S	L	K	E	A	L	S	N	C	E	U
A	O	P	P	I	E	O	S	X	P	O	H	R	J	T	N	F	M	H	G
L	L	P	Z	G	S	D	U	H	G	W	K	A	U	E	L	O	M	V	R
U	Y	B	M	G	M	E	E	D	D	E	O	Q	W	D	E	R	Y	Q	E
T	G	G	R	A	F	M	S	F	A	S	N	T	P	L	A	E	O	Q	A
A	H	E	I	G	G	K	U	L	Q	T	J	E	R	R	P	V	K	M	T
T	O	D	D	H	T	N	N	A	S	A	R	W	R	Q	E	E	M	I	T
I	S	L	A	E	Z	G	I	P	M	T	O	O	V	A	D	R	H	G	H
O	T	R	O	O	N	E	R	F	J	E	Y	D	H	B	T	Y	U	H	I
N	U	M	Y	N	Q	M	V	E	Y	M	E	R	C	Y	Y	I	W	T	N
F	E	A	R	S	C	A	T	T	E	R	E	D	L	V	V	J	O	Y	G
K	L	Q	H	B	U	C	P	E	R	F	O	R	M	A	N	C	E	N	S
O	G	H	M	T	S	T	R	E	N	G	T	H	C	I	W	G	O	Q	O
M	Y	H	A	I	S	M	E	Q	U	R	E	J	O	I	C	E	D	H	E
N	J	G	P	M	Q	O	F	I	Y	G	Q	A	Q	A	R	M	W	V	K

BABE
FILLED
PERFORMANCE
REJOICED
MIGHTY
GREAT THINGS
GENERATION
ARM
PROUD
SALUTATION
LEAPED
HOLY GHOST
MAGNIFY
LOW ESTATE
MERCY
FEAR
STRENGTH
SCATTERED
EXALTED
FOREVER

15. SIMEON AND ANNA: LUKE 2:21–38

His name was called JESUS, which was so named of the angel before He was conceived in the womb. And... [his parents] brought Him to Jerusalem, to present *Him* to the Lord;...And, behold, there was a man in Jerusalem, whose name *was* Simeon.... And it was revealed to him by the Holy Ghost, that he should not see death, before he had seen the Lord's Christ. And he came by the Spirit into the temple: and when the parents brought in the child Jesus, to do for Him after the custom of the law, then took he Him up in his arms, and blessed God, and said, Lord, now let You Your servant depart in peace, according to Your word: for my eyes have seen Your salvation, which You have prepared before the face of all people; a light to lighten the Gentiles, and the glory of your people Israel....

And Simeon blessed them, and said to Mary His mother, Behold, this *Child* is set for the fall and rising again of many in Israel; and for a sign which shall be spoken against; (yea, a sword shall pierce through your own soul also,) that the thoughts of many hearts may be revealed.

And there was one Anna, a prophetess, the daughter of Phanuel, of the tribe of Aser: she was of a great age, and had lived with a husband seven years from her virginity; and she *was* a widow of about fourscore and four years, which departed not from the temple, but served *God* with fastings and prayers night and day. And she coming in that instant gave thanks likewise to the Lord, and spoke of Him to all them that looked for redemption in Jerusalem.

C	P	R	E	P	A	R	E	D	M	P	Z	P	O	P	P	S	V	S	W
C	P	O	Z	M	G	Y	Y	O	N	V	L	R	J	B	U	I	M	E	A
R	R	J	Q	B	P	F	O	T	P	D	P	E	S	O	R	M	T	I	K
P	O	N	S	A	L	V	A	T	I	O	N	S	R	J	I	E	T	G	S
I	P	O	J	C	G	S	C	I	Z	A	B	E	R	F	F	O	D	H	A
M	H	J	S	U	L	N	Z	M	M	V	D	N	F	T	I	N	P	T	C
M	E	Z	B	S	O	V	Q	H	B	V	M	T	I	S	C	G	R	I	R
U	T	O	J	T	R	E	D	E	M	P	T	I	O	N	A	C	E	J	I
V	E	S	Y	O	Y	J	Z	P	E	A	C	E	J	H	T	H	V	B	F
Y	S	X	E	M	H	E	W	X	D	A	N	N	A	H	I	R	E	S	I
C	S	D	F	R	S	G	C	T	H	A	N	K	S	I	O	I	A	M	C
L	I	G	H	T	V	K	L	O	L	P	S	B	Q	Y	N	S	L	S	E
Y	K	A	Y	Z	I	E	J	E	R	U	S	A	L	E	M	T	E	P	C
I	F	M	D	Z	A	N	D	P	Z	W	V	C	V	T	V	A	D	T	Y
Z	T	U	R	T	L	E	D	O	V	E	S	M	U	O	Z	P	T	W	J

EIGHT
PRESENT
SIMEON
ANNA
CUSTOM
PEACE
GLORY
LIGHT
THANKS
SERVED
PURIFICATION
JERUSALEM
SACRIFICE
TURTLEDOVES
CHRIST
PROPHETESS
PREPARED
REDEMPTION
REVEALED
SALVATION

16. MARY PONDERED THESE THINGS: LUKE 2:8–20

Jesus fulfilled prophecy in every aspect of His life. The song "Mary Did You Know?" asks if Mary understood the implications of giving birth to the Messiah.[1] *We do know "Mary kept all these things, and pondered them in her heart" (Luke 2:19).*

And there were in the same country shepherds abiding in the field, keeping watch over their flock by night. And, lo, the angel of the Lord came upon them, and the glory of the Lord shone round about them: and they were sore afraid. And the angel said to them, Fear not: for, behold, I bring you good tidings of great joy, which shall be to all people. For to you is born this day in the city of David a Savior, which is Christ the Lord. And this shall be a sign to you; You shall find the babe wrapped in swaddling clothes, lying in a manger. And suddenly there was with the angel a multitude of the heavenly host praising God, and saying Glory to God in the highest, and on earth peace, good will toward men....

The shepherds said one to another, Let us now go even to Bethlehem, and see this thing which is come to pass, which the Lord has made known to us. And they came with haste, and found Mary, and Joseph, and the babe lying in a manger. And when they had seen it, they made known abroad the saying which was told them concerning this Child. And all they that heard it wondered at those things which were told them by the shepherds. But Mary kept all these things, and pondered them in her heart. And the shepherds returned, glorifying and praising God.

M	X	H	S	G	I	M	W	H	D	O	D	G	Y	V	F
W	U	Q	E	W	L	G	P	T	M	W	C	R	G	O	K
G	V	L	S	A	A	O	U	D	C	H	E	E	Z	D	E
T	O	Q	T	F	V	D	R	G	D	B	E	A	L	Y	E
G	B	O	B	I	L	E	D	I	Q	Y	S	T	T	P	P
Z	P	T	D	E	T	O	N	L	F	W	V	J	H	O	I
M	A	T	H	T	T	U	C	L	I	Y	E	O	E	N	N
I	A	B	A	I	I	H	D	K	Y	N	I	Y	D	D	G
S	Q	N	I	E	S	D	L	E	H	H	G	N	W	E	W
E	C	I	G	D	W	C	I	E	W	J	O	Z	G	R	A
F	S	T	D	E	I	Z	H	N	H	L	D	S	T	E	T
B	B	R	P	D	R	N	N	I	G	E	J	Z	T	D	C
U	L	Z	U	M	W	P	G	L	L	S	M	L	C	H	H
R	O	U	N	D	A	B	O	U	T	D	J	P	E	I	W
N	L	S	J	U	H	E	G	O	O	D	W	I	L	L	R
S	H	O	N	E	S	O	R	E	A	F	R	A	I	D	W
B	T	X	S	H	E	P	H	E	R	D	S	L	D	Z	M
B	A	B	E	F	G	L	O	R	Y	T	O	G	O	D	M

SHEPHERDS	ABIDING
KEEPING WATCH	GOOD TIDINGS
SHONE	ROUND ABOUT
SORE AFRAID	FLOCK
GREAT JOY	GOOD WILL
SWADDLING	MANGER
MULTITIDE	BETHLEHEM
GLORY TO GOD	HEAVENLY HOST
BABE	THIS CHILD
PONDERED	GLORIFYING

1. Michael English, "Mary, Did You Know?", on *Michael English* (Curb Records, 1991).

17. MARY IN JESUS'S MINISTRY: JOHN 2:1–11

There was a marriage in Cana of Galilee; and the mother of Jesus was there: and both Jesus was called, and His disciples, to the marriage. And when they wanted wine, the mother of Jesus said to Him, They have no wine. Jesus said to her, Woman, what have I to do with you? My hour is not yet come. His mother said to the servants, Whatsoever He says to you, do it. And there were set there six water-pots of stone, after the manner of the purifying of the Jews, containing two or three firkins apiece. Jesus said to them, Fill the water-pots with water. And they filled them up to the brim. And He said to them, Draw out now, and bear to the governor of the feast. And they bore it. When the ruler of the feast had tasted the water that was made wine, and knew not where it was: (but the servants which drew the water knew;) the governor of the feast called the bridegroom, and said to him, Every man at the beginning does set forth good wine; and when men have well drunk, then that which is worse: but you have kept the good wine until now. This beginning of miracles did Jesus in Cana of Galilee, and manifested forth His glory; and His disciples believed on Him.

LUKE 8:19–21

Then came to Him His mother and His brethren, and could not come to Him for the press. And it was told Him by certain which said, Your mother and Your brethren stand outside, desiring to see You. And He answered and said to them, My mother and My brethren are these which hear the word of God, and do it.

JOHN 19:25–27

Now there stood by the cross of Jesus His mother, and His mother's sister, Mary the wife of Cleophas, and Mary Magdalene. When Jesus therefore saw His mother, and the disciple standing by, whom He loved, He said to His mother, Woman, behold your son! Then said He to the disciple, Behold your mother! And from that hour that disciple took her to his own home.

Q	C	T	C	N	D	Z	N	W	J	D	M	N	C	H	F	X	F	F	H
I	Q	K	O	F	S	P	R	A	A	R	E	S	I	P	M	F	M	E	Z
B	C	F	W	K	I	H	B	D	L	T	I	H	E	Q	I	B	W	A	E
I	B	N	Q	O	R	L	H	E	R	N	E	O	U	F	H	N	O	S	E
X	A	R	R	G	B	Q	L	I	G	A	R	R	I	A	B	T	R	T	T
M	G	H	C	K	H	R	M	E	P	I	Z	V	P	E	X	F	D	R	Z
K	I	A	R	N	U	W	I	H	D	B	N	V	L	O	O	D	O	S	A
O	Q	R	L	X	P	W	K	M	W	Z	D	N	J	X	T	I	F	P	L
X	M	C	A	I	U	O	S	V	L	V	T	E	I	G	Z	S	G	K	N
G	A	P	T	C	L	Z	B	L	P	K	H	Z	T	N	O	C	O	O	Q
I	R	K	A	Q	L	E	L	U	J	R	Q	G	E	B	G	I	D	O	I
T	Y	H	V	X	F	E	E	Q	V	Z	E	C	D	V	D	P	W	B	B
Z	H	K	U	N	P	M	A	N	I	F	E	S	T	E	D	L	T	R	E
X	E	X	E	Y	A	V	R	H	D	N	E	C	S	C	E	E	V	E	H
B	R	I	D	E	G	R	O	O	M	U	T	A	X	Z	Y	Q	Y	T	O
I	C	L	E	O	P	H	A	S	I	V	F	N	T	M	Z	J	A	H	L
N	M	A	R	R	I	A	G	E	P	C	P	A	A	D	N	E	M	R	D
E	M	D	M	N	D	B	R	D	M	R	O	L	Y	C	D	W	O	E	E
F	R	O	M	T	H	A	T	H	O	U	R	M	G	U	S	Y	A	N	Q
P	X	C	G	C	T	D	K	L	W	J	P	W	X	A	W	I	N	E	L

MARRIAGE
CANA
GALILEE
WINE
WATERPOTS
FILLED
BRIM
FEAST
BRIDEGROOM
MIRACLE
BRETHREN
WORD OF GOD
BEHOLD
CLEOPHAS
FROM THAT HOUR
MARY
MANIFESTED
DISCIPLE
PRESS
BEGINNING

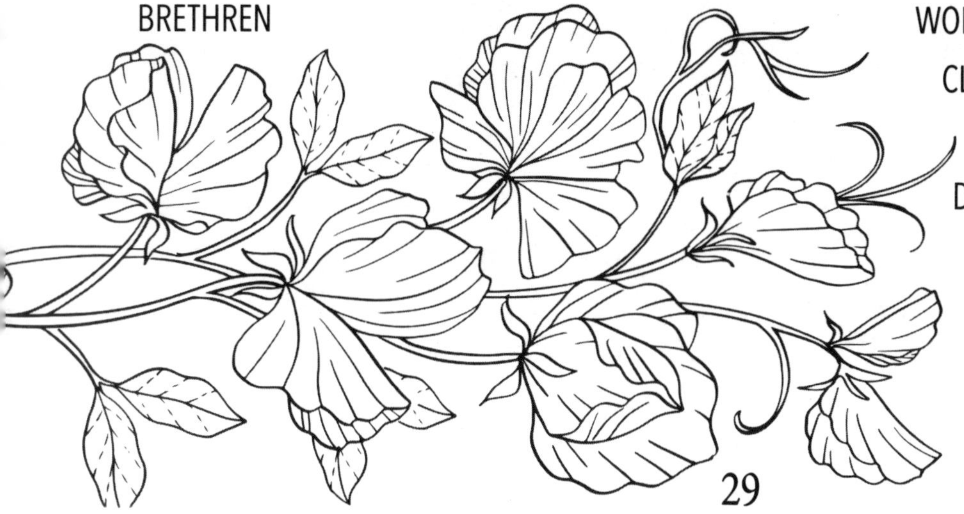

18. EVE: THE CREATION OF MAN AND WOMAN: GENESIS 2:1–24

Thus the heavens and the earth were finished, and all the host of them. And on the seventh day God ended His work which He had made; and He rested on the seventh day from all His work which He had made. And God blessed the seventh day, and sanctified it: because that in it He had rested from all His work which God created and made....

And the Lord God formed man of the dust of the ground, and breathed into his nostrils the breath of life; and man became a living soul. And the Lord God planted a garden eastward in Eden; and there He put the man whom He had formed. And out of the ground made the Lord God to grow every tree that is pleasant to the sight, and good for food; the tree of life also in the midst of the garden, and the tree of knowledge of good and evil. And a river went out of Eden to water the garden; and from there it was parted, and became into four heads....

And the Lord God took the man, and put him into the garden of Eden to dress it and to keep it. And the Lord God commanded the man, saying, Of every tree of the garden you may freely eat: but of the tree of the knowledge of good and evil, you shall not eat of it: for in the day that you eat thereof you shall surely die. And the Lord God said, It is not good that the man should be alone; I will make him a help meet for him. And out of the ground the Lord God formed every beast of the field, and every fowl of the air; and brought them to Adam to see what he would call them: and whatsoever Adam called every living creature, that was the name thereof. And Adam gave names to all cattle, and to the fowl of the air, and to every beast of the field; but for Adam there was not found a help meet for him.

And the Lord God caused a deep sleep to fall upon Adam, and he slept: and He took one of his ribs, and closed up the flesh instead thereof; and the rib, which the Lord God had taken from man, made He a woman, and brought her to the man. And Adam said, This is now bone of my bones, and flesh of my flesh: she shall be called Woman, because she was taken out of Man. Therefore shall a man leave his father and his mother, and shall cling to his wife: and they shall be one flesh.

O	Z	L	I	N	H	I	R	W	J	U	Y	K	B	S	H	I	Y	I	Y
C	N	O	S	A	D	W	E	G	C	D	U	S	E	C	C	U	W	Z	A
Q	Y	Z	R	M	U	O	S	A	L	N	R	C	X	S	D	R	Y	O	V
B	S	P	V	E	W	S	T	R	A	I	U	C	I	J	Y	I	B	N	J
G	Q	K	P	S	Q	E	E	D	E	T	V	V	C	H	U	B	O	O	P
J	T	I	L	L	G	V	D	E	O	F	L	I	V	I	B	I	N	S	L
D	F	U	O	Q	G	E	E	N	O	T	Q	H	N	K	O	F	E	T	O
E	P	O	F	J	C	N	H	O	I	Y	P	N	B	G	C	W	A	R	N
E	B	N	R	A	H	T	V	F	A	X	H	C	G	L	S	T	E	I	Q
P	A	T	S	J	B	H	A	E	R	L	P	Q	X	S	D	O	R	L	H
S	P	T	W	R	A	D	M	D	B	G	O	L	S	X	K	C	U	S	E
L	V	N	E	J	H	A	I	E	L	G	W	N	A	L	S	I	H	L	L
E	A	V	J	N	I	Y	A	N	D	V	P	W	E	N	C	V	L	Y	P
E	A	Y	C	L	I	N	G	S	F	W	B	D	A	H	T	J	L	Z	M
P	N	Z	N	C	R	E	A	T	U	R	E	S	W	E	F	E	X	E	E
E	B	G	Q	W	T	I	N	E	I	S	C	J	F	L	E	S	H	K	E
Z	H	E	A	V	E	N	S	A	N	D	E	A	R	T	H	F	N	W	T
G	A	B	R	E	A	T	H	O	F	L	I	F	E	U	L	V	J	G	L
D	U	S	T	O	F	T	H	E	G	R	O	U	N	D	E	I	I	X	P
H	V	P	G	O	O	Q	C	H	E	R	B	G	R	B	E	B	Q	H	O

HEAVENS AND EARTH	HERB	BREATH OF LIFE	NAMES	FLESH
RESTED	TILL	LIVING SOUL	HELP MEET	RIB
SEVENTH DAY	NOSTRILS	GARDEN OF EDEN	CREATURES	BONE
PLANT	DUST OF THE GROUND	ALONE	DEEP SLEEP	CLING

19. THE TEMPTATION AND FALL OF MANKIND: GENESIS 3:1–20

Now the serpent was more subtle than any beast of the field which the LORD God had made. And he said to the woman, Yea, has God said, You shall not eat of every tree of the garden? And the woman said to the serpent, We may eat of the fruit of the trees of the garden: but of the fruit of the tree which is in the midst of the garden, God has said You shall not eat of it, neither shall you touch it, lest you die. And the serpent said to the woman, You shall not surely die: for God does know that in the day you eat thereof, then your eyes shall be opened, and you shall be as gods, knowing good and evil.

And when the woman saw that the tree was good for food, and that it was pleasant to the eyes, and a tree to be desired to make one wise, she took of the fruit thereof, and did eat, and gave also to her husband with her and he did eat. And the eyes of them both were opened, and they knew that they were naked; and they sewed fig leaves together, and made themselves aprons. And they heard the voice of the LORD God walking in the garden in the cool of the day: and Adam and his wife hid themselves from the presence of the LORD God among the trees of the garden. And the LORD God called to Adam, and said to him, Where are you? And he said, I heard your voice in the garden, and I was afraid, because I was naked; and I hid myself.

And He said, Who told you that you were naked? Have you eaten of the tree, whereof I commanded you that you should not eat? And the man said, The woman whom You gave to be with me, she gave me of the tree, and I did eat. And the LORD God said to the woman, What is this that you have done? And the woman said, The serpent beguiled me, and I did eat....

To the woman He said, I will greatly multiply your sorrow and your conception; in sorrow you shall bring forth children; and your desire shall be to your husband, and he shall rule over you. And to Adam He said, Because you have hearkened to the voice of your wife, and have eaten of the tree, of which I commanded you, saying, You shall not eat of it: cursed is the ground for your sake; in sorrow shall you eat of it all the days of your life; thorns also and thistles shall it bring forth to you; and you shall eat the herb of the field; in the sweat of your face shall you eat bread, till you return to the ground; for out of it were you taken: for dust you are, and to dust shall you return. And Adam called his wife's name Eve; because she was the mother of all living.

B	Y	S	N	W	G	A	R	D	E	N	B	J	D	U	L	G	R	I	B
H	N	T	Q	S	F	W	B	V	F	B	N	R	S	U	H	B	I	Q	E
C	E	D	F	C	Z	I	Z	S	Y	Q	Y	U	U	B	S	P	J	V	L
I	H	E	O	R	D	P	G	N	U	C	I	M	Q	I	N	T	G	A	L
B	Y	L	L	A	E	Y	Q	L	D	B	I	B	G	M	S	J	W	R	Y
D	D	C	I	W	S	W	P	L	E	R	T	L	T	K	T	E	V	R	M
B	M	P	R	L	I	U	U	L	R	A	I	L	M	C	F	G	O	F	K
N	F	A	H	Q	R	T	B	D	E	F	V	E	E	Y	R	D	I	S	D
A	S	J	Z	S	E	V	X	X	N	A	F	E	M	O	U	I	C	U	E
M	S	T	S	Z	D	U	A	A	P	Y	S	D	S	J	I	A	E	L	J
A	F	N	G	U	H	T	W	C	B	I	B	A	B	R	T	Q	O	M	X
P	X	S	G	R	R	W	I	S	E	T	L	Q	N	B	H	E	F	V	F
R	I	Y	O	U	T	E	D	N	X	A	E	C	H	T	N	C	G	B	O
O	P	I	Y	R	K	C	L	F	E	J	T	A	W	M	I	H	O	E	V
N	A	E	C	V	R	S	H	Y	N	K	G	B	C	T	S	V	D	A	V
S	M	S	G	Z	Y	O	U	L	D	O	K	T	M	E	S	G	C	S	G
A	B	U	D	J	V	T	W	D	V	I	R	K	M	B	L	R	U	T	B
P	Q	W	G	F	W	D	O	L	T	W	E	I	G	R	O	U	N	D	Z
N	M	U	L	T	I	P	L	Y	U	D	W	Y	Q	P	J	B	A	X	W
R	R	Y	Y	Z	I	S	E	R	P	E	N	T	D	D	Y	N	S	N	R

SERPENT	SUBTLE	BEAST	FRUIT	GARDEN
SURELY DIE	PLEASANT	DESIRED	WISE	FIG LEAVES
APRONS	VOICE OF GOD	CRAWL	BELLY	BRUISE
HEEL	MULTIPLY	SORROW	GROUND	DUST

20. SARAH GETS A NEW NAME: GENESIS 17:1–6, 16–22

When Abram was ninety years old and nine, the LORD appeared to Abram, and said to him, I am the Almighty God; walk before Me, and be you perfect. And I will make My covenant between Me and you, and will multiply you exceedingly...and you shall be a father of many nations. Neither shall your name any more be called Abram, but your name shall be Abraham; for a father of many nations have I made you. And I will make you exceeding fruitful, and I will make nations of you...

As for Sarai your wife, you shall not call her name Sarai, but Sarah shall her name be. And I will bless her, and give you a son also of her: yea, I will bless her, and she shall be a mother of nations; kings of people shall be of her. Then Abraham fell upon his face, and laughed, and said in his heart, Shall a child be born to him that is a hundred years old? and shall Sarah, that is ninety years old, bear?...

And God said, Sarah your wife shall bear you a son indeed; and you shall call his name Isaac: and I will establish My covenant with him for an everlasting covenant, and with his seed after him....My covenant will I establish with Isaac, which Sarah shall bear to you at this set time in the next year.

T	F	A	T	H	E	R	O	F	N	A	T	I	O	N	S	H	Y
E	O	E	D	T	K	I	E	S	T	A	B	L	I	S	H	F	A
V	L	X	I	N	A	P	F	A	Z	X	F	C	X	F	A	R	D
E	C	C	D	N	L	L	H	L	B	W	E	N	T	U	P	U	K
R	O	E	N	H	E	G	K	E	A	R	N	B	H	U	M	I	T
L	V	E	I	S	U	X	M	I	B	U	A	E	W	T	Z	T	M
A	E	D	N	Z	A	N	T	J	N	R	G	M	L	T	T	F	U
S	N	I	E	W	C	R	D	Y	Z	G	A	H	D	K	M	U	L
T	A	N	T	Z	V	M	A	R	E	O	D	R	E	H	P	L	T
I	N	G	Y	B	E	A	R	I	E	A	J	B	Z	D	L	W	I
N	T	L	L	F	X	R	B	I	J	D	R	Y	R	S	Y	X	P
G	L	Y	I	S	A	A	C	E	P	I	S	H	M	A	E	L	L
U	A	L	M	I	G	H	T	Y	T	W	E	L	V	E	A	R	Y

ABRAM	SARAI	LAUGHED	BEAR	EVERLASTING
NINETY	ALMIGHTY	ISHMAEL	TALKING	ISAAC
MULTIPLY	EXCEEDINGLY	COVENANT	HUNDRED	NEXT YEAR
FATHER OF NATIONS	FRUITFUL	TWELVE	ESTABLISH	WENT UP

21. SARAH LAUGHS: GENESIS 18:1–15; 21:1–7

And the Lord appeared to him [Abraham] in the plains of Mamre: and he sat in the tent door in the heat of the day; and he lifted up his eyes and looked, and, lo, three men stood by him....And Abraham hastened into the tent to Sarah, and said, Make ready quickly three measures of fine meal, knead it, and make cakes upon the hearth. And Abraham ran to the herd, and brought a calf tender and good, and gave it to a young man; and he hasted to dress it. And he took butter, and milk, and the calf which he had dressed, and set it before them; and he stood by them under the tree, and they did eat.

And they said to him, Where is Sarah your wife? And he said, Behold, in the tent. And he said, I will certainly return to you according to the time of life; and, lo, Sarah your wife shall have a son.

And Sarah heard it in the tent door, which was behind him. Now Abraham and Sarah were old and well stricken in age; and it ceased to be with Sarah after the manner of women. Therefore Sarah laughed within herself, saying, After I am waxed old shall I have pleasure, my lord being old also?

And the Lord said to Abraham, Wherefore did Sarah laugh, saying, Shall I of a surety bear a child, which am old? Is any thing too hard for the Lord? At the time appointed I will return to you, according to the time of life, and Sarah shall have a son. Then Sarah denied, saying, I laughed not; for she was afraid. And He said, Nay; but you did laugh…

And the Lord visited Sarah as He had said, and the Lord did to Sarah as He had spoken. For Sarah conceived, and bore Abraham a son in his old age, at the set time of which God had spoken to him. And Abraham called the name of his son that was born to him, whom Sarah bore to him, Isaac. And Abraham circumcised his son Isaac being eight days old, as God had commanded him. And Abraham was a hundred years old, when his son Isaac was born to him. And Sarah said, God has made me to laugh, so that all that hear will laugh with me. And she said, Who would have said to Abraham, that Sarah should have given children suck? for I have born him a son in his old age.

Y	G	A	V	Y	S	U	R	E	T	Y	U	U	W	U	D	H	M	N	U
Q	D	A	C	A	K	E	S	B	Z	Q	G	G	U	A	L	P	A	C	L
W	U	H	U	T	K	T	M	E	A	S	U	R	E	S	A	L	P	O	A
T	I	J	Y	O	M	R	R	L	B	U	H	S	J	Q	C	E	B	M	U
N	B	O	F	O	C	O	N	C	E	I	V	E	D	X	R	A	S	M	G
D	D	M	F	A	U	B	E	A	R	A	S	O	N	F	F	S	I	A	H
X	E	U	P	A	Y	J	M	F	O	W	D	L	F	E	P	U	T	N	X
V	Q	O	S	O	V	D	H	Y	Z	J	E	Y	D	Y	T	R	I	D	X
G	V	M	Y	W	N	O	T	K	W	A	G	K	S	Q	G	E	M	E	L
F	Q	O	U	G	A	A	R	T	A	A	K	A	F	I	G	P	E	D	Q
R	P	Z	A	J	R	F	D	T	X	Q	L	N	Z	H	U	J	O	O	V
N	B	S	I	T	V	Y	Z	M	E	I	G	L	E	D	L	D	F	H	I
X	G	Z	T	A	E	F	P	X	D	A	F	R	G	A	N	K	L	B	S
M	T	N	L	R	K	N	R	C	O	H	E	P	B	V	D	J	I	U	L
W	M	H	N	M	I	Q	T	D	L	W	T	D	H	M	X	T	F	T	M
D	A	I	R	D	Q	C	T	D	D	K	X	U	F	S	C	M	E	T	D
K	M	A	P	E	G	Z	K	V	O	W	P	U	S	O	A	W	D	E	W
M	R	S	U	Q	E	B	R	E	G	O	Q	M	E	V	L	M	E	R	X
Q	E	Y	E	R	D	Y	W	S	N	L	R	C	Q	N	F	A	V	A	W
U	R	O	L	D	Y	Y	H	E	A	T	O	F	D	A	Y	L	T	R	U

MAMRE	TENT DOOR	HEAT OF DAY	PLEASURE	BUTTER
MEASURES	KNEAD	CAKES	SURETY	THREE
STRICKEN	OLD	TIME OF LIFE	WAXED OLD	FAVOR
CONCEIVED	BEAR A SON	COMMANDED	LAUGH	CALF

22. HAGAR AND ISHMAEL: GENESIS 16:1–16

Isaac was born to Sarah and Abraham when they were well advanced in years. It isn't surprising that they grew tired of waiting for God's timing and tried to take matters into their own hands. While Ishmael also became a father of nations, he was not the promised offspring.

Now Sarai Abram's wife bore him no children: and she had a handmaid, an Egyptian, whose name was Hagar. And Sarai said to Abram, Behold now, the LORD has restrained me from bearing: I pray you, go in to my maid; it may be that I may obtain children by her. And Abram hearkened to the voice of Sarai.

And Sarai Abram's wife took Hagar her maid the Egyptian, after Abram had dwelt ten years in the land of Canaan, and gave her to her husband Abram to be his wife. And he went in to Hagar, and she conceived: and when she saw that she had conceived, her mistress was despised in her eyes. And Sarai said to Abram, My wrong be upon you: I have given my maid into your bosom; and when she saw that she had conceived, I was despised in her eyes: the LORD judge between me and you. But Abram said to Sarai, Behold, your maid is in your hand; do to her as it pleases you. And when Sarai dealt hardly with her, she fled from her face.

And the angel of the LORD found her by a fountain of water in the wilderness, by the fountain in the way to Shur. And He said, Hagar, Sarai's maid, where came you? and where will you go? And she said, I flee from the face of my mistress Sarai. And the angel of the LORD said to her, Return to your mistress, and submit yourself under her hands. And the angel of the LORD said to her, I will multiply your seed exceedingly, that it shall not be numbered for multitude. And the angel of the LORD said to her, Behold, you are with child, and shall bear a son, and shall call his name Ishmael; because the LORD has heard your affliction. And he will be a wild man; his hand will be against every man, and every man's hand against him; and he shall dwell in the presence of all his brethren. And she called the name of the LORD that spoke to her, You God see me: for she said, Have I also here looked after Him that sees me?...

And Hagar bore Abram a son: and Abram called his son's name, which Hagar bore, Ishmael. And Abram was fourscore and six years old, when Hagar bore Ishmael to Abram.

H	F	O	V	K	M	L	D	C	A	N	A	A	N	W	I	L	D	C	Q
O	B	T	A	I	N	D	W	D	P	Q	C	L	A	C	Z	W	L	M	V
J	A	W	M	V	R	F	D	E	J	K	H	S	H	Y	R	U	M	F	F
M	W	Z	D	Q	Z	J	I	S	E	K	I	R	T	O	S	G	Z	C	Y
G	C	P	I	C	R	L	V	P	W	D	L	B	X	U	M	U	D	G	M
W	J	G	E	S	K	E	D	I	T	C	D	T	L	G	U	J	T	Z	I
H	C	L	C	Y	H	Q	J	S	M	D	R	S	B	O	L	D	D	X	S
V	A	B	I	V	K	M	T	E	L	S	E	T	J	D	T	E	O	Z	T
U	T	G	E	B	I	V	A	D	S	O	N	S	P	S	I	A	O	O	R
Y	Z	S	A	N	W	M	D	E	T	L	V	I	X	E	P	L	N	E	E
B	S	Y	V	R	X	Q	E	V	L	G	T	C	T	E	L	T	X	I	S
U	F	R	E	S	T	R	A	I	N	E	D	W	Z	M	Y	G	X	B	S
G	O	C	R	U	R	H	L	G	K	Z	O	H	J	E	D	G	F	V	S
J	U	R	Q	E	X	C	E	E	D	I	N	G	L	Y	X	F	E	M	E
Y	N	M	N	Z	B	E	K	O	W	W	I	C	W	H	Q	N	Z	P	E
T	T	X	P	W	W	Z	M	U	L	T	I	T	U	D	E	U	R	F	D
H	A	R	D	L	Y	R	C	B	O	E	G	Y	P	T	I	A	N	V	Y
J	I	G	L	F	O	H	B	E	A	F	F	L	I	C	T	I	O	N	H
Q	N	K	K	V	Z	Q	I	W	O	K	T	J	B	L	D	U	K	Y	V
Y	X	B	E	A	R	I	N	G	A	D	S	U	D	V	M	V	D	H	O

RESTRAINED	BEARING	OBTAIN	SEED	FOUNTAIN
CANAAN	DESPISED	DEALT	EXCEEDINGLY	EGYPTIAN
MISTRESS	MULTIPLY	ISHMAEL	CHILDREN	WILD
MULTITIUDE	YOU GOD SEE ME	HARDLY	AFFLICTION	HAGAR

23. THE LORD PROTECTS HAGAR: GENESIS 21:8–21

Sarah saw the son of Hagar the Egyptian, which she had born to Abraham, mocking [Isaac]. Wherefore she said to Abraham, Cast out this bondwoman and her son: for the son of this bondwoman shall not be heir with my son, even with Isaac....Abraham rose up early in the morning, and took bread, and a bottle of water, and gave it to Hagar, putting it on her shoulder, and the child, and sent her away: and she departed, and wandered in the wilderness of Beersheba. And the water was spent in the bottle, and she cast the child under one of the shrubs. And she went, and sat her down opposite him a good way off, as it were a bowshot: for she said, Let me not see the death of the child. And she sat opposite him, and lifted up her voice, and wept.

And God heard the voice of the lad; and the angel of God called to Hagar out of heaven, and said to her, What ails you, Hagar? fear not; for God has heard the voice of the lad where he is. Arise, lift up the lad, and hold him in your hand; for I will make him a great nation. And God opened her eyes, and she saw a well of water; and she went, and filled the bottle with water, and gave the lad drink. And God was with the lad; and he grew, and dwelt in the wilderness, and became an archer. And he dwelt in the wilderness of Paran: and his mother took him a wife out of the land of Egypt.

D	N	J	M	S	L	E	X	I	A	H	K	J	M	P	L	L	M
B	S	N	A	T	I	O	N	I	U	F	E	A	C	W	O	G	J
O	H	A	W	B	W	F	E	A	S	T	V	I	H	S	P	O	E
N	R	B	R	W	R	E	T	N	W	F	O	B	R	G	P	D	B
D	U	V	V	C	Y	E	A	I	T	J	I	O	X	R	O	H	O
W	B	M	F	L	H	A	A	N	K	Z	C	W	E	I	S	A	T
O	S	O	P	U	J	E	R	D	E	S	E	S	E	E	I	S	T
M	A	C	M	A	W	H	R	I	A	D	J	H	L	V	T	H	L
A	U	K	X	H	R	E	L	N	S	V	V	O	N	O	E	E	E
N	G	I	F	N	B	A	P	D	F	E	V	T	I	U	O	A	M
O	H	N	W	Q	Y	X	N	T	V	D	J	M	M	S	M	R	X
V	O	G	W	A	T	E	R	L	A	D	L	C	Y	D	B	D	X

FEAST	WEANED	BOTTLE	LAD	OPPOSITE
MOCKING	BONDWOMAN	WATER	WEPT	ARISE
HEIR	GRIEVOUS	SHRUBS	ARCHER	PARAN
NATION	BREAD	BOWSHOT	GOD HAS HEARD	VOICE

24. ABRAHAM AND KETURAH: GENESIS 25:1–6

Then again Abraham took a wife, and her name was Keturah. And she bore him Zimran, and Jokshan, and Medan, and Midian, and Ishbak, and Shuah. And Jokshan fathered Sheba, and Dedan. And the sons of Dedan were Asshurim, and Letushim, and Leummim. And the sons of Midian; Ephah, and Epher, and Hanoch, and Abidah, and Eldaah. All these were the children of Keturah. And Abraham gave all that he had to Isaac. But to the sons of the concubines, which Abraham had, Abraham gave gifts, and sent them away from Isaac his son, while he yet lived, eastward, to the east country.

K	X	I	Q	D	Z	M	K	M	B	G	V	N	Q	A	A	L	N
L	F	U	N	N	Z	F	E	L	R	Z	R	K	O	L	Q	H	O
D	U	Y	I	O	G	U	L	D	U	Y	V	S	P	A	O	A	V
X	W	P	R	Q	I	C	E	J	A	I	F	Y	A	B	F	N	P
V	S	D	D	S	V	S	Q	W	E	N	U	L	P	R	V	O	E
U	H	I	Z	K	G	X	H	Q	H	A	Y	Z	M	A	Z	C	Q
F	E	Y	R	Z	A	Y	N	B	G	L	S	N	S	H	K	H	R
C	B	D	B	I	S	L	F	M	A	L	V	T	H	A	R	U	E
N	A	Y	S	J	Y	I	L	H	P	K	Q	E	W	M	Z	P	Z
R	C	Z	V	Q	A	S	S	H	U	R	I	M	Y	A	A	R	S
B	U	O	I	T	F	K	Q	T	E	X	E	X	T	H	R	K	S
S	S	Q	N	M	C	K	X	Y	Z	H	S	J	K	F	P	D	G
G	H	M	I	C	R	X	M	A	L	D	A	I	J	H	N	O	F
Q	I	U	K	M	U	A	L	A	K	C	K	D	N	Q	Z	L	M
T	P	F	A	T	Y	B	N	F	I	X	J	D	G	O	C	H	I
A	S	Y	T	H	E	R	I	Q	D	J	B	D	E	D	A	N	D
U	E	B	T	S	H	V	E	N	G	Q	L	D	H	Q	S	S	I
J	B	X	D	J	Y	V	V	M	E	R	B	S	M	N	S	P	A
O	J	V	H	C	O	F	V	A	Q	S	B	V	A	W	S	R	N
K	E	A	S	T	C	O	U	N	T	R	Y	Y	M	B	D	C	M
S	Y	C	I	O	H	A	G	O	K	I	X	B	S	J	H	V	X
H	I	D	G	V	X	S	E	N	T	A	W	A	Y	V	J	L	W
A	V	N	Z	L	E	T	U	S	H	I	M	M	J	Q	A	M	D
N	B	Q	E	I	Z	X	K	E	T	U	R	A	H	N	P	S	J
J	G	Q	T	S	K	P	D	L	Y	I	S	A	A	C	J	I	Y

KETURAH
EASTWARD
JOKSHAN
SHEBA
SENT AWAY
ISAAC
ISHBAK
HANOCH
MIDIAN
ABRAHAM
SHUAH

ALL HE HAD
EAST COUNTRY
MEDAN
DEDAN
ZIMRAN
GIFTS
LETUSHIM
CONCUBINES
ASSHURIM

25. AND 26. REBEKAH: GOD'S BRIDE FOR ISAAC: GENESIS 24:1–67

And Abraham was old, and well stricken in age: and the Lord had blessed Abraham in all things. And Abraham said to his eldest servant of his house, that ruled over all that he had,...Go to my country, and to my kindred, and take a wife to my son Isaac.... The servant...swore to him concerning that matter...and he arose, and went to Mesopotamia, to the city of Nahor.

And he made his camels to kneel down outside the city by a well of water at the time of the evening, even the time that women go out to draw water. And he said, O Lord God of my master Abraham, I pray You, send me good speed this day, and show kindness to my master Abraham. Behold, I stand here by the well of water; and the daughters of the men of the city come out to draw water: and let it come to pass, that the damsel to whom I shall say, Let down your pitcher, I pray you, that I may drink; and she shall say, Drink, and I will give your camels drink also: let the same be she that You have appointed for your servant Isaac; and thereby shall I know that You have showed kindness to my master.

And it came to pass, before he had done speaking, that, behold, Rebekah came out, who was born to Bethuel, son of Milcah, the wife of Nahor, Abraham's brother, with her pitcher upon her shoulder. And the damsel was very fair to look upon, a virgin, neither had any man known her: and she went down to the well, and filled her pitcher, and came up. And the servant ran to meet her, and said, Let me, I pray you, drink a little water of your pitcher. And she said, Drink, my lord: and she hasted, and let down her pitcher upon her hand, and gave him drink. And when she had done giving him drink, she said, I will draw water for your camels also, until they have done drinking. And she hasted, and emptied her pitcher into the trough, and ran again to the well to draw water, and drew for all his camels. And the man wondering at her held his peace, to know whether the Lord had made his journey prosperous or not. And it came to pass, as the camels had done drinking, that the man took a golden earring of half a shekel weight, and two bracelets for her hands of ten shekels weight of gold; and said, Whose daughter are you? tell me, I pray you: is there room in your father's house for us to lodge in? And she said to him, I am the daughter of Bethuel the son of Milcah, which she bore to Nahor. She said moreover to him, We have both straw and provender enough, and room to lodge in.

And the man bowed down his head, and worshipped the Lord. And he said, Blessed be the Lord God of my master Abraham, who has not left destitute my master of His mercy and His truth: I being in the way, the Lord led me to the house of my master's brethren. And the damsel ran, and told them of her mother's house these things. And Rebekah had a brother, and his name was Laban: and Laban ran out to the man, to the well.... And he said, Come in, you blessed of the Lord; wherefore stand you outside? for I have prepared the house, and room for the camels. And the man came into the house: and he ungirded his camels, and gave straw and provender for the camels, and water to wash his feet, and the men's feet that were with him. And there was set meat before him to eat: but he said, I will not eat, until I have told my errand.... And now if you will deal kindly and truly with my master, tell me: and if not, tell me; that I may turn to the right hand, or to the left.

Then Laban and Bethuel answered and said, The thing proceeds from the Lord: we cannot speak to you bad or good. Behold, Rebekah is before you, take her, and go, and let her be your master's son's wife, as the

Lord has spoken. And it came to pass, that, when Abraham's servant heard their words, he worshipped the Lord, bowing himself to the earth. And the servant brought forth jewels of silver, and jewels of gold, and raiment, and gave them to Rebekah: he gave also to her brother and to her mother precious things. And they did eat and drink, he and the men that were with him, and tarried all night; and they rose up in the morning, and he said, Send me away to my master. And her brother and her mother said,...We will call the damsel, and inquire at her mouth. And they called Rebekah, and said to her, Will you go with this man? And she said, I will go....And they blessed Rebekah, and said to her, You are our sister, be you the mother of thousands of millions, and let your seed possess the gate of those which hate them. And Rebekah arose, and her damsels, and they rode upon the camels, and followed the man: and the servant took Rebekah, and went his way.

And Isaac came from the way of the well Lahairoi; for he dwelt in the south country. And Isaac went out to meditate in the field at the evening: and he lifted up his eyes, and saw, and, behold, the camels were coming. And Rebekah lifted up her eyes, and when she saw Isaac, she lighted off the camel. For she had said to the servant, What man is this that walks in the field to meet us? And the servant had said, It is my master: therefore she took a veil, and covered herself. And the servant told Isaac all things that he had done. And Isaac brought her into his mother Sarah's tent, and took Rebekah, and she became his wife; and he loved her: and Isaac was comforted after his mother's death.

B	Q	C	P	M	N	D	S	E	C	U	P	D	G	M	A	M	G
Q	L	S	H	I	E	C	L	X	P	Q	E	R	N	N	I	T	O
Y	P	E	B	H	T	S	A	A	X	B	A	I	E	X	W	O	D
W	N	R	S	J	D	C	O	M	T	B	C	N	X	B	K	Y	S
E	W	Y	O	S	F	R	H	P	E	R	E	K	R	Q	I	O	A
A	L	D	V	S	E	S	A	E	O	L	O	W	U	P	N	U	N
F	I	D	P	K	P	D	E	W	R	T	S	U	A	W	D	R	G
A	N	Z	E	J	D	E	R	R	W	F	A	L	G	R	R	S	E
I	A	I	F	S	H	F	R	V	V	A	U	M	B	H	E	E	L
R	H	G	G	O	T	B	W	O	Q	A	T	T	I	Q	D	E	B
Z	O	J	T	G	Q	M	V	S	U	A	N	E	H	A	K	D	E
N	R	O	J	O	U	R	N	E	Y	S	J	T	R	M	Z	J	O
L	D	A	M	S	E	L	P	Z	T	H	I	G	H	H	D	V	F

BLESSED	ELDEST	NAHOR	PEACE	DAMSEL
SERVANT	THIGH	CAMELS	PROSPEROUS	FAIR
KINDRED	BEWARE	PITCHER	MESOPOTAMIA	JOURNEY
TO YOUR SEED	GOD'S ANGEL	DRINK	DRAW WATER	TROUGH

N	Z	E	D	O	K	M	C	D	K	E	A	R	R	I	N	G	D
K	A	S	H	O	U	L	D	E	R	P	N	U	R	S	E	K	B
N	I	I	J	L	X	F	Z	Z	N	G	B	H	R	N	F	U	I
P	B	P	F	U	K	Y	O	S	H	X	R	Z	K	P	B	M	M
J	S	E	V	E	N	I	N	G	D	C	A	L	L	O	O	A	I
F	O	L	U	O	U	W	O	E	V	H	C	H	B	S	C	S	L
G	U	S	I	L	V	E	R	W	R	E	E	E	J	S	O	T	L
O	T	H	O	U	S	A	N	D	S	J	L	A	K	E	V	E	I
L	H	X	I	N	U	R	K	W	K	K	E	R	X	S	E	R	O
D	E	H	F	O	L	L	O	W	E	D	T	T	Q	S	R	K	N
L	A	H	A	I	R	O	I	C	O	M	F	O	R	T	E	D	S
A	L	I	F	T	E	D	H	I	S	E	Y	E	S	C	D	D	I
J	E	W	E	L	S	V	L	D	M	E	D	I	T	A	T	E	P

GOLD	NURSE	SHOULDER	HEART	EARRING
THOUSANDS	MILLIONS	LIFTED HIS EYES	JEWELS	BRACELET
POSSESS	LAHAIROI	MEDITATE	EVENING	SILVER
		SOUTH	COVERED	MASTER
			FOLLOWED	COMFORTED

27. ISAAC BLESSES JACOB: GENESIS 27:1–29

When Isaac was old, and his eyes were dim, so that he could not see, he called Esau his eldest son, and said to him,...Behold now, I am old, I know not the day of my death: now therefore take, I pray you, your weapons, your quiver and your bow, and go out to the field, and take me some venison; and make me savory meat, such as I love, and bring it to me, that I may eat; that my soul may bless you before I die.

And Rebekah heard when Isaac spoke to Esau his son. And Esau went to the field to hunt for venison, and to bring it. And Rebekah spoke to Jacob her son, saying, Behold, I heard your father speak to Esau your brother, saying, Bring me venison, and make me savory meat, that I may eat, and bless you before the LORD before my death. Now therefore, my son, obey my voice according to that which I command you. Go now to the flock, and bring me from there two good kids of the goats; and I will make them savory meat for your father, such as he loves: and you shall bring it to your father, that he may eat, and that he may bless you before his death.

And Jacob said to Rebekah his mother, Behold, Esau my brother is a hairy man, and I am a smooth man: my father perhaps will feel me, and I shall seem to him as a deceiver; and I shall bring a curse upon me, and not a blessing. And his mother said to him, Upon me be your curse, my son: only obey my voice, and go bring me them. And he went, and brought, and brought them to his mother: and his mother made savory meat, such as his father loved.

And Rebekah took goodly raiment of her eldest son Esau, which were with her in the house, and put them upon Jacob her younger son: and she put the skins of the kids of the goats upon his hands, and upon the smooth of his neck: and she gave the savory meat and the bread, which she had prepared, into the hand of her son Jacob.

And he came to his father, and said, My father: and he said, Here am I; who are you, my son? And Jacob said to his father, I am Esau your firstborn; I have done according as you bid me: arise, I pray you, sit and eat of my venison, that your soul may bless me...

And Isaac said to Jacob, Come near, I pray you, that I may feel you, my son, whether you be my very son Esau or not. And Jacob went near to Isaac his father; and he felt him, and said, The voice is Jacob's voice, but the hands are the hands of Esau. And he discerned him not, because his hands were hairy, as his brother Esau's hands: so he blessed him. And he said, Are you my very son Esau? And he said, I am. And he said, Bring it near to me, and I will eat of my son's venison, that my soul may bless you....And his father Isaac said to him, Come near now, and kiss me, my son. And he came near, and kissed him: and he smelled the smell of his raiment, and blessed him, and said, See, the smell of my son is as the smell of a field which the LORD has blessed: therefore God give you of the dew of heaven, and the fatness of the earth, and plenty of corn and wine: let people serve you, and nations bow down to you: be lord over your brethren, and let your mother's sons bow down to you: cursed be every one that curses you, and blessed be he that blesses you.

H	W	I	G	E	Q	U	I	V	E	R	O	B	E	Y	Y	W	P	C	F
Y	E	C	Y	U	V	Y	R	K	X	Z	T	W	W	A	R	H	B	I	A
M	W	N	B	B	L	E	S	S	E	S	L	D	K	H	A	C	C	P	T
C	R	Y	O	D	D	V	E	N	I	S	O	N	M	J	F	S	O	R	N
C	D	X	W	E	D	P	K	T	O	Z	J	P	G	V	N	J	R	E	E
J	A	Q	D	W	X	T	I	N	H	O	O	B	U	N	Z	K	N	P	S
K	D	C	O	O	K	Z	S	I	U	O	O	Y	B	H	H	T	A	A	S
W	A	C	W	F	C	U	S	K	N	N	Z	P	Z	J	R	O	N	R	O
M	T	B	N	H	S	X	M	N	P	M	H	I	J	H	C	V	D	E	F
Q	V	H	J	E	D	C	E	B	F	T	M	S	G	A	L	A	W	D	E
S	C	Y	A	A	I	Z	E	P	W	G	P	M	U	I	Z	S	I	H	A
E	E	F	Z	V	L	O	R	D	O	V	E	R	T	R	E	N	N	V	R
R	F	Q	Z	E	O	U	Q	Z	B	U	G	G	L	Y	Z	T	E	O	T
V	K	C	T	N	S	M	O	O	T	H	N	Y	Y	F	E	W	I	I	H
E	D	P	Q	B	G	Q	G	Y	A	S	Z	E	Y	W	U	Z	R	C	H
K	P	B	B	A	U	A	N	X	R	D	E	C	E	I	V	E	R	E	L
C	P	B	S	Z	S	Q	S	A	V	O	R	Y	Q	W	E	T	X	Q	F
O	X	Z	B	G	K	X	U	B	H	Q	V	J	E	K	D	J	R	C	G
F	C	R	U	R	A	V	X	S	Z	U	P	K	G	P	U	C	K	T	C
G	O	A	T	S	C	U	R	S	E	S	G	O	O	D	K	I	D	S	N

VENISON	GOATS	OBEY	CORN AND WINE	BLESSES
QUIVER	HAIRY	KISS ME	SERVE	LORD OVER
SAVORY	SMOOTH	DEW OF HEAVEN	BOW DOWN	VOICE
GOOD KIDS	DECEIVER	FATNESS OF EARTH	CURSES	PREPARED

28. "SHE IS MY SISTER": GENESIS 12:10–20

There are three times in the Bible when Abraham and Isaac tell their wives to say, "I am his sister" to avoid conflict with a ruler. Do they not trust God to provide? Do they not learn their lesson? Or does it seem easier to rely worldly wisdom, rather than faith?

Abram went down into Egypt to sojourn there; for the famine was grievous in the land. And it came to pass, when he was come near to enter into Egypt, that he said to Sarai his wife, Behold now, I know that you are a fair woman to look upon: therefore it shall come to pass, when the Egyptians shall see you, that they shall say, This is his wife: and they will kill me, but they will save you alive. Say, I pray you, you are my sister: that it may be well with me for your sake; and my soul shall live because of you. And it came to pass, that, when Abram was come into Egypt, the Egyptians beheld the woman that she was very fair. The princes also of Pharaoh saw her, and commended her before Pharaoh: and the woman was taken into Pharaoh's house. And he entreated Abram well for her sake: and he had sheep, and oxen, and he asses, and menservants, and maidservants, and she asses, and camels. And the LORD plagued Pharaoh and his house with great plagues because of Sarai Abram's wife. And Pharaoh called Abram, and said, What is this that you have done to me? why did you not tell me that she was your wife? Why said you, She is my sister? so I might have taken her to me as a wife: now therefore behold your wife, take her, and go your way.

H	X	S	K	B	Y	Y	S	K	K	D	T	S	O	U	L	O	H
F	G	R	E	E	V	Y	Y	E	A	O	E	H	Z	E	H	X	C
S	A	R	G	R	A	C	G	O	N	P	W	V	A	F	X	E	O
F	O	I	I	F	V	O	O	E	U	T	L	G	Z	V	U	N	M
R	A	J	R	E	S	A	S	V	G	R	A	A	N	P	Y	C	M
X	W	M	O	D	V	A	N	H	K	Y	W	W	G	T	N	Y	A
E	U	G	I	U	A	O	K	T	E	C	P	I	A	U	Y	F	N
V	D	T	G	N	R	N	U	E	S	E	U	T	F	Y	E	V	D
J	W	Y	J	W	E	N	O	S	A	R	P	Y	I	E	J	D	E
E	S	A	V	E	A	L	I	V	E	C	R	U	V	A	V	V	D
S	M	C	A	M	E	L	S	T	A	K	E	H	E	R	N	T	X
E	N	T	R	E	A	T	E	D	A	N	C	R	R	F	R	S	M
C	V	P	R	I	N	C	E	S	I	S	T	E	R	P	B	D	S

SOJOURN
FAIR
SAVE ALIVE
SAKE
PRINCES
SHEEP
SERVANTS
PLAGUED
COMMANDED
YOUR WIFE
FAMINE
GRIEVOUS
EGYPTIANS
SISTER
SOUL
ENTREATED
OXEN
CAMELS
TAKE HER
SENT AWAY

29. ABRAHAM, SARAH, AND ABIMELECH: GENESIS 20:1–18

And Abraham journeyed from there toward the south country, and...sojourned in Gerar. And Abraham said of Sarah his wife, She is my sister: and Abimelech king of Gerar sent, and took Sarah. But God came to Abimelech in a dream by night, and said to him, Behold, you are but a dead man, for the woman which you have taken; for she is a man's wife. But Abimelech had not come near her: and he said, Lord, will You slay also a righteous nation? Said he not to me, She is my sister? and she, even she herself said, He is my brother: in the integrity of my heart and innocency of my hands have I done this.

And God said to him in a dream, Yea, I know that you did this in the integrity of your heart; for I also withheld you from sinning against Me: therefore allowed I you not to touch her. Now therefore restore the man his wife; for he is a prophet, and he shall pray for you, and you shall live: and if you restore her not, know you that you shall surely die, you, and all that are yours....

Then Abimelech called Abraham, and said to him, What have you done to us? and what have I offended you, that you have brought on me and on my kingdom a great sin? you have done deeds to me that ought not to be done. And Abimelech said to Abraham, What saw you, that you have done this thing? And Abraham said, Because I thought, Surely the fear of God is not in this place; and they will slay me for my wife's sake. And yet indeed she is my sister; she is the daughter of my father, but not the daughter of my mother; and she became my wife. And it came to pass, when God caused me to wander from my father's house, that I said to her, This is your kindness which you shall show to me; at every place where we shall come, say of me, he is my brother. And Abimelech took sheep, and oxen, and menservants, and womenservants, and gave them to Abraham, and restored him Sarah his wife.

And Abimelech said, Behold, my land is before you: dwell where it pleases you. And to Sarah he said, Behold, I have given your brother a thousand pieces of silver: behold, he is to you a covering of the eyes, to all that are with you, and with all other: thus she was reproved. So Abraham prayed to God: and God healed Abimelech, and his wife, and his maidservants; and they bore children. For the Lord had fast closed up all the wombs of the house of Abimelech, because of Sarah Abraham's wife.

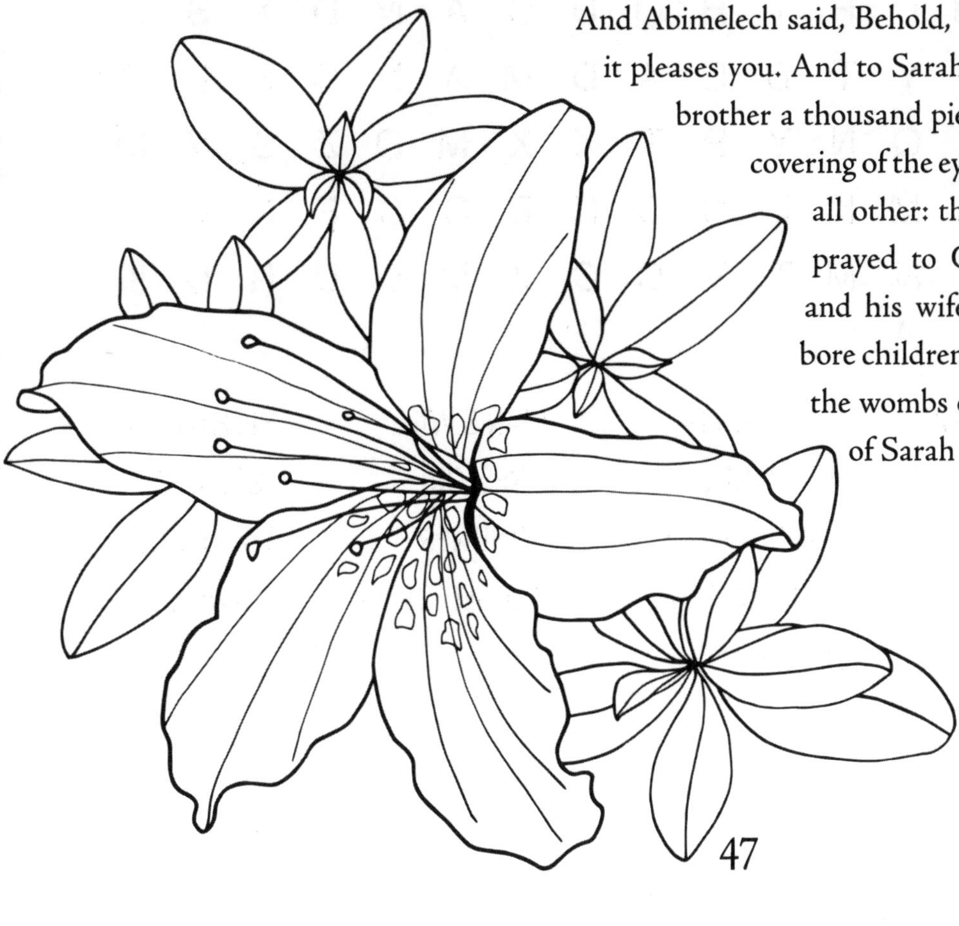

F	R	R	N	C	M	E	M	J	C	O	V	E	R	I	N	G	C	T	R
E	B	R	T	C	W	H	M	P	W	I	V	P	F	W	S	I	L	U	E
C	I	I	N	N	F	N	S	G	B	F	N	R	I	A	E	B	O	O	P
C	K	G	B	T	E	C	P	Y	G	D	N	O	I	N	P	P	S	R	R
A	F	H	V	K	A	U	S	I	R	P	V	P	M	D	T	U	E	U	O
B	R	T	A	C	R	E	E	L	E	B	W	H	M	E	V	R	D	V	V
I	B	E	U	K	O	V	N	U	A	H	E	E	T	R	W	L	U	M	E
M	S	O	K	U	F	A	K	E	T	Y	E	T	K	Q	C	B	P	U	D
E	J	U	X	U	G	M	F	X	S	H	X	M	J	X	I	S	S	T	F
L	I	S	G	J	O	E	J	L	I	C	X	X	H	T	V	N	Z	J	I
E	H	N	S	X	D	X	Q	L	N	E	A	Z	V	U	K	C	K	J	B
C	Z	E	T	R	E	S	T	O	R	E	U	G	O	C	N	Y	N	W	D
H	A	L	G	E	V	U	L	A	I	N	N	O	C	E	N	C	Y	O	G
V	U	B	Q	P	G	D	S	M	A	N	S	W	I	F	E	Q	H	M	P
S	O	U	T	H	Q	R	P	Y	T	G	P	Y	K	O	I	K	X	B	M
H	E	A	L	E	D	M	I	F	T	H	O	U	S	A	N	D	X	S	I
E	M	R	M	W	H	B	Y	T	D	E	A	D	M	A	N	C	B	E	G
F	P	N	W	C	G	F	Q	N	Y	P	T	X	X	M	O	Z	S	V	M
N	P	Q	J	Q	K	R	M	K	I	N	D	N	E	S	S	R	X	W	Z
C	R	J	Z	S	J	X	N	M	T	V	C	C	X	M	L	U	R	U	K

REPROVED	FEAR OF GOD	HEALED	MAN'S WIFE	RIGHTEOUS
SLAY	INTEGRITY	WANDER	RESTORE	GREAT SIN
COVERING	ABIMELECH	INNOCENCY	KINDNESS	THOUSAND
PROPHET	SOUTH	DEAD MAN	CLOSED UP	WOMBS

30. ISAAC, ABIMELECH, AND REBEKAH: GENESIS 26:6–13

And Isaac dwelt in Gerar: and the men ofthe place asked him of his wife; and he said, She is my sister: for he feared to say, She is my wife; lest, said he, the men of the place should kill me for Rebekah; because she was fair to look upon. And it came to pass, when he had been there a long time, that Abimelech king of the Philistines looked out at a window, and saw, and, behold, Isaac was sporting with Rebekah his wife. And Abimelech called Isaac, and said, Behold, of a surety she is your wife: and how said you, She is my sister? And Isaac said to him, Because I said, Lest I die for her. And Abimelech said, What is this you have done to us? one of the people might lightly have lain with your wife, and you should have brought guiltiness upon us. And Abimelech charged all his people, saying, He that touches this man or his wife shall surely be put to death. Then Isaac sowed in that land, and received in the same year a hundredfold: and the Lord blessed him.

Q	J	A	C	F	T	T	H	O	O	Y	U	O	I	A
L	Q	S	N	P	F	O	U	Z	K	L	V	I	K	P
E	C	P	D	Z	I	U	N	U	L	P	R	F	F	G
S	Q	H	E	L	Q	C	D	O	O	N	W	H	P	U
T	J	I	W	O	Q	H	R	H	O	M	K	C	V	I
I	L	L	X	A	G	E	E	U	K	S	Z	I	F	L
D	X	I	F	D	I	S	D	R	U	L	R	M	Q	T
I	F	S	Q	C	E	A	F	J	P	W	F	H	Q	I
E	A	T	Q	L	P	W	O	Y	O	P	S	L	Z	N
H	I	I	U	R	H	N	L	X	N	Q	W	F	M	E
G	R	N	X	R	A	V	D	T	T	X	M	P	D	S
D	C	E	Y	P	G	J	D	Z	P	Z	W	J	Z	S
J	P	S	G	U	G	B	E	G	A	R	Q	S	R	I
I	P	O	U	C	H	E	X	O	S	O	W	E	D	S
S	P	O	R	T	I	N	G	L	L	A	I	N	Z	

FAIR
LOOK UPON
PHILISTINES
SPORTING
LEST I DIE
LAIN
GUILTINESS
TOUCHES
SOWED
HUNDREDFOLD

31. RACHEL AND JACOB MEET: GENESIS 29:1–14

Then Jacob...came into the land of the people of the east. And he looked, and behold a well in the field, and, lo, there were three flocks of sheep lying by it; for out of that well they watered the flocks: and a great stone was upon the well's mouth. And there were all the flocks gathered: and they rolled the stone from the well's mouth, and watered the sheep, and put the stone again upon the well's mouth in its place. And Jacob said to them, My brethren, where be you? And they said, Of Haran are we. And he said to them, Know you Laban the son of Nahor? And they said, We know him. And he said to them, Is he well? And they said, He is well: and, behold, Rachel his daughter comes with the sheep....And while he yet spoke with them, Rachel came with her father's sheep: for she kept them. And it came to pass, when Jacob saw Rachel the daughter of Laban his mother's brother, and the sheep of Laban his mother's brother, that Jacob went near, and rolled the stone from the well's mouth, and watered the flock of Laban his mother's brother. And Jacob kissed Rachel, and lifted up his voice, and wept. And Jacob told Rachel that he was her father's brother, and that he was Rebekah's son: and she ran and told her father. And it came to pass, when Laban heard the tidings of Jacob his sister's son, that he ran to meet him, and embraced him, and kissed him, and brought him to his house....And Laban said to him, Surely you are my bone and my flesh. And he abode with him the space of a month.

R	Y	J	O	U	R	N	E	Y	G	E	T	P	U	D	Y	C	W
A	T	K	B	G	W	H	O	Z	B	A	A	L	N	A	L	M	E
C	T	I	D	E	J	A	T	R	O	F	T	S	Z	X	S	O	N
H	D	M	D	K	H	S	T	Y	N	H	U	H	T	U	N	N	T
E	S	N	O	I	V	O	A	E	E	S	R	Z	E	N	R	T	N
L	V	H	X	U	N	Q	L	B	R	F	T	C	E	R	L	H	E
D	Q	L	E	D	T	G	O	D	O	E	J	O	G	F	E	H	A
F	P	M	O	E	J	H	S	L	G	D	D	Z	N	Z	V	D	R
L	O	J	M	W	P	H	X	A	W	F	E	Y	X	E	N	Z	R
E	P	R	O	L	L	E	D	B	V	C	A	T	T	L	E	G	P
S	J	S	N	D	E	L	J	A	I	W	O	A	D	U	A	Z	B
H	F	L	O	C	K	S	O	N	E	M	B	R	A	C	E	D	O

JOURNEY	EAST	CATTLE	ABODE	WENT NEAR
FLOCKS	STONE	ROLLED	GATHERED	FLESH
MOUTH	LABAN	TIDINGS	WATERED	MONTH
BEHOLD	RACHEL	BONE	EMBRACED	SHEEP

32. JACOB MARRIES LEAH AND RACHEL: GENESIS 29:16–30

Laban had two daughters: the name of the elder was Leah, and the name of the younger was Rachel. Leah was tender eyed; but Rachel was beautiful and well favored. And Jacob loved Rachel; and said, I will serve you seven years for Rachel your younger daughter....

And Jacob served seven years for Rachel; and they seemed to him but a few days, for the love he had to her. And Jacob said to Laban, Give me my wife, for my days are fulfilled, that I may go in to her....And it came to pass in the evening, that [Laban] took Leah his daughter, and brought her to him; and he went in to her.... In the morning, behold, it was Leah: and he said to Laban, What is this you have done to me? did not I serve with you for Rachel? wherefore then have you beguiled me?

And Laban said, It must not be so done in our country, to give the younger before the firstborn. Fulfill her week, and we will give you this also for the service which you shall serve with me yet seven other years. And Jacob did so, and fulfilled her week: and he gave him Rachel his daughter as a wife also.... And he went in also to Rachel, and he loved also Rachel more than Leah, and served with him yet seven other years.

F	Y	D	A	U	G	H	T	E	R	S	G	U	J	Y	X	Q	W
S	V	O	K	W	U	B	B	E	T	T	E	R	W	Y	R	H	F
N	E	B	U	K	Y	W	O	S	W	P	Y	M	E	R	E	Y	U
L	D	V	E	N	D	C	P	E	D	E	S	B	L	R	J	T	L
G	I	H	E	A	G	N	J	R	W	T	P	R	L	A	O	E	F
G	H	Z	Q	N	U	E	F	V	X	D	Q	O	F	C	J	N	I
N	Q	Z	E	M	Y	T	R	E	L	R	V	U	A	H	I	D	L
V	J	X	Q	L	V	E	I	B	W	K	J	G	V	E	S	E	L
Q	O	B	E	R	D	Z	A	F	I	G	Q	H	O	L	E	R	E
A	J	M	A	I	D	E	R	R	U	L	B	T	R	Y	E	E	D
F	E	W	D	A	Y	S	R	W	S	L	H	E	E	U	M	Y	R
Z	L	D	W	R	L	E	A	H	Q	D	D	A	D	Y	E	E	Y
G	A	T	I	S	K	N	Y	S	W	E	E	K	H	R	D	D	J
E	W	E	N	T	I	N	J	Z	I	L	P	A	H	G	Y	T	U

DAUGHTERS	ELDER	BILHAH	WENT IN	SEEMED
LEAH	YOUNGER	WEEK	BROUGHT	SEVEN YEARS
RACHEL	TENDER EYED	MAID	FULFILLED	BETTER
BEAUTIFUL	WELL FAVORED	ZILPAH	FEW DAYS	SERVE

33. RACHEL STEALS THE HOUSEHOLD IDOLS: GENESIS 31:22–42

And it was told Laban on the third day that Jacob was fled. And he took his brethren with him, and pursued after him seven days' journey; and they overtook him in the mount Gilead. And God came to Laban the Syrian in a dream by night, and said to him, Take heed that you speak not to Jacob either good or bad. Then Laban overtook Jacob....

And Laban said to Jacob, What have you done, that you have stolen away unawares to me, and carried away my daughters, as captives taken with the sword? Wherefore did you flee away secretly, and steal away from me; and did not tell me...? And have not allowed me to kiss my sons and my daughters? you have now done foolishly in so doing.... Yet wherefore have you stolen my gods?

And Jacob answered and said to Laban, Because I was afraid: for I said, Perhaps you would take by force your daughters from me. With whomsoever you find your gods, let him not live: before our brethren discern you what is yours with me, and take it to you. For Jacob knew not that Rachel had stolen them. And Laban went into Jacob's tent, and into Leah's tent, and into the two maidservants' tents; but he found them not. Then went he out of Leah's tent, and entered into Rachel's tent.

Now Rachel had taken the images, and put them in the camel's furniture, and sat upon them. And Laban searched all the tent, but found them not. And she said to her father, Let it not displease my lord that I cannot rise up before you; for the custom of women is upon me. And he searched, but found not the images. And Jacob was angry, and chode with Laban: and Jacob answered and said to Laban, What is my trespass? what is my sin, that you have so hotly pursued after me?... This twenty years have I been with you; your ewes and your she goats have not cast their young, and the rams of your flock have I not eaten. That which was torn of beasts I brought not to you; I bore the loss of it; of my hand did you require it, whether stolen by day, or stolen by night. Thus I was; in the day the drought consumed me, and the frost by night; and my sleep departed from my eyes. Thus have I been twenty years in your house; I served you fourteen years for your two daughters, and six years for your cattle: and you have changed my wages ten times. Except the God of my father, the God of Abraham, and the fear of Isaac, had been with me, surely you had sent me away now empty. God has seen my affliction and the labor of my hands.

T	W	A	G	E	S	F	C	U	K	S	N	N	S	E	M	P	T	Y	F
D	A	A	M	S	J	R	N	M	A	A	R	P	J	S	O	C	E	I	I
F	G	B	I	M	J	O	U	D	O	F	H	A	L	Q	V	Q	P	M	F
H	H	D	R	Q	E	S	U	B	A	U	F	T	Z	C	U	F	H	A	U
O	L	S	T	E	O	T	B	P	L	Y	N	L	O	E	F	W	E	G	R
T	L	O	H	U	T	X	A	H	E	I	D	T	I	V	V	W	I	E	N
L	D	J	C	A	B	D	R	O	U	G	H	T	G	C	V	O	S	S	I
Y	H	H	S	R	J	L	U	T	S	C	H	L	V	I	T	Q	R	P	T
I	X	E	W	T	H	C	A	D	Y	L	J	I	K	C	L	I	A	R	U
P	S	V	U	D	O	T	S	B	S	G	N	M	H	G	C	E	O	P	R
U	X	H	S	N	U	L	E	L	T	O	B	T	C	K	U	S	A	N	E
S	Q	O	M	C	E	E	E	Q	P	T	N	W	F	N	L	E	Y	D	Z
C	A	P	T	I	V	E	S	N	R	U	K	G	L	Y	M	C	E	A	F
Y	U	O	C	Y	E	P	K	B	A	T	U	V	S	L	K	R	F	V	V
I	R	M	E	A	J	A	K	D	M	W	E	T	Z	E	S	E	B	C	O
D	C	N	Q	R	M	E	X	C	S	Y	A	J	R	P	H	T	L	R	L
B	Y	D	R	S	K	E	B	O	V	U	P	Y	P	I	Z	L	Q	X	G
G	V	Q	C	P	D	R	L	F	E	W	E	S	I	A	W	Y	K	D	O
B	K	T	M	A	L	N	F	T	V	C	O	N	L	A	B	O	R	W	Y
A	A	M	F	S	F	J	V	J	U	H	A	R	P	H	E	W	J	P	R

MOUNT GILEAD	STOLEN AWAY	CAPTIVES	SECRETLY	MIRTH
SONGS	TABRET	HARP	IMAGES	CAMEL
FURNITURE	HOTLY	EWES	RAMS	DROUGHT
FROST	WAGES	EMPTY	AFFLICTION	LABOR

34. THE CHILDREN OF JACOB: GENESIS 29:31–30:24

And when the LORD saw that Leah was hated, He opened her womb: but Rachel was barren. And Leah conceived, and bore a son, and she called his name Reuben: for she said, Surely the LORD has looked upon my affliction; now therefore my husband will love me. And she conceived again, and bore a son; and said, Because the LORD has heard that I was hated, He has therefore given me this son also: and she called his name Simeon. And she conceived again, and bore a son; and said, Now this time will my husband be joined to me, because I have born him three sons: therefore was his name called Levi. And she conceived again, and bore a son: and she said, Now will I praise the LORD: therefore she called his name Judah; and left bearing.

And when Rachel saw that she bore Jacob no children, Rachel envied her sister; and said to Jacob, Give me children, or else I die. And Jacob's anger was kindled against Rachel: and he said, Am I in God's stead, who has withheld from you the fruit of the womb? And she said, Behold my maid Bilhah, go in to her; and she shall bear upon my knees, that I may also have children by her. And she gave him Bilhah her handmaid as a wife: and Jacob went in to her.

And Bilhah conceived, and bore Jacob a son. And Rachel said, God has judged me, and has also heard my voice, and has given me a son: therefore called she his name Dan. And Bilhah Rachel's maid conceived again, and bore Jacob a second son. And Rachel said, With great wrestlings have I wrestled with my sister, and I have prevailed: and she called his name Naphtali. When Leah saw that she had left bearing, she took Zilpah her maid, and gave her Jacob as a wife.

And Zilpah Leah's maid bore Jacob a son. And Leah said, A troop comes: and she called his name Gad. And Zilpah Leah's maid bore Jacob a second son. And Leah said, Happy am I, for the daughters will call me blessed: and she called his name Asher. And Reuben went in the days of wheat harvest, and found mandrakes in the field, and brought them to his mother Leah.... And Jacob came out of the field in the evening, and Leah went out to meet him, and said, You must come in to me; for surely I have hired you with my son's mandrakes. And he lay with her that night. And God hearkened to Leah, and she conceived, and bore Jacob the fifth son. And Leah said, God has given me my hire, because I have given my maiden to my husband: and she called his name Issachar. And Leah conceived again, and bore Jacob the sixth son. And Leah said, God has endued me with a good dowry; now will my husband dwell with me, because I have born him six sons: and she called his name Zebulun. And afterwards she bore a daughter, and called her name Dinah.

And God remembered Rachel, and God hearkened to her, and opened her womb. And she conceived, and bore a son; and said, God has taken away my reproach: and she called his name Joseph; and said, The LORD shall add to me another son.

W	W	D	A	N	N	A	O	Z	U	G	T	Y	T	L	J	P	M	K	V
O	Z	Q	W	V	R	Q	Q	J	I	F	H	S	I	F	U	D	K	D	Y
M	Z	H	M	W	V	E	L	R	Y	I	C	A	M	S	D	C	A	H	G
B	E	E	H	S	C	B	U	K	L	O	E	P	O	P	A	I	M	W	N
Q	N	G	B	I	M	Z	Q	B	A	L	M	X	O	N	H	Z	T	M	P
F	A	W	T	U	O	Q	F	O	E	D	Z	V	G	O	D	Y	K	J	D
W	F	H	M	P	L	Y	K	R	W	N	Q	J	J	P	Y	S	S	P	O
Z	A	K	A	Q	T	U	T	A	A	N	Y	D	G	A	D	P	Q	R	W
Y	D	U	N	E	K	V	N	N	A	P	S	F	N	W	E	B	B	A	R
W	N	S	D	N	I	D	B	L	S	B	T	R	D	I	N	A	H	I	Y
R	E	D	R	M	A	V	N	H	H	Z	T	R	O	O	P	I	Z	S	A
E	L	U	A	O	C	Q	F	R	E	M	M	E	G	S	U	D	Y	E	E
S	T	A	K	W	O	H	P	I	R	A	W	T	T	F	A	S	C	S	N
T	O	T	E	X	S	I	M	E	O	N	L	U	C	S	Q	V	E	K	D
L	Q	P	S	Y	L	M	I	E	R	O	H	R	P	C	L	E	V	I	U
I	J	M	B	C	W	B	H	K	S	X	V	J	O	S	E	P	H	C	E
N	F	T	C	F	F	Z	V	Z	I	D	N	A	P	H	T	A	L	I	D
G	G	N	M	W	A	T	A	V	X	I	R	H	N	K	V	O	K	M	W
S	B	A	R	R	E	N	A	P	R	B	P	H	E	S	U	K	Z	L	D
Y	I	S	S	A	C	H	A	R	L	D	U	X	Q	V	Y	R	L	D	H

WOMB	LEVI	WRESTLINGS	ASHER	ENDUED
BARREN	PRAISE	NAPHTALI	MANDRAKES	DOWRY
REUBEN	JUDAH	TROOP	ISSACHAR	DINAH
SIMEON	DAN	GAD	ZEBULUN	JOSEPH

35. LOT'S WIFE AND DAUGHTERS: GENESIS 19:1–11

And there came two angels to Sodom at evening;...and Lot seeing them rose up to meet them; and he bowed himself with his face toward the ground; and he said, Behold now, my lords, turn in, I pray you, into your servant's house, and tarry all night, and wash your feet, and you shall rise up early, and go on your ways. And they said, Nay; but we will abide in the street all night. And he pressed upon them greatly; and they turned in to him, and entered into his house.... But before they lay down, the men of the city, even the men of Sodom, compassed the house round, both old and young, all the people from every quarter: and they called to Lot, and said to him, Where are the men which came in to you this night? bring them out to us, that we may know them.

And Lot went out at the door to them, and shut the door after him, and said, I pray you, brethren, do not so wickedly. Behold now, I have two daughters which have not known man; let me, I pray you, bring them out to you, and do you to them as is good in your eyes: only to these men do nothing; for therefore came they under the shadow of my roof. And they said, Stand back.... And they pressed sore upon the man, even Lot, and came near to break the door. But the men put forth their hand, and pulled Lot into the house to them, and shut to the door. And they smote the men that were at the door of the house with blindness, both small and great: so that they wearied themselves to find the door.

L	B	B	M	U	Q	T	G	R	E	A	T	R	Y	T	J	A	Z
C	I	R	L	E	M	B	X	B	J	X	J	S	N	B	H	B	E
J	C	N	E	I	N	U	D	G	U	F	Y	U	D	Q	H	I	C
O	O	P	T	A	N	O	N	J	D	F	E	A	S	T	W	D	F
A	P	K	A	H	D	D	F	L	G	H	S	C	K	M	I	E	O
V	R	W	Y	W	E	A	N	T	E	P	C	T	V	K	C	L	Q
R	E	W	I	B	L	S	S	E	H	A	M	G	O	Q	K	S	U
S	S	F	Q	S	O	S	T	H	S	E	V	E	O	W	E	M	A
O	S	Y	L	T	T	J	O	R	A	S	C	E	Z	S	D	A	R
D	E	C	O	M	P	A	S	S	E	D	R	I	N	R	L	L	T
O	D	E	W	E	A	R	I	E	D	E	O	I	T	E	Y	L	E
M	R	R	Y	S	O	J	O	U	R	N	T	W	D	Y	D	S	R
U	C	D	O	O	R	O	F	T	H	E	H	O	U	S	E	S	I

SODOM	LOT	ABIDE	COMPASSED	GREAT
MEN OF THE CITY	IN THE STREET	QUARTER	WICKEDLY	SMALL
PRESSED	FEAST	SHADOW	SOJOURN	WEARIED
UNLEAVENED	BREAD	JUDGE	BLINDNESS	DOOR OF THE HOUSE

36. SODOM AND GOMORRAH DESTROYED: GENESIS 19:12–26

And the men said to Lot, Have you here any besides? son in law, and your sons, and your daughters, and whatsoever you have in the city, bring them out of this place: for we will destroy this place, because the cry of them is waxed great before the face of the LORD; and the LORD has sent us to destroy it. And Lot went out, and spoke to his sons in law, which married his daughters, and said, Up, get you out of this place; for the LORD will destroy this city. But he seemed as one that mocked to his sons in law.

And when the morning arose, then the angels hastened Lot, saying, Arise, take your wife, and your two daughters, which are here; lest you be consumed in the iniquity of the city. And while he lingered, the men laid hold upon his hand, and upon the hand of his wife, and upon the hand of his two daughters; the LORD being merciful to him: and they brought him forth, and set him outside the city. And it came to pass, when they had brought them forth abroad, that He said, Escape for your life; look not behind you, neither stay you in all the plain; escape to the mountain, lest you be consumed....

Then the LORD rained upon Sodom and upon Gomorrah brimstone and fire from the LORD out of heaven; and He overthrew those cities, and all the plain, and all the inhabitants of the cities, and that which grew upon the ground. But his wife looked back from behind him, and she became a pillar of salt.

V	Q	U	J	W	Q	L	M	O	C	K	E	D	L	A	O	C	R	Y	K
B	B	W	T	L	I	N	G	E	R	E	D	O	L	Y	D	L	M	L	Q
I	N	H	A	B	I	T	A	N	T	S	F	U	V	E	I	O	T	W	P
J	F	W	P	G	G	E	L	T	E	N	R	T	D	T	K	O	V	Y	Q
D	A	P	N	H	W	C	U	W	N	X	P	S	T	G	P	K	X	D	N
B	B	R	I	M	S	T	O	N	E	R	I	I	A	O	B	N	N	A	J
C	L	X	U	S	Q	C	X	I	T	X	C	D	P	E	U	O	N	Q	O
C	J	U	F	U	Q	Y	M	W	X	T	O	E	I	F	J	T	M	R	B
Q	J	C	F	B	R	P	Q	G	U	A	N	B	L	I	J	D	E	N	R
J	S	D	E	S	T	R	O	Y	P	M	S	C	L	I	Z	N	R	R	I
R	P	Q	Q	K	L	B	J	A	D	O	U	P	A	N	O	H	C	Z	N
W	X	I	C	G	L	Y	A	W	E	U	M	O	R	I	A	D	I	K	G
A	A	T	P	X	Z	C	N	E	D	N	E	T	O	Q	R	G	F	P	T
X	T	B	P	S	D	X	N	Q	H	T	D	C	F	U	C	C	U	B	H
E	G	O	R	A	W	G	N	O	X	A	N	J	S	I	T	U	L	E	E
D	A	X	A	O	L	M	S	I	B	I	N	K	A	T	N	F	H	H	M
X	V	Z	K	C	A	P	S	W	A	N	Y	M	L	Y	I	N	G	I	O
G	D	R	N	D	Y	D	B	X	B	V	P	P	T	O	D	E	N	N	U
C	P	V	I	M	A	G	N	I	F	I	E	D	D	O	S	Q	J	D	T
J	P	L	A	I	N	Y	Z	U	K	R	T	J	X	L	P	G	G	A	J

DESTROY	CRY	BRING THEM OUT	WAXED	MOUNTAIN
CONSUMED	INIQUITY	LINGERED	MERCIFUL	PLAIN
ABROAD	LOOK NOT	BEHIND	MOCKED	INHABITANTS
MAGNIFIED	ZOAR	BRIMSTONE	OUTSIDE	PILLAR OF SALT

37. AND 38. DINAH, JACOB, AND LEAH'S DAUGHTER: GENESIS 34:1–31

And Dinah the daughter of Leah, which she bore to Jacob, went out to see the daughters of the land. And when Shechem the son of Hamor the Hivite, prince of the country, saw her, he took her, and lay with her, and defiled her. And his soul clung to Dinah the daughter of Jacob, and he loved the damsel, and spoke kindly to the damsel. And Shechem spoke to his father Hamor, saying, Get me this damsel as a wife....

And Hamor the father of Shechem went out to Jacob to commune with him. And the sons of Jacob came out of the field when they heard it: and the men were grieved, and they were very angry, because he had wrought folly in Israel in lying with Jacob's daughter; which thing ought not to be done. And Hamor communed with them, saying, The soul of my son Shechem longs for your daughter: I pray you give her him as a wife. And make you marriages with us, and give your daughters to us, and take our daughters to you. And you shall dwell with us: and the land shall be before you; dwell and trade you therein, and get your possessions therein. And Shechem said to her father and to her brethren, Let me find grace in your eyes, and what you shall say to me I will give. Ask me never so much dowry and gift, and I will give according as you shall say to me: but give me the damsel as a wife.

And the sons of Jacob answered Shechem and Hamor his father deceitfully, and said, because he had defiled Dinah their sister: and they said to them, We cannot do this thing, to give our sister to one that is uncircumcised; for that were a reproach to us: but in this will we consent to you: If you will be as we be, that every male of you be circumcised; then will we give our daughters to you, and we will take your daughters to us, and we will dwell with you, and we will become one people. But if you will not hearken to us, to be circumcised; then will we take our daughter, and we will be gone. And their words pleased Hamor, and Shechem Hamor's son. And the young man deferred not to do the thing, because he had delight in Jacob's daughter: and he was more honorable than all the house of his father....

And to Hamor and to Shechem his son hearkened all that went out of the gate of his city; and every male was circumcised, all that went out of the gate of his city. And it came to pass on the third day, when they were sore, that two of the sons of Jacob, Simeon and Levi, Dinah's brethren, took each man his sword, and came upon the city boldly, and slew all the males. And they slew Hamor and Shechem his son with the edge of the sword, and took Dinah out of Shechem's house, and went out. The sons of Jacob came upon the slain, and spoiled the city, because they had defiled their sister. They took their sheep, and their oxen, and their asses, and that which was in the city, and that which was in the field, and all their wealth, and all their little ones, and their wives took they captive, and spoiled even all that was in the house. And Jacob said to Simeon and Levi, You have troubled me to make me to stink among the inhabitants of the land, among the Canaanites and the Perizzites: and I being few in number, they shall gather themselves together against me, and slay me; and I shall be destroyed, I and my house. And they said, Should he deal with our sister as with a harlot?

H	O	N	E	P	E	O	P	L	E	Q	C	S	U	H	M	B	D
B	P	O	S	S	E	S	S	I	O	N	S	N	F	C	P	G	K
I	Y	Z	B	S	H	B	H	F	Q	W	X	B	I	X	I	J	I
J	D	W	E	L	L	W	I	T	H	U	S	R	N	R	F	C	D
U	N	C	I	R	C	U	M	S	I	S	E	D	D	F	M	L	D
W	R	E	P	R	O	A	C	H	V	V	Z	E	G	Y	A	U	E
Q	B	R	N	H	D	A	M	S	E	L	F	L	R	A	R	N	F
V	Y	I	H	R	R	J	U	U	K	K	F	Y	A	G	R	G	I
J	S	O	U	L	X	V	C	A	T	T	L	E	C	V	I	F	L
F	S	H	O	N	O	R	A	B	L	E	M	N	E	C	A	P	E
G	G	M	E	Y	B	U	P	R	I	N	C	E	V	C	G	Q	D
T	T	S	C	Z	U	D	D	O	W	R	Y	G	M	S	E	R	R
M	Y	O	I	L	S	V	X	O	L	G	S	M	L	K	S	E	Y

PRINCE	DAMSEL	POSSESSIONS	ONE PEOPLE	CLUNG
DEFILED	CATTLE	FIND GRACE	HONORABLE	DWELL WITH US
SOUL	MARRIAGES	DOWRY	UNCIRCUMSISED	REPROACH

F	Z	L	S	Q	N	S	T	I	W	D	S	B	Z	C	V	S	A
C	A	P	T	I	V	E	J	L	I	I	L	H	G	J	M	O	W
H	Y	W	V	U	W	N	C	L	C	H	A	J	H	W	A	N	P
V	A	Q	E	N	O	K	K	S	F	S	I	I	G	Z	T	S	E
B	Q	R	B	A	O	Q	B	U	H	A	N	V	G	A	W	O	A
Q	Y	B	L	P	L	F	M	B	A	R	K	T	Y	E	Q	F	C
M	S	N	E	O	I	T	W	S	Q	O	H	D	M	F	H	J	E
R	M	W	J	A	T	U	H	T	D	S	I	M	E	O	N	A	A
Y	D	J	O	N	S	T	L	A	U	W	R	L	E	V	I	C	B
G	L	V	P	R	G	T	Q	N	P	E	E	L	Y	Z	I	O	L
X	B	L	P	Z	D	F	C	C	C	R	G	L	X	Z	N	B	E
S	P	O	I	L	E	D	C	E	E	L	H	D	L	A	L	E	L
U	K	Q	C	O	N	S	E	N	T	L	E	D	I	N	A	H	N

PEACEABLE
DWELL
CONSENT
SUBSTANCE
BEAST
SIMEON
LEVI
SWORD
DINAH
SLAIN
SPOILED
SONS OF JACOB
WEALTH
CAPTIVE
HARLOT

39. POTIPHAR'S WIFE: GENESIS 39:1–21

And Joseph was brought down to Egypt; and Potiphar, an officer of Pharaoh, captain of the guard, an Egyptian, bought him of the hands of the Ishmeelites, which had brought him down there. And the LORD was with Joseph, and he was a prosperous man; and he was in the house of his master the Egyptian. And his master saw that the LORD was with him, and that the LORD made all that he did to prosper in his hand. And Joseph found grace in his sight, and he served him: and he made him overseer over his house, and all that he had he put into his hand. And it came to pass from the time that he had made him overseer in his house, and over all that he had, that the LORD blessed the Egyptian's house for Joseph's sake; and the blessing of the LORD was upon all that he had in the house, and in the field. And he left all that he had in Joseph's hand; and he knew not anything he had, save the bread which he did eat.

And Joseph was a goodly person, and well favored. And it came to pass after these things, that his master's wife cast her eyes upon Joseph; and she said, Lie with me. But he refused, and said to his master's wife, Behold, my master knows not what is with me in the house, and he has committed all that he has to my hand; there is none greater in this house than I; neither has he kept back any thing from me but you, because you are his wife: how then can I do this great wickedness, and sin against God? And it came to pass, as she spoke to Joseph day by day, that he hearkened not to her, to lie by her, or to be with her.

And it came to pass about this time, that Joseph went into the house to do his business; and there was none of the men of the house there inside. And she caught him by his garment, saying, Lie with me: and he left his garment in her hand, and fled, and got him out. And it came to pass, when she saw that he had left his garment in her hand, and was fled forth, that she called to the men of her house, and spoke to them, saying, See, he has brought in a Hebrew to us to mock us; he came in to me to lie with me, and I cried with a loud voice: and it came to pass, when he heard that I lifted up my voice and cried, that he left his garment with me, and fled, and got him out. And she laid up his garment by her, until his lord came home. And she spoke to him according to these words, saying, The Hebrew servant, which you have brought to us, came in to me to mock me: and it came to pass, as I lifted up my voice and cried, that he left his garment with me, and fled out. And it came to pass, when his master heard the words of his wife, which she spoke to him, saying, After this manner did your servant to me; that his wrath was kindled. And Joseph's master took him, and put him into the prison, a place where the king's prisoners were bound.

X	P	F	G	C	A	P	T	A	I	N	S	B	O	J	R	R	P	K	F
H	P	K	M	G	U	A	B	B	N	C	M	N	H	A	E	W	I	G	L
I	H	O	I	Z	Q	T	B	Z	W	W	A	R	N	R	E	U	W	U	I
B	Q	P	T	N	Y	T	Y	U	S	B	S	F	D	G	M	P	I	A	E
F	I	I	R	I	D	U	N	B	T	V	T	Q	C	O	F	G	C	R	W
O	J	I	K	O	P	L	I	Q	Z	V	E	Z	H	O	M	A	K	D	I
Q	V	O	H	Q	S	H	E	R	C	K	R	V	F	D	X	R	E	N	T
I	Y	E	S	A	S	P	A	D	N	J	S	F	L	L	Z	M	D	Z	H
O	E	E	R	E	Z	W	E	R	L	D	W	R	E	Y	G	E	N	S	M
V	G	T	O	S	P	A	E	R	Q	Y	I	C	M	S	O	N	E	Z	E
T	Y	A	X	E	E	H	Y	L	O	L	F	T	Q	S	Z	T	S	U	C
E	P	L	N	T	F	E	U	S	L	U	E	O	R	N	C	C	S	W	D
J	T	L	G	I	L	A	R	U	F	F	S	W	Y	N	J	L	P	C	Q
S	H	D	E	P	E	S	N	M	V	S	A	Y	B	Y	K	F	R	M	A
Y	X	Z	K	P	D	M	T	O	J	L	D	V	Q	G	H	T	I	M	A
B	G	B	L	E	S	S	I	N	G	I	T	Y	O	J	S	D	S	K	W
E	F	Y	P	O	A	M	F	M	A	S	T	E	R	R	W	J	O	H	T
H	N	W	R	Z	D	V	H	U	I	Q	Q	X	R	U	E	C	N	J	V
S	M	P	R	E	F	U	S	E	D	K	O	K	P	S	V	D	E	W	M
J	J	V	C	G	R	A	C	E	K	I	C	O	N	B	U	B	I	O	O

EGYPT	OVERSEER	GARMENT	PROSPEROUS	LIE WITH ME
CAPTAIN	GOODLY	KINDLED	GRACE	WICKEDNESS
JOSEPH	MASTER'S WIFE	POTIPHAR	BLESSING	FLED
MASTER	REFUSED	GUARD	WELL FAVORED	PRISON

40. THE MIDWIVES OF EGYPT: EXODUS 1:15–22

And the king of Egypt spoke to the Hebrew midwives, of which the name of the one was Shiphrah, and the name of the other Puah: and he said, When you do the office of a midwife to the Hebrew women, and see them upon the stools; if it be a son, then you shall kill him: but if it be a daughter, then she shall live. But the midwives feared God, and did not as the king of Egypt commanded them, but saved the men children alive. And the king of Egypt called for the midwives, and said to them, Why have you done this thing, and have saved the men children alive? And the midwives said to Pharaoh, Because the Hebrew women are not as the Egyptian women; for they are lively, and are delivered before the midwives come in to them. Therefore God dealt well with the midwives: and the people multiplied, and waxed very mighty. And it came to pass, because the midwives feared God, that He made them houses. And Pharaoh charged all his people, saying, Every son that is born you shall cast into the river, and every daughter you shall save alive.

S	F	D	Z	S	S	W	V	K	T	D	I	R	Q	B	C	C	C	M	B
Y	K	D	A	P	T	A	U	M	Q	V	B	V	D	M	H	K	A	G	R
K	Z	L	O	C	I	O	V	Q	Y	W	Q	B	S	U	A	Q	S	I	N
X	D	U	O	D	A	H	O	E	M	K	D	J	J	L	R	O	T	T	V
S	O	M	S	E	B	G	C	L	D	X	W	G	J	T	G	H	X	L	H
L	T	E	B	N	W	A	Z	I	S	A	T	W	O	I	E	E	O	H	B
W	L	N	N	K	G	D	W	Y	N	S	L	D	C	P	D	B	G	H	Q
I	R	C	I	L	Z	W	Z	L	A	Q	D	I	R	L	I	R	K	P	B
Y	K	H	D	E	L	I	V	E	R	E	D	Q	V	I	Y	E	S	E	G
D	U	I	M	I	D	W	I	V	E	S	H	C	W	E	V	W	H	T	K
T	C	L	V	I	C	L	I	V	E	L	Y	C	D	D	X	E	L	H	S
C	D	D	W	A	X	E	D	M	I	G	H	T	I	L	Y	I	R	O	V
M	L	R	F	C	L	T	P	V	M	Z	U	X	L	V	L	T	H	U	H
D	P	E	B	E	T	K	E	H	O	E	U	S	I	P	Q	D	T	S	C
V	G	N	J	H	A	G	F	E	I	P	T	B	W	X	R	L	P	E	X
B	M	H	L	K	S	R	N	E	E	E	U	X	L	W	U	Y	A	S	T
U	I	A	A	L	I	N	E	X	Q	Q	T	A	D	E	A	L	T	N	I
R	V	I	X	T	U	N	L	D	I	I	S	Y	H	R	S	T	F	A	Y
O	F	F	I	C	E	U	G	S	H	I	P	H	R	A	H	D	L	E	K
P	I	Z	T	C	O	M	M	A	N	D	E	D	D	Q	D	T	P	Y	W

KING
MIDWIVES
SHIPHRAH
PUAH
OFFICE
STOOLS
FEARED
COMMANDED
SAVED ALIVE
MEN CHILDREN
HEBREW
LIVELY
DELIVERED
DEALT
MULTIPLIED
WAXED MIGHTILY
HOUSES
CHARGED
CAST
RIVER

41. MOSES'S MOTHER AND PHAROAH'S DAUGHTER: EXODUS 2:1–10

There went a man of the house of Levi, and took as a wife a daughter of Levi. And the woman conceived, and bore a son: and when she saw him that he was a goodly child, she hid him three months. And when she could not longer hide him, she took for him an ark of bulrushes, and daubed it with slime and with pitch, and put the child therein; and she laid it in the flags by the river's brink. And his sister stood afar off, to know what would be done to him. And the daughter of Pharaoh came down to wash herself at the river; and her maidens walked along by the river's side; and when she saw the ark among the flags, she sent her maid to bring it. And when she had opened it, she saw the child: and, behold, the babe wept. And she had compassion on him, and said, This is one of the Hebrews' children. Then said his sister to Pharaoh's daughter, Shall I go and call to you a nurse of the Hebrew women, that she may nurse the child for you? And Pharaoh's daughter said to her, Go. And the maid went and called the child's mother. And Pharaoh's daughter said to her, Take this child away, and nurse it for me, and I will give you your wages. And the woman took the child, and nursed it. And the child grew, and she brought him to Pharaoh's daughter, and he became her son. And she called his name Moses: and she said, Because I drew him out of the water.

T	J	F	Y	K	W	H	L	T	Y	W	E	P	T	P	P	U	A
H	A	R	K	U	L	D	S	J	Z	U	S	N	O	J	L	U	F
R	H	I	D	D	E	N	K	G	C	O	B	F	U	D	N	M	A
E	M	D	C	O	N	C	E	I	V	E	D	M	F	R	M	V	R
E	D	A	U	B	E	D	U	A	Q	O	X	O	L	E	S	X	O
M	O	C	O	M	P	A	S	S	I	O	N	S	A	W	B	E	F
O	U	W	A	G	E	S	A	S	Y	U	S	E	G	H	B	G	F
N	H	O	U	S	E	O	F	L	E	V	I	S	S	I	R	H	P
T	T	G	O	O	D	L	Y	I	U	W	X	D	V	M	I	L	I
H	N	T	X	Q	R	S	O	M	Z	I	R	A	C	O	N	P	T
S	E	M	N	P	M	H	Z	E	H	C	T	T	A	U	K	M	C
T	H	E	R	E	I	N	K	E	O	G	W	I	S	T	Q	V	H
Y	P	W	R	W	P	B	U	L	R	U	S	H	E	S	A	U	O

HOUSE OF LEVI	CONCEIVED	SLIME	NURSE	BRINK
GOODLY	THREE MONTHS	THEREIN	MOSES	COMPASSION
HIDDEN	ARK	AFAR OFF	PITCH	WAGES
BULRUSHES	DAUBED	WEPT	FLAGS	DREW HIM OUT

42. ZIPPORAH: EXODUS 2:11–22

When Moses was grown, that he went out to his brethren, and looked on their burdens: and he spied an Egyptian smiting a Hebrew, one of his brethren. And he looked this way and that way, and when he saw that there was no man, he slew the Egyptian, and hid him in the sand.... Now when Pharaoh heard this thing, he sought to slay Moses. But Moses fled from the face of Pharaoh, and dwelt in the land of Midian: and he sat down by a well. Now the priest of Midian had seven daughters: and they came and drew water, and filled the troughs to water their father's flock. And the shepherds came and drove them away: but Moses stood up and helped them, and watered their flock. And when they came to Reuel their father, he said, How is it that you are come so soon to day? And they said, An Egyptian delivered us out of the hand of the shepherds, and also drew water enough for us, and watered the flock. And he said to his daughters, And where is he? why is it that you have left the man? call him, that he may eat bread. And Moses was content to dwell with the man: and he gave Moses Zipporah his daughter. And she bore him a son, and he called his name Gershom: for he said, I have been a stranger in a strange land.

G	X	Y	S	X	O	B	S	H	I	D	D	E	N	R	K	I	F
B	R	S	Z	P	J	B	U	A	B	Q	U	L	Z	R	O	M	A
R	I	S	M	R	U	W	F	R	N	J	A	K	E	C	V	R	C
E	G	T	F	I	D	S	H	R	D	D	H	Z	S	V	M	Z	E
T	T	R	L	N	G	D	X	L	U	E	O	E	X	M	I	I	O
H	R	A	O	C	E	S	M	I	T	E	N	V	W	O	T	P	F
R	O	N	C	E	D	G	S	P	U	X	N	S	C	S	R	P	P
E	U	G	K	G	B	C	A	G	R	O	W	N	M	E	E	O	H
N	G	E	S	E	A	T	B	R	E	A	D	W	Q	S	U	R	A
S	H	R	K	T	D	R	G	E	R	S	H	O	M	O	E	A	R
Q	S	E	V	E	N	D	A	U	G	H	T	E	R	S	L	H	A
M	L	P	F	I	G	S	T	R	A	N	G	E	L	A	N	D	O
B	M	P	R	I	E	S	T	O	F	M	I	D	I	A	N	D	H

MOSES	GROWN	TROUGHS	ZIPPORAH	FLOCK
BRETHREN	BURDENS	PRIEST OF MIDIAN	JUDGE	SEVEN DAUGHTERS
HIDDEN	SAND	STRANGER	STRANGE LAND	EAT BREAD
SMITE	PRINCE	REUEL	FACE OF PHARAOH	GERSHOM

43. MOSES RETURNS TO EGYPT: EXODUS 4:18–26

Moses took his wife and his sons, and set them upon an ass, and he returned to the land of Egypt: and Moses took the rod of God in his hand. And the LORD said to Moses, When you go to return into Egypt, see that you do all those wonders before Pharaoh, which I have put in your hand: but I will harden his heart, that he shall not let the people go. And you shall say to Pharaoh, Thus says the LORD, Israel is My son, even My firstborn: and I say to you, Let My son go, that he may serve Me: and if you refuse to let him go, behold, I will slay your son, even your firstborn. And it came to pass by the way in the inn, that the LORD met him, and sought to kill him. Then Zipporah took a sharp stone, and cut off the foreskin of her son, and cast it at his feet, and said, Surely a bloody husband are you to me. So He let him go: then she said, A bloody husband you are, because of the circumcision.

K	J	F	P	J	W	J	L	I	R	M	O	C	S	B	M	P	L	S	U
W	U	R	O	I	B	R	X	D	U	N	G	G	P	G	G	L	E	L	P
S	Q	I	N	N	C	I	E	U	V	X	W	G	C	Z	P	K	T	E	Q
D	L	Y	X	B	A	S	H	T	F	E	M	H	U	D	N	E	M	F	O
A	H	A	N	G	A	R	G	Z	U	U	H	Q	N	R	O	B	Y	O	C
V	E	L	Y	P	R	A	E	A	A	R	J	Q	S	E	W	N	P	R	S
A	R	G	A	A	T	E	P	N	R	T	N	B	G	A	M	G	E	E	O
F	A	D	N	P	X	L	T	I	K	W	N	D	U	G	Y	C	O	S	U
E	L	T	H	U	S	S	A	Y	S	T	H	E	L	O	R	D	P	K	G
M	Q	D	W	V	B	G	F	R	B	I	A	I	J	K	Z	S	L	I	H
K	H	S	J	R	S	G	U	W	O	X	U	Q	I	I	N	H	E	N	T
T	Y	T	Y	L	X	X	E	U	N	D	U	C	O	U	V	A	G	V	H
P	X	O	Q	Q	J	Q	G	R	E	T	O	M	I	G	Q	R	O	F	A
W	O	N	D	E	R	S	Y	Y	G	N	J	F	D	P	H	P	M	P	R
O	Q	E	L	Z	F	D	P	T	Q	G	C	E	G	E	E	L	H	D	D
K	Q	B	Z	T	S	M	T	U	X	P	L	R	T	O	S	A	S	X	E
R	K	T	F	A	T	H	E	R	I	N	L	A	W	H	D	P	C	X	N
L	F	I	R	S	T	B	O	R	N	R	R	R	O	T	R	K	V	E	N
T	C	I	R	C	U	M	C	I	S	I	O	N	W	G	D	O	S	F	S
K	Q	L	A	H	B	L	O	O	D	Y	P	X	X	Y	G	A	Y	L	W

FATHER IN LAW
RETURN
SOUGHT
WONDERS
LET MY PEOPLE GO
ISRAEL
FIRSTBORN
SHARP
FORESKIN
CIRCUMCISION
JETHRO
PEACE
EGYPT
ROD OF GOD
THUS SAYS THE LORD
HARDEN
SLAY
INN
STONE
BLOODY

44. AND 45. THE SONGS OF MIRIAM AND MOSES: EXODUS 15:1–21

Then sang Moses and the children of Israel this song to the LORD..., I will sing to the LORD, for He has triumphed gloriously: the horse and its rider has He thrown into the sea. The LORD is my strength and song, and He is become my salvation: He is my God, and I will prepare Him a habitation; my father's God, and I will exalt him. The LORD is a man of war: the LORD is His name. Pharaoh's chariots and his host has He cast into the sea: his chosen captains also are drowned in the Red sea. The depths have covered them: they sank into the bottom as a stone. Your right hand, O LORD, is become glorious in power: Your right hand, O LORD, has dashed in pieces the enemy. And in the greatness of your excellency You have overthrown them that rose up against You: You sent forth your wrath, which consumed them as stubble. And with the blast of your nostrils the waters were gathered together, the floods stood upright as a heap, and the depths were congealed in the heart of the sea.... You did blow with your wind, the sea covered them: they sank as lead in the mighty waters.

Who is like to You, O LORD, among the gods? who is like You, glorious in holiness, fearful in praises, doing wonders? You stretched out your right hand, the earth swallowed them. You in your mercy have led forth the people which You have redeemed: You have guided them in Your strength to Your holy habitation. The people shall hear, and be afraid.... Fear and dread shall fall upon them; by the greatness of Your arm they shall be as still as a stone; till Your people pass over, O LORD, till the people pass over, which You have purchased. You shall bring them in, and plant them in the mountain of Your inheritance, in the place, O LORD, which You have made for You to dwell in, in the Sanctuary, O LORD, which Your hands have established. The LORD shall reign for ever and ever. For the horse of Pharaoh went in with his chariots and with his horsemen into the sea, and the LORD brought again the waters of the sea upon them; but the children of Israel went on dry land in the midst of the sea.

And Miriam the prophetess, the sister of Aaron, took a timbrel in her hand; and all the women went out after her with timbrels and with dances. And Miriam answered them, Sing you to the Lord, for He has triumphed gloriously; the horse and its rider has He thrown into the sea.

E	G	Z	F	H	B	V	T	B	Z	C	P	Y	E	G	W	L	T	O	Q
A	R	T	G	I	O	F	H	L	L	D	Z	F	X	B	Z	H	U	T	M
A	E	C	D	M	N	R	R	V	B	O	P	O	W	E	R	G	C	O	J
P	A	C	G	Y	Y	S	S	I	D	C	V	R	C	B	Z	L	Q	T	E
U	T	Y	C	C	I	O	W	E	D	O	Y	F	D	Q	A	O	S	H	W
R	N	N	A	H	R	I	V	H	K	E	Q	R	X	W	D	R	T	E	X
S	E	E	D	Y	A	X	F	N	L	Q	R	G	R	D	W	I	U	L	P
U	S	K	Z	S	T	R	E	N	G	T	H	U	C	E	S	O	B	O	L
E	S	W	O	J	H	L	I	A	E	U	K	D	C	U	D	U	B	R	W
B	G	L	L	V	U	Y	J	O	B	H	Z	M	I	B	J	S	L	D	B
P	I	R	I	H	O	S	T	K	T	L	P	T	N	H	V	T	E	T	N
M	B	C	B	G	P	X	C	N	F	S	M	W	H	I	I	H	V	A	Q
Q	A	J	F	H	Z	J	J	M	Q	W	K	O	E	B	Q	R	S	F	P
S	U	N	H	D	E	X	C	E	L	L	E	N	C	Y	B	O	R	R	S
C	N	B	O	I	R	S	S	E	R	S	J	W	O	R	E	W	C	E	J
D	V	V	X	F	S	A	L	V	A	T	I	O	N	G	X	N	T	S	N
C	K	U	G	N	W	K	R	J	S	F	Q	M	I	K	A	J	O	I	U
Z	S	H	C	G	H	A	V	I	T	A	T	I	O	N	L	R	X	N	Y
S	V	T	F	A	P	T	R	Z	E	Q	D	R	P	L	T	Z	M	G	J
P	G	A	C	A	P	T	A	I	N	S	T	B	F	R	M	A	M	I	O

TO THE LORD	MAN OF WAR	GREATNESS	SING	CAPTAINS
RIDER	HOST	PURSUE	HORSE	GLORIOUS
STRENGTH	RED SEA	SALVATION	THROWN	STUBBLE
HABITATION	POWER	EXALT	CHARIOTS	EXCELLENCY

V	F	R	C	W	K	T	X	G	S	S	D	D	E	F	K	M	P	K	E
M	E	E	C	Z	N	R	M	M	B	T	L	E	N	H	J	T	R	P	R
Q	A	D	A	S	A	I	W	I	F	R	Y	Z	E	S	K	R	O	S	N
M	R	E	T	X	I	U	R	R	V	E	S	D	D	M	E	U	P	A	O
P	F	E	V	Z	C	M	Y	J	H	T	H	V	P	Y	P	Y	H	N	S
R	U	M	K	I	J	P	S	Z	G	C	F	I	E	Y	F	B	E	C	T
A	L	E	K	P	R	H	V	M	T	H	W	M	H	L	G	S	T	T	R
I	M	D	M	V	E	E	O	K	U	E	D	D	S	F	D	W	E	U	I
S	K	P	U	B	I	D	C	I	C	D	M	R	C	Y	R	A	S	A	L
E	U	R	M	H	A	B	I	T	A	T	I	O	N	Q	Y	L	S	R	S
S	T	W	P	Y	H	E	A	R	T	W	H	C	I	U	L	L	D	Y	E
B	M	P	K	N	A	V	O	L	X	T	O	Q	B	I	A	O	N	M	H
O	I	N	F	P	Z	O	E	J	Y	N	K	N	L	E	N	W	J	Z	C
Y	Y	W	P	V	T	I	M	B	R	E	L	S	D	B	D	E	I	L	H
C	O	N	G	E	A	L	E	D	D	J	M	E	J	E	R	D	Y	O	P
J	E	S	T	A	B	L	I	S	H	E	D	H	E	W	R	Z	E	I	M
H	A	B	G	Q	G	C	F	H	U	R	C	I	E	W	J	S	C	J	G
H	R	O	V	E	R	T	A	K	E	J	D	R	K	I	R	T	I	Q	K
A	U	O	G	D	A	N	C	E	S	F	Y	A	A	Z	G	J	W	L	C
L	J	Y	E	X	H	U	X	Z	H	O	L	I	N	E	S	S	P	F	D

OVERTAKE	STRETCHED	PROPHETESS	FEARFUL	SANCTUARY
CONGEALED	MERCY	DANCES	WONDERS	DRY LAND
HOLINESS	HABITATION	NOSTRILS	SWALLOWED	TIMBRELS
PRAISES	ESTABLISHED	HEART	REDEEMED	TRIUMPHED

46. MIRIAM PUNISHED: NUMBERS 12:1–15

Miriam and Aaron spoke against Moses because of the Ethiopian woman whom he had married:.... And they said, Has the Lord indeed spoken only by Moses? has He not spoken also by us? And the Lord heard it. (Now the man Moses was very meek, above all the men which were upon the face of the earth.) And the Lord spoke suddenly to Moses, and to Aaron, and to Miriam, Come out you three to the tabernacle of the congregation. And they three came out.... And He said, Hear now My words: If there be a prophet among you, I the Lord will make Myself known to him in a vision, and will speak to him in a dream. My servant Moses is not so, who is faithful in all My house. With him will I speak mouth to mouth, even apparently, and not in dark speeches; and the similitude of the Lord shall he behold: wherefore then were you not afraid to speak against My servant Moses? And the anger of the Lord was kindled against them; and He departed. And the cloud departed from off the tabernacle; and, behold, Miriam became leprous, white as snow.... And Moses cried to the Lord, saying, Heal her now, O God, I beseech You. And the Lord said to Moses,...let her be shut out from the camp seven days, and after that let her be received in again. And Miriam was shut out from the camp seven days: and the people journeyed not till Miriam was brought in again.

MEEK
TABERNACLE
PILLAR
DOOR
VISION
SPEECHES
LEPROUS
SNOW
SHUT OUT
JOURNEYED
EARTH
CONGREGATION
CLOUD
PROPHET
FAITHFUL
WHITE
FOOLISHLY
SEVEN DAYS
BROUGHT IN
MY SERVANT MOSES

C	M	H	G	Q	O	S	P	E	E	C	H	E	S	S	X	L	U
O	Y	U	Q	T	G	X	K	E	W	O	A	X	U	E	J	E	O
N	S	Y	T	C	H	F	G	A	K	L	V	I	D	V	O	P	T
G	E	A	P	I	L	L	A	R	F	Q	I	Q	R	E	U	R	A
R	R	R	Q	V	S	F	Z	T	I	A	S	L	F	N	R	O	B
E	V	G	Z	V	H	J	T	H	T	C	I	F	O	D	N	U	E
G	A	W	P	D	U	J	T	I	Q	N	O	A	O	A	E	S	R
A	N	H	E	R	T	Y	G	K	W	D	N	I	L	Y	Y	H	N
T	T	I	B	R	O	U	G	H	T	I	N	T	I	S	E	S	A
I	M	T	Y	W	U	P	O	E	U	E	Q	H	S	E	D	N	C
O	O	E	K	H	T	W	H	S	G	H	T	F	H	T	O	O	L
N	S	O	N	U	X	J	Z	E	A	M	L	U	L	I	V	W	E
D	E	L	R	S	D	O	O	R	T	G	G	L	Y	P	B	E	U
G	S	W	V	C	L	O	U	D	Y	N	R	M	E	E	K	G	L

47. THE DAUGHTERS OF ZELOPHEHAD: NUMBERS 27:1–7

Then came the daughters of Zelophehad, the son of Hepher, the son of Gilead, the son of Machir, the son of Manasseh, of the families of Manasseh the son of Joseph: and these are the names of his daughters; Mahlah, Noah, and Hoglah, and Milcah, and Tirzah. And they stood before Moses, and before Eleazar the priest, and before the princes and all the congregation, by the door of the tabernacle of the congregation, saying, Our father died in the wilderness, and he was not in the company of them that gathered themselves together against the Lord in the company of Korah; but died in his own sin, and had no sons. Why should the name of our father be done away from among his family, because he has no son? Give to us therefore a possession among the brethren of our father. And Moses brought their cause before the Lord. And the Lord spoke to Moses, saying, The daughters of Zelophehad speak right: you shall surely give them a possession of an inheritance among their father's brethren; and you shall cause the inheritance of their father to pass to them.

NUMBERS 36:10–12

Even as the Lord commanded Moses, so did the daughters of Zelophehad: for Mahlah, Tirzah, and Hoglah, and Milcah, and Noah, the daughters of Zelophehad, were married to their father's brothers' sons: and they were married into the families of the sons of Manasseh the son of Joseph, and their inheritance remained in the tribe of the family of their father.

JOSHUA 17:3–6

But Zelophehad, the son of Hepher, the son of Gilead, the son of Machir, the son of Manasseh, had no sons, but daughters: and these are the names of his daughters, Mahlah, and Noah, Hoglah, Milcah, and Tirzah. And they came near before Eleazar the priest, and before Joshua the son of Nun, and before the princes, saying, The Lord commanded Moses to give us an inheritance among our brethren. Therefore according to the commandment of the Lord he gave them an inheritance among the brethren of their father. And there fell ten portions to Manasseh, beside the land of Gilead and Bashan, which were on the other side Jordan; because the daughters of Manasseh had an inheritance among his sons: and the rest of Manasseh's sons had the land of Gilead.

X	L	W	J	Z	S	I	K	R	R										
Z	M	I	R	N	Y	N	L	Q	Y										
V	Q	L	J	P	U	H	T	S	X	P	B	N							
G	O	D	G	O	R	E	A	T	F	B	E	M	D			E	E	P	A
N	U	E	V	S	H	R	B	B	U	V	F	I	E	T	R	I	B	E	N
R	R	R	H	S	U	I	E	B	S	O	O	L	Q	O	X	H	J	Y	X
K	F	N	C	E	I	T	R	I	O	M	R	C	E	O	L	W	G	I	E
A	A	E	A	S	Z	A	N	K	T	A	E	A	W	U	S	P	R	T	L
Y	T	S	U	S	E	N	A	N	O	N	T	H	F	E	E	Z	N	E	E
Z	H	S	S	I	W	C	C	K	E	A	H	B	G	N	M	B	O	N	A
A	E	D	E	O	S	E	L	A	J	S	E	X	N	D	D	U	S	P	Z
B	R	V	Z	N	S	H	E	L	F	S	L	F	Z	A	G	J	O	O	A
Z	G	Q	I	M	I	P	P	H	S	E	O	J	S	M	E	F	N	R	R
Y	F	T	T	R	Y	G	H	B	X	H	R	F	P	P	F	Y	S	T	E
G	I	L	E	A	D	U	O	G	A	I	D	X	D	N	Q	G	B	I	S
V	R	X	Q	X	X	Y	G	P	I	E	X	M	Q	F	G	H	D	O	I
K	T	G	Q	S	C	V	L	D	U	R	N	B	E	J	H	O	A	N	L
K	O	R	A	H	L	H	A	P	T	I	R	Z	A	H	P	R	R	S	E
D	E	N	O	A	H	Y	H	G	Z	E	L	O	P	H	E	H	A	D	D
K	H	Q	C	L	N	O	L	Q	X	M	T	M	A	H	L	A	H	M	F

ZELOPHEHAD	MAHLAH	NOAH	HOGLAH	MILCAH
TIRZAH	ELEAZAR	TABERNACLE	WILDERNESS	KORAH
NO SONS	OUR FATHER	POSSESSION	CAUSE	BEFORE THE LORD
INHERITANCE	MANASSEH	GILEAD	TRIBE	TEN PORTIONS

48. DEBORAH AND JAEL: JUDGES 4:4–24

And Deborah, a prophetess, the wife of Lapidoth, she judged Israel at that time...and the children of Israel came up to her for judgment. And she sent and called Barak the son of Abinoam out of Kedeshnaphtali, and said to him, Has not the Lord God of Israel commanded, saying, Go and draw toward mount Tabor, and take with you ten thousand men of the children of Naphtali and of the children of Zebulun? And I will draw to you to the river Kishon Sisera, the captain of Jabin's army, with his chariots and his multitude; and I will deliver him into your hand. And Barak said to her, If you will go with me, then I will go: but if you will not go with me, then I will not go. And she said, I will surely go with you: notwithstanding the journey that you take shall not be for your honor for the Lord shall sell Sisera into the hand of a woman.

And Deborah arose and went with Barak to Kedesh.... He went up with ten thousand men at his feet: and Deborah went up with him. Now Heber the Kenite, which was of the children of Hobab the father in law of Moses, had severed himself from the Kenites, and pitched his tent to the plain of Zaanaim, which is by Kedesh. And they showed Sisera that Barak the son of Abinoam was gone up to mount Tabor. And Sisera gathered together all his chariots, even nine hundred chariots of iron, and all the people that were with him, from Harosheth of the Gentiles to the river of Kishon.

And Deborah said to Barak, Up; for this is the day in which the Lord has delivered Sisera into your hand: is not the Lord gone out before you? So Barak went down from mount Tabor, and ten thousand men after him. And the Lord discomfited Sisera, and all his chariots, and all his host with the edge of the sword before Barak; so that Sisera lighted down off his chariot, and fled away on his feet. But Barak pursued after the chariots, and after the host, to Harosheth of the Gentiles: and all the host of Sisera fell upon the edge of the sword; and there was not a man left.

However Sisera fled away on his feet to the tent of Jael the wife of Heber the Kenite: for there was peace between Jabin the king of Hazor and the house of Heber the Kenite. And Jael went out to meet Sisera, and said to him, Turn in, my lord, turn in to me; fear not. And when he had turned in to her into the tent, she covered him with a mantle. And he said to her, Give me, I pray you, a little water to drink; for I am thirsty. And she opened a bottle of milk, and gave him drink, and covered him. Again he said to her, Stand in the door of the tent, and it shall be, when any man does come and inquire of you, and say, Is there any man here? that you shall say, No. Then Jael Heber's wife took a nail of the tent, and took a hammer in her hand, and went softly to him, and smote the nail into his temples, and fastened it into the ground: for he was fast asleep and weary. So he died.

And, behold, as Barak pursued Sisera, Jael came out to meet him, and said to him, Come, and I will show you the man whom you seek. And when he came into her tent, behold, Sisera lay dead, and the nail was in his temples. So God subdued on that day Jabin the king of Canaan before the children of Israel.

E	S	S	R	S	C	L	U	W	Z	Z	L	A	L	E	K	W	G	H	J
B	U	W	H	P	N	B	A	Q	V	E	J	S	F	R	B	T	U	X	T
X	O	F	N	U	V	A	U	P	A	R	H	U	G	J	X	G	G	Z	E
H	A	F	Q	E	A	R	J	R	I	Y	I	B	D	V	R	W	O	G	N
D	V	T	A	J	N	A	N	I	S	D	B	V	B	G	X	G	N	C	T
G	T	G	R	W	M	K	W	V	I	Y	O	O	E	U	E	F	E	C	H
T	A	Q	K	S	O	V	N	Y	S	I	I	T	Z	R	M	D	O	H	O
P	Z	H	H	I	I	M	N	J	E	N	J	I	H	F	Q	M	U	A	U
M	O	U	T	M	N	R	A	E	R	T	D	I	M	Y	N	H	T	R	S
M	N	T	X	B	F	Z	O	N	A	O	T	I	E	V	T	J	Y	I	A
Y	A	Z	P	N	A	T	B	N	N	T	S	U	P	D	T	B	I	O	N
K	X	F	K	E	H	I	V	F	G	H	Z	C	H	E	R	E	G	T	D
T	E	N	T	N	A	I	L	Q	A	E	W	I	R	L	Q	X	W	S	A
M	B	E	F	O	R	E	Y	O	U	H	D	I	A	I	J	G	S	I	V
A	L	B	Q	G	L	S	X	O	H	A	R	I	I	V	O	L	W	T	Y
M	J	A	C	B	I	C	K	T	W	N	P	X	M	E	K	J	X	D	J
I	G	U	Q	G	H	Q	C	F	A	D	E	C	E	R	F	A	A	T	Z
O	P	P	R	E	S	S	E	D	F	K	Y	W	Z	E	G	E	E	H	G
E	G	E	N	T	I	L	E	S	A	C	K	D	N	D	B	L	N	P	Y
T	D	E	B	O	R	A	H	I	S	T	H	I	R	S	T	Y	U	L	P

LAPIDOTH
JUDGED
EPHRAIM
SISERA
GENTILES
CHARIOTS
OPPRESSED
DEBORAH
BARAK
INTO THE HAND
OF A WOMAN
TEN THOUSAND
IRON
RIVER
DELIVERED
GONE OUT
BEFORE YOU
THIRSTY
JAEL
TENT NAIL

49. THE SONG OF DEBORAH: JUDGES 5:1–31

The story of Barak, Deborah, and Jael shows that God will accomplish His plans, even if the source of deliverance is unexpected. In this case, He saved Israel using two women who acted to protect their people.

Then sang Deborah and Barak the son of Abinoam on that day, saying, Praise you the Lord for the avenging of Israel, when the people willingly offered themselves. Hear, O you kings; give ear, O you princes; I, even I, will sing to the Lord: I will sing praise to the Lord God of Israel. Lord, when You went out of Seir, when You marched out of the field of Edom, the earth trembled, and the heavens dropped, the clouds also dropped water. The mountains melted from before the Lord, even that Sinai from before the Lord God of Israel. In the days of Shamgar the son of Anath, in the days of Jael, the highways were unoccupied, and the travellers walked through byways. The inhabitants of the villages ceased, they ceased in Israel, until that I Deborah arose, that I arose a mother in Israel. They chose new gods; then was war in the gates: was there a shield or spear seen among forty thousand in Israel? My heart is toward the governors of Israel, that offered themselves willingly among the people. Bless you the Lord. Speak, you that ride on white asses, you that sit in judgment, and walk by the way. They that are delivered from the noise of archers in the places of drawing water, there shall they rehearse the righteous acts of the Lord, even the righteous acts toward the inhabitants of His villages in Israel: then shall the people of the Lord go down to the gates. Awake, awake, Deborah: awake, awake, utter a song: arise, Barak, and lead your captivity captive, you son of Abinoam. Then he made him that remains have dominion over the nobles among the people: the Lord made me have dominion over the mighty....

Blessed above women shall Jael the wife of Heber the Kenite be, blessed shall she be above women in the tent. He asked water, and she gave him milk; she brought forth butter in a lordly dish. She put her hand to the nail, and her right hand to the workmen's hammer; and with the hammer she smote Sisera, she smote off his head, when she had pierced and stricken through his temples. At her feet he bowed, he fell, he lay down: at her feet he bowed, he fell: where he bowed, there he fell down dead. The mother of Sisera looked out at a window, and cried through the lattice, Why is his chariot so long in coming? why tarry the wheels of his chariots? Her wise ladies answered her, yea, she returned answer to herself, Have they not sped? have they not divided the prey; to every man a damsel or two; to Sisera a prey of divers colors, a prey of divers colors of needlework, of divers colors of needlework on both sides, meet for the necks of them that take the spoil? So let all your enemies perish, O Lord: but let them that love Him be as the sun when it goes forth in his might.

K	B	P	A	Z	X	Z	Y	I	P	B	L	G	S	H	F	T	Y	N	O
T	R	A	V	E	L	L	E	R	S	D	S	L	G	K	F	I	J	R	B
T	G	Z	N	O	M	P	V	H	L	O	I	F	U	Z	L	P	Y	O	Y
C	O	M	Q	J	K	D	T	F	S	M	L	Q	I	M	C	O	L	O	W
A	D	R	O	P	P	E	D	L	P	I	N	X	X	Q	Q	N	O	T	A
K	F	A	A	B	S	P	N	T	H	N	G	S	A	L	W	R	R	D	Y
F	F	I	W	D	V	M	K	W	F	I	G	V	R	X	H	H	D	S	S
T	D	D	Y	K	C	Y	D	N	K	O	U	E	C	D	B	Q	G	C	C
B	D	I	S	N	C	Y	C	H	D	N	F	U	H	H	G	B	O	G	B
P	K	V	J	L	T	S	Q	E	S	S	C	A	E	R	T	K	D	O	S
R	D	I	A	W	A	K	E	A	P	E	X	Y	R	O	R	Z	L	V	I
I	H	S	J	A	C	T	A	V	R	Y	L	D	S	H	E	E	L	E	N
N	O	I	H	A	V	I	B	E	A	Z	U	A	Y	L	M	J	Q	R	G
C	A	O	I	X	G	E	L	N	I	Z	K	Y	I	A	B	A	W	N	P
E	D	N	X	U	G	H	G	S	S	T	B	E	U	B	L	S	R	O	R
S	Y	S	I	W	H	A	M	M	E	R	D	O	M	G	E	F	I	R	A
R	I	G	H	T	E	O	U	S	Z	R	S	Q	U	N	D	I	T	S	I
P	R	I	F	M	N	E	E	D	L	E	W	O	R	K	L	F	E	J	S
P	K	R	Q	Q	Z	U	M	Y	P	J	P	L	R	J	Z	I	R	T	E
O	E	D	P	B	V	P	R	E	H	E	A	R	S	E	A	H	T	V	Z

PRAISE	TREMBLED	BYWAYS	AWAKE	WRITER
PRINCES	HEAVENS	ARCHERS	DOMINION	DIVISIONS
SING PRAISE	DROPPED	REHEARSE	ROOT	HAMMER
LORD GOD	TRAVELLERS	RIGHTEOUS	GOVERNOR	NEEDLEWORK

50. JEPHTHAH'S DAUGHTER: JUDGES 11:29–40

Then the Spirit of the Lord came upon Jephthah.... And Jephthah vowed a vow to the Lord, and said, If You shall without fail deliver the children of Ammon into my hands, then it shall be, that whatsoever comes forth of the doors of my house to meet me, when I return in peace from the children of Ammon, shall surely be the Lord's, and I will offer it up for a burned offering. So Jephthah passed over to the children of Ammon to fight against them; and the Lord delivered them into his hands. And he smote them from Aroer, even till you come to Minnith, even twenty cities, and to the plain of the vineyards, with a very great slaughter. Thus the children of Ammon were subdued before the children of Israel.

And Jephthah came to Mizpeh to his house, and, behold, his daughter came out to meet him with timbrels and with dances: and she was his only child; beside her he had neither son nor daughter. And it came to pass, when he saw her, that he rent his clothes, and said, Alas, my daughter! you have brought me very low, and you are one of them that trouble me: for I have opened my mouth to the Lord, and I cannot go back. And she said to him, My father, if you have opened your mouth to the Lord, do to me according to that which has proceeded out of your mouth; forasmuch as the Lord has taken vengeance for you of your enemies, even of the children of Ammon. And she said to her father, Let this thing be done for me: let me alone two months, that I may go up and down upon the mountains, and bewail my virginity, I and my fellows. And he said, Go. And he sent her away for two months: and she went with her companions, and bewailed her virginity upon the mountains. And it came to pass at the end of two months, that she returned to her father, who did with her according to his vow which he had vowed: and she knew no man. And it was a custom in Israel, that the daughters of Israel went yearly to lament the daughter of Jephthah the Gileadite four days in a year.

Y	N	I	V	O	W	E	D	A	V	O	W	W	B	V	G	S	A	C	F
Y	T	J	A	T	T	R	R	P	V	S	P	P	Z	A	M	B	L	N	O
V	W	Q	P	B	B	E	W	A	I	L	H	U	C	B	O	Q	K	G	U
C	O	I	R	K	O	H	G	D	T	P	M	X	O	R	U	J	E	C	R
Y	M	Z	O	J	Y	A	T	Z	B	N	V	H	N	V	N	E	H	U	D
A	O	K	C	K	B	K	L	L	O	L	R	U	L	X	T	P	I	S	A
I	N	C	E	Z	N	X	E	A	N	D	K	N	Y	T	A	H	W	T	Y
Z	T	L	E	R	E	E	B	Y	M	P	A	K	C	S	I	T	I	O	S
E	H	P	D	U	L	R	W	X	H	E	B	P	H	I	N	H	E	M	Y
V	S	A	E	Q	L	F	K	N	Z	T	N	W	I	R	S	A	N	I	I
R	A	E	D	A	Q	M	S	O	O	S	V	T	L	A	H	H	D	N	J
C	W	K	I	K	A	A	E	A	G	M	C	H	D	C	Q	V	I	I	C
Z	K	Z	N	H	B	I	R	C	K	A	A	J	C	B	E	R	V	S	H
A	R	O	E	R	E	M	I	Z	P	E	H	N	X	G	T	P	P	R	G
F	Q	O	F	F	E	R	I	T	U	P	O	Y	B	H	N	B	B	A	Y
X	N	L	A	O	H	C	U	S	P	R	G	I	H	S	M	O	T	E	N
A	G	B	L	T	I	S	U	B	D	U	E	D	G	H	K	Z	E	L	W
K	D	A	N	C	E	S	M	I	D	C	B	V	A	M	M	O	N	L	P
H	R	Q	Q	L	A	W	Z	U	S	T	I	M	B	R	E	L	S		
E	N	Q	O	P	E	N	M	Y	M	O	U	T	H	J	R	F	B		

JEPHTHAH
AROER
ONLY CHILD
BEWAIL
FOUR DAY
LAMENT
TWO MONTHS
AMMON
SUBDUED
OPEN MY MOUTH
KNEW NO MAN
SMOTE
DANCES
MOUNTAINS
VOWED A VOW
MIZPEH
PROCEEDED
CUSTOM IN ISRAEL
OFFER IT UP
TIMBRELS

51. THE LEVITE'S CONCUBINE: JUDGES 19:1–29

This biblical story is seldom used in sermons, but it highlights the problem of sin and evil in this world. After the woman committed adultery, her husband, a Levite, let the men of Gibeah abuse her to the point of death.

And it came to pass in those days, when there was no king in Israel, that there was a certain Levite sojourning on the side of mount Ephraim, who took to him a concubine out of Bethlehemjudah. And his concubine played the whore against him, and went away from him to her father's house to Bethlehemjudah, and was there four whole months. And her husband arose, and went after her, to speak friendly to her, and to bring her again, having his servant with him, and a couple of asses: and she brought him into her father's house: and when the father of the damsel saw him, he rejoiced to meet him. And his father in law, the damsel's father, retained him; and he abode with him three days: so they did eat and drink, and lodged there....

But the man would not tarry that night, but he rose up and departed, and came opposite Jebus, which is Jerusalem; and there were with him two asses saddled, his concubine also was with him. And when they were by Jebus, the day was far spent; and the servant said to his master, Come, I pray you, and let us turn in into this city of the Jebusites, and lodge in it. And his master said to him, We will not turn aside here into the city of a stranger, that is not of the children of Israel; we will pass over to Gibeah. And he said to his servant, Come, and let us draw near to one of these places to lodge all night, in Gibeah, or in Ramah. And they passed on and went their way; and the sun went down upon them when they were by Gibeah, which belongs to Benjamin. And they turned aside there, to go in and to lodge in Gibeah: and when he went in, he sat him down in a street of the city: for there was no man that took them into his house to lodging.

And, behold, there came an old man from his work out of the field at evening, which was also of mount Ephraim; and he sojourned in Gibeah: but the men of the place were Benjamites. And when he had lifted up his eyes, he saw a wayfaring man in the street of the city: and the old man said, Where go you? And where come you? And he said to him, We are passing from Bethlehemjudah toward the side of mount Ephraim; from there am I: and I went to Bethlehemjudah, but I am now going to the house of the Lord; and there is no man that receives me to house. Yet there is both straw and provender for our asses; and there is bread and wine also for me, and for your handmaid, and for the young man which is with your servants: there is no want of any thing. And the old man said, Peace be with you; howsoever let all your wants lie upon me; only lodge not in the street. So he brought him into his house, and gave provender to the asses: and they washed their feet, and did eat and drink.

Now as they were making their hearts merry, behold, the men of the city, certain sons of Belial, beset the house round about, and beat at the door, and spoke to the master of the house, the old man, saying, Bring forth the man that came into your house, that we may know him. And the man, the master of the house, went out to them, and said to them, Nay, my brethren, nay, I pray you, do not so wickedly; seeing that this man is come into my house, do not this folly. Behold, here is my daughter a maiden, and his concubine; them I will bring out now, and humble you them, and do with them what seems good to you: but to this man do not so vile a thing. But the men would not hearken to him: so the man took his concubine, and brought her forth to them; and they knew her, and abused her all the night until the morning: and when the day began to spring, they let her go. Then came the woman in the dawning of the day, and fell down at the door of the man's house where her lord was, till it was light. And her lord rose up in the morning, and opened the doors of the house, and went out to go his way: and, behold, the woman his concubine was fallen down at the door of the house, and her hands were upon the threshold. And he said to her, Up, and let us be going. But none answered. Then the man took her up upon an ass, and the man rose up, and got him to his place. And when he was come into his house, he took a knife, and laid hold on his concubine, and divided her, together with her bones, into twelve pieces, and sent her into all the coasts of Israel.

O	O	C	Z	T	W	Z	G	C	S	I	K	N	S	W	F	E	W	F	M
D	J	L	E	V	I	T	E	G	O	H	H	O	T	F	W	O	J	L	A
Z	Z	L	O	D	G	E	X	W	J	W	G	K	V	A	G	T	X	Q	I
E	J	R	S	G	F	U	X	X	O	W	M	X	F	T	T	A	B	A	D
A	V	D	I	V	I	D	E	D	U	M	H	Y	P	H	I	H	T	A	E
N	E	E	U	A	V	P	E	B	R	C	B	Z	D	E	G	S	A	E	N
S	F	U	N	V	B	E	C	E	N	Q	E	I	K	R	I	K	R	V	C
P	N	M	Z	I	H	R	M	X	I	W	T	T	C	I	C	H	R	K	I
D	R	N	K	Q	N	H	T	V	N	C	H	A	R	N	B	C	Y	P	T
K	V	O	H	N	G	G	L	I	G	Q	L	P	F	L	L	O	E	O	Y
B	F	T	V	N	Y	N	F	U	U	G	E	O	R	A	R	N	J	J	S
D	A	M	S	E	L	Y	J	P	G	B	H	D	L	W	E	C	U	S	T
F	J	B	W	P	N	J	C	B	E	M	E	R	R	Y	T	U	T	F	R
P	O	S	U	L	Q	D	G	E	G	R	M	P	X	T	A	B	T	T	E
E	X	L	N	S	D	D	E	Q	N	E	J	K	K	X	I	I	N	L	E
I	Z	Q	Q	Y	E	V	X	R	E	B	U	F	V	S	N	N	N	E	T
G	S	R	X	A	X	D	Z	J	C	N	D	T	V	Z	E	E	M	D	Q
J	F	J	Q	D	B	E	L	I	A	L	A	O	Q	A	D	D	K	M	N
T	S	T	R	A	W	K	Z	H	I	B	H	Q	N	O	K	I	N	G	R
F	A	J	B	J	E	R	U	S	A	L	E	M	W	K	U	O	F	M	R

NO KING	LEVITE	SOJOURNING	BETHLEHEMJUDAH	CONCUBINE
DAMSEL	FATHER IN LAW	RETAINED	BE MERRY	TARRY
PROVENDER	LODGE	JERUSALEM	CITY STREET	STRAW
EVENING	BELIAL	MAIDEN	ABUSED	DIVIDED

52. WIVES FOR THE BENJAMITES: JUDGES 21:1–23

Now the men of Israel had sworn in Mizpeh, saying, There shall not any of us give his daughter to Benjamin as a wife. And the people came to the house of God, and abode there till evening before God, and lifted up their voices, and wept sore.... And the children of Israel repented them for Benjamin their brother, and said, There is one tribe cut off from Israel this day. How shall we do for wives for them that remain, seeing we have sworn by the Lord that we will not give them of our daughters to wives? And they said, What one is there of the tribes of Israel that came not up to Mizpeh to the Lord? And, behold, there came none to the camp from Jabeshgilead to the assembly.... And they found among the inhabitants of Jabeshgilead four hundred young virgins, that had known no man by lying with any male: and they brought them to the camp to Shiloh, which is in the land of Canaan....

And Benjamin came again at that time; and they gave them wives which they had saved alive of the women of Jabeshgilead: and yet so they sufficed them not. And the people repented them for Benjamin, because that the Lord had made a breach in the tribes of Israel. Then the elders of the congregation said, How shall we do for wives for them that remain, seeing the women are destroyed out of Benjamin? And they said, There must be an inheritance for them that be escaped of Benjamin, that a tribe be not destroyed out of Israel. However we may not give them wives of our daughters: for the children of Israel have sworn, saying, Cursed be he that gives a wife to Benjamin.

Then they said, Behold, there is a feast of the Lord in Shiloh yearly in a place which is on the north side of Bethel, on the east side of the highway that goes up from Bethel to Shechem, and on the south of Lebonah. Therefore they commanded the children of Benjamin, saying, Go and lie in wait in the vineyards; and see, and, behold, if the daughters of Shiloh come out to dance in dances, then come you out of the vineyards, and catch you every man his wife of the daughters of Shiloh, and go to the land of Benjamin. And it shall be, when their fathers or their brethren come to us to complain, that we will say to them, Be favorable to them for our sakes: because we reserved not to each man his wife in the war: for you did not give to them at this time, that you should be guilty. And the children of Benjamin did so, and took them wives, according to their number, of them that danced, whom they caught: and they went and returned to their inheritance, and repaired the cities, and dwelled in them.

Y	M	X	T	C	A	S	R	E	P	A	I	R	E	D	R	V	W	U	S
F	W	D	X	O	O	F	G	D	A	N	C	E	S	C	V	I	N	X	R
B	R	K	G	M	Q	Y	K	J	C	P	N	O	F	U	V	N	Z	P	E
O	S	R	F	P	Q	S	F	E	Z	M	V	A	E	J	E	E	R	E	P
Q	Y	D	M	L	Y	T	A	A	J	I	B	T	P	O	H	Y	X	A	E
B	S	E	F	A	K	Y	J	N	V	J	Y	H	D	L	I	A	D	C	N
D	E	H	N	I	M	F	V	H	F	O	N	M	W	P	R	R	W	E	T
E	C	C	I	N	F	T	Q	A	R	X	R	B	X	G	V	D	E	A	E
B	G	C	Q	L	T	D	M	Q	L	R	L	A	A	S	N	S	L	B	D
E	H	K	D	K	O	R	I	D	T	I	B	T	B	B	Y	S	L	L	S
N	Z	D	I	O	R	H	B	E	D	C	A	R	H	L	M	U	E	Y	Y
J	K	F	N	R	N	M	T	T	F	E	T	N	K	B	E	Q	D	V	Q
A	C	L	A	C	K	I	N	G	F	O	N	E	T	R	I	B	E	V	U
M	N	F	H	H	D	Z	O	I	W	C	U	W	A	E	R	X	R	D	T
I	O	Z	I	Z	H	P	Q	M	Y	Z	O	O	G	J	S	X	P	W	W
N	P	R	O	N	D	E	O	P	T	Y	Y	F	V	G	O	T	E	Y	C
V	U	W	R	K	Y	H	B	N	C	U	T	O	F	F	D	R	Q	B	W
B	S	O	A	O	V	N	A	B	K	T	S	R	Y	K	D	M	R	L	M
D	B	T	T	I	W	I	W	T	E	V	A	C	A	U	G	H	T	X	K
S	D	E	S	T	R	O	Y	E	D	N	E	S	C	A	P	E	D	H	O

MIZPEH
MORROW
VALIANTEST
PEACEABLY
FAVORABLE
BENJAMIN
OATH
REPENTED
VINEYARDS
CAUGHT
ONE TRIBE
CUT OFF
ESCAPED
DANCES
REPAIRED
LACKING
SHILOH
DESTROYED
COMPLAIN
DWELLED

53. HANNAH: 1 SAMUEL 1:1–7

Like the Virgin Mary's cousin Elisabeth, Hannah in the Old Testament hoped and prayed for a child, and God granted her request.

There was a certain man..., and his name was Elkanah...: and he had two wives; the name of the one was Hannah, and the name of the other Peninnah: and Peninnah had children, but Hannah had no children. And this man went up out of his city yearly to worship and to sacrifice to the LORD of hosts in Shiloh. And the two sons of Eli, Hophni and Phinehas, the priests of the LORD, were there. And when the time was that Elkanah offered, he gave to Peninnah his wife, and to all her sons and her daughters, portions: but to Hannah he gave a worthy portion; for he loved Hannah: but the LORD had shut up her womb. And her adversary also provoked her sore, for to make her fret, because the LORD had shut up her womb. And as he did so year by year, when she went up to the house of the LORD, so she provoked her; therefore she wept, and did not eat.

T	M	A	V	J	E	R	O	H	A	M	I	W	P	R	W	R	C	U	X
S	P	S	J	O	R	Z	S	D	O	R	V	L	O	E	Q	Y	H	C	X
G	M	B	S	J	S	L	I	W	S	F	E	R	R	F	M	D	I	R	Y
H	K	P	B	D	K	Z	U	O	T	K	P	T	T	S	P	Z	L	L	I
N	K	P	S	B	V	D	M	R	D	R	H	Q	I	M	F	P	D	Z	M
C	U	N	Y	J	X	V	V	S	C	H	R	P	O	W	P	G	R	O	B
M	C	F	Q	F	N	J	G	H	X	F	A	P	N	H	E	Q	E	V	S
L	O	V	E	D	I	N	M	I	D	R	I	S	S	S	T	P	N	S	V
K	C	Y	E	A	R	L	Y	P	N	E	M	V	V	M	S	D	T	H	M
V	C	L	U	J	X	O	Z	C	Z	T	L	Y	Z	U	A	S	I	I	R
P	U	U	W	J	G	T	D	A	L	I	J	F	D	A	C	J	C	L	W
E	N	L	K	C	Z	B	U	F	J	P	V	W	D	C	R	R	C	O	P
N	P	N	Z	I	O	I	X	N	D	A	D	E	W	A	I	K	S	H	R
I	I	R	W	O	R	T	H	Y	X	K	C	N	I	X	F	P	D	J	I
N	Q	C	X	L	O	R	D	O	F	H	O	S	T	S	I	J	Q	W	E
N	W	S	M	X	Y	H	A	E	B	R	Z	W	Q	Z	C	K	F	S	S
A	E	L	K	A	N	A	H	P	S	S	V	P	K	C	E	N	U	J	T
H	H	P	R	O	V	O	K	E	D	H	A	N	N	A	H	Y	X	B	S
A	I	K	X	R	T	Y	H	N	C	A	D	V	E	R	S	A	R	Y	
S	H	U	T	U	P	C	R	E	M	Q	M	Y	Q	U	X	H	T	U	

EPHRAIM	ELKANAH
JEROHAM	HANNAH
PENINNAH	CHILDREN
YEARLY	WORSHIP
SACRIFICE	LOVED
SHILOH	PRIESTS
ADVERSARY	FRET
WORTHY	SHUT UP
PROVOKED	WEPT
PORTIONS	LORD OF HOSTS

54. HANNAH'S VOW: 1 SAMUEL 1:8–18

Then said Elkanah her husband to her, Hannah, why weep you? and why eat you not? and why is your heart grieved? am not I better to you than ten sons? So Hannah rose up after they had eaten in Shiloh, and after they had drunk. Now Eli the priest sat upon a seat by a post of the temple of the Lord. And she was in bitterness of soul, and prayed to the Lord, and wept sore. And she vowed a vow, and said, O Lord of hosts, if You will indeed look on the affliction of your handmaid, and remember me, and not forget your handmaid, but will give to your handmaid a man child, then I will give him to the Lord all the days of his life, and there shall no razor come upon his head....

Now Hannah, she spoke in her heart; only her lips moved, but her voice was not heard: therefore Eli thought she had been drunken. And Eli said to her, How long will you be drunken? put away your wine from you. And Hannah answered and said, No, my lord, I am a woman of a sorrowful spirit: I have drunk neither wine nor strong drink, but have poured out my soul before the Lord. Count not your handmaid for a daughter of Belial: for out of the abundance of my complaint and grief have I spoken until now. Then Eli answered and said, Go in peace: and the God of Israel grant you your petition that you have asked of Him. And she said, Let your handmaid find grace in your sight. So the woman went her way, and did eat, and her countenance was no more sad.

G	R	A	N	T	G	P	S	Z	R	A	Z	O	R	H	V	S	O
M	A	G	G	M	F	F	O	S	K	J	C	F	G	D	L	W	A
A	F	W	O	B	G	J	R	X	W	X	O	D	Q	G	D	M	B
N	F	P	D	R	C	T	R	O	C	C	U	P	I	O	R	P	U
C	L	R	O	E	Q	M	O	S	P	O	N	F	Z	I	U	O	N
H	I	Z	F	M	F	A	W	T	R	M	T	T	F	N	N	U	D
I	C	Z	I	E	B	R	F	X	O	P	E	Z	H	P	K	R	A
L	T	V	S	M	E	K	U	Q	E	L	N	X	S	E	E	E	N
D	I	O	R	B	T	E	L	E	L	A	A	Z	O	A	N	D	C
I	O	W	A	E	T	D	I	N	O	I	N	J	U	C	P	H	E
O	N	E	E	R	E	S	Y	S	V	N	C	I	L	E	C	Z	K
O	K	D	L	T	R	O	N	Y	M	T	E	G	R	I	E	F	P
X	A	S	I	G	H	T	I	C	O	N	T	I	N	U	E	D	L

SOUL
AFFLICTION
MAN CHILD
MARKED
SORROWFUL
ABUNDANCE
GRIEF
GRANT
COUNTENANCE
GOD OF ISRAEL
BETTER
VOWED
REMEMBER
RAZOR
DRUNKEN
POURED
COMPLAINT
GO IN PEACE
SIGHT
CONTINUED

55. HANNAH GIVES BIRTH TO SAMUEL: 1 SAMUEL 1:19–28

And Elkanah knew Hannah his wife; and the Lord remembered her. Wherefore it came to pass, when the time was come about after Hannah had conceived, that she bore a son, and called his name Samuel, saying, Because I have asked him of the Lord. And the man Elkanah, and all his house, went up to offer to the Lord the yearly sacrifice, and his vow. But Hannah went not up; for she said to her husband, I will not go up until the child be weaned, and then I will bring him, that he may appear before the Lord, and there abide for ever....

And when she had weaned him, she took him up with her..., and brought him to the house of the Lord in Shiloh: and the child was young. And they slew a bullock, and brought the child to Eli. And she said, Oh my lord, as your soul lives, my lord, I am the woman that stood by you here, praying to the Lord. For this child I prayed; and the Lord has given me my petition which I asked of Him: therefore also I have lent him to the Lord; as long as he lives he shall be lent to the Lord.

E	E	U	W	J	Y	J	A	J	B	H	I	S	W	O	R	D	W
E	S	R	E	A	J	D	F	B	O	T	T	L	E	W	S	A	A
B	T	Z	A	E	I	A	M	B	T	Q	A	Z	G	O	I	B	S
U	A	H	N	R	E	R	O	S	E	Y	R	K	X	R	L	I	K
L	B	D	E	D	D	P	X	A	A	E	R	O	U	S	Y	D	E
L	L	S	D	Q	H	E	U	J	I	A	Y	I	Q	H	H	E	D
O	I	R	E	T	U	R	N	E	D	R	Y	P	M	I	G	E	O
C	S	M	O	R	N	I	N	G	Y	L	X	L	I	P	D	P	F
K	H	Z	R	V	H	E	M	P	O	Y	W	M	Y	E	E	H	H
S	D	U	F	J	E	F	L	O	U	R	G	Q	N	D	I	A	I
T	O	T	H	E	L	O	R	D	N	X	Z	B	Y	P	N	H	M
L	W	Z	Z	C	L	R	B	X	G	O	W	O	L	E	N	T	W
G	A	P	P	E	A	R	C	Z	H	X	N	C	H	I	L	D	D

ROSE
WORSHIPED
BOTTLE
WEANED
ABIDE
ESTABLISH
EPHAH

MORNING
RETURNED
YEARLY
APPEAR
TARRY
BULLOCKS
FLOUR

TO THE LORD
ASKED OF HIM
HIS WORD
LENT
YOUNG
CHILD

56. HANNAH REJOICES: 1 SAMUEL 2:1–11

Hannah prayed, and said, My heart rejoices in the LORD, my horn is exalted in the LORD: my mouth is enlarged over my enemies; because I rejoice in your salvation. There is none holy as the LORD: for there is none beside You: neither is there any rock like our God. Talk no more so exceeding proudly; let not arrogancy come out of your mouth: for the LORD is a God of knowledge, and by Him actions are weighed. The bows of the mighty men are broken, and they that stumbled are girded with strength. They that were full have hired out themselves for bread; and they that were hungry ceased: so that the barren has born seven; and she that has many children is waxed feeble. The LORD kills, and makes alive: He bring down to the grave, and brings up. The LORD makes poor, and makes rich: He brings low, and lifts up. He raises up the poor out of the dust, and lifts up the beggar from the dunghill, to set them among princes, and to make them inherit the throne of glory: for the pillars of the earth are the LORD's, and He has set the world upon them. He will keep the feet of His saints, and the wicked shall be silent in darkness; for by strength shall no man prevail. The adversaries of the LORD shall be broken to pieces; out of heaven shall He thunder upon them: the LORD shall judge the ends of the earth; and He shall give strength to His king, and exalt the horn of His anointed.... And the child did minister to the LORD before Eli the priest.

HORN
ENLARGED
SALVATION
BESIDE
EXCEEDING
ARROGANCE
ACTION
BOWS
LIFTS UP
ANOINTED
MOUTH
ENEMIES
NONE
ROCK
PROUDLY
KNOWLEDGE
WEIGHED
MIGHTY
PILLARS
MINISTER

T	T	L	L	B	E	N	L	A	R	G	E	D	L	E	H	K	A
D	M	C	R	X	S	M	I	N	I	S	T	E	R	N	O	T	R
I	O	O	O	X	O	E	X	E	P	N	W	K	C	E	R	M	R
O	U	U	C	F	I	N	O	N	E	D	E	N	M	M	N	Q	O
X	T	D	K	M	P	Y	N	K	C	A	I	O	M	I	A	L	G
W	H	G	G	U	V	V	S	L	Y	N	G	W	I	E	C	I	A
B	C	B	P	R	O	U	D	L	Y	O	H	L	G	S	T	F	N
O	D	A	W	A	Y	F	X	B	A	I	E	E	H	L	I	T	C
W	C	U	L	A	T	F	U	P	R	N	D	D	T	S	O	S	E
S	A	L	V	A	T	I	O	N	L	T	Q	G	Y	Y	N	U	P
E	X	C	E	E	D	I	N	G	T	E	N	E	G	R	L	P	Q
T	S	M	J	V	L	B	E	S	I	D	E	C	Y	H	H	T	W
T	D	P	I	L	L	A	R	S	J	T	U	K	M	B	S	F	Y

57. SAUL AND THE MEDIUM: 1 SAMUEL 28:3–25

Now Samuel was dead, and all Israel had lamented him, and buried him in Ramah, even in his own city. And Saul had put away those that had familiar spirits [mediums], and the wizards, out of the land. And the Philistines gathered themselves together.... And when Saul saw the host of the Philistines, he was afraid, and his heart greatly trembled. And when Saul inquired of the LORD, the LORD answered him not, neither by dreams, nor by Urim, nor by prophets.

Then said Saul to his servants, Seek me a woman that has a familiar spirit, that I may go to her, and inquire of her. And his servants said to him, Behold, there is a woman that has a familiar spirit at Endor. And Saul disguised himself, and put on other raiment, and he went, and two men with him, and they came to the woman by night: and he said, I pray you, divine to me by the familiar spirit, and bring me him up, whom I shall name to you.

And the woman said to him, Behold, you know what Saul has done, how he has cut off those that have familiar spirits, and the wizards, out of the land: wherefore then lay you a snare for my life, to cause me to die? And Saul swore to her by the LORD, saying, As the LORD lives, there shall no punishment happen to you for this thing. Then said the woman, Whom shall I bring up to you? And he said, Bring me up Samuel.

And when the woman saw Samuel, she cried with a loud voice: and the woman spoke to Saul, saying, Why have you deceived me? for you are Saul. And the king said to her, Be not afraid: for what saw you? And the woman said to Saul, I saw gods ascending out of the earth. And he said to her, What form is he of? And she said, An old man comes up; and he is covered with a mantle. And Saul perceived that it was Samuel, and he stooped with his face to the ground, and bowed himself.

And Samuel said to Saul, Why have you disquieted me, to bring me up? And Saul answered, I am sore distressed; for the Philistines make war against me, and God is departed from me, and answers me no more, neither by prophets, nor by dreams: therefore I have called you, that you may make known to me what I shall do. Then said Samuel, Why then do you ask of me, seeing the LORD is departed from you, and is become your enemy? And the LORD has done to him, as He spoke by me: for the LORD has rent the kingdom out of your hand, and given it to your neighbor, even to David: because you obeyed not the voice of the LORD.... Moreover the LORD will also deliver Israel with you into the hand of the Philistines....

Then Saul fell immediately all along on the earth, and was sore afraid, because of the words of Samuel: and there was no strength in him; for he had eaten no bread all the day, nor all the night. And the woman came to Saul, and saw that he was sore troubled, and said to him, Behold, your handmaid has obeyed your voice, and I have put my life in my hand, and have hearkened to your words which you spoke to me. Now therefore, I pray you, hearken you also to the voice of your handmaid, and let me set a morsel of bread before you; and eat, that you may have strength, when you go on your way.

G	W	F	A	M	I	L	I	A	R	S	P	I	R	I	T	S	F	D	H
O	M	P	D	Y	B	J	R	M	W	Y	O	N	R	K	V	J	V	I	X
P	M	R	L	T	H	B	A	S	C	E	N	D	I	N	G	G	M	S	Q
T	X	O	Q	M	V	R	A	I	M	E	N	T	N	S	H	W	E	Q	D
C	L	P	L	M	O	R	S	E	L	F	H	I	I	M	Y	L	D	U	B
Z	S	H	H	B	E	V	P	H	V	O	T	K	T	M	Z	Z	I	I	X
C	T	E	C	T	E	M	B	L	E	D	U	R	I	M	D	D	U	E	C
W	C	T	H	A	Y	O	L	Q	E	Z	Z	S	V	L	U	X	M	T	K
Q	U	S	L	Q	I	S	A	M	U	E	L	L	L	L	E	X	B	E	B
D	Z	S	A	U	L	H	X	F	P	L	E	L	U	N	G	E	H	D	F
V	E	C	M	Y	L	E	C	J	H	X	I	Z	H	U	J	Z	D	D	I
V	F	S	E	Q	I	L	Y	H	I	H	N	J	X	V	Y	C	R	P	E
I	P	U	N	I	S	H	M	E	N	T	S	G	H	J	U	F	E	I	R
Y	E	J	T	B	M	J	S	E	I	W	I	Z	A	R	D	S	A	U	C
V	A	S	E	C	X	X	D	P	N	A	L	X	L	M	T	B	M	K	E
L	E	H	D	I	M	Q	M	T	D	L	L	H	V	Z	Z	E	S	U	X
J	Z	O	Z	U	X	S	R	I	V	C	V	X	W	P	E	H	B	X	P
R	C	C	P	O	M	K	U	N	L	E	A	V	E	N	E	D	D	D	N
M	R	U	O	S	N	A	R	E	M	H	S	X	H	N	B	Q	U	E	Q
K	D	I	S	G	U	I	S	E	D	M	N	F	A	T	C	A	L	F	B

SAUL	WIZARDS	PROPHETS	PUNISHMENT	ASCENDING
LAMENTED	TREMBLED	DISGUISED	SAMUEL	MORSEL
MEDIUM	DREAMS	RAIMENT	DISQUIETED	FAT CALF
FAMILIAR SPIRITS	URIM	SNARE	FIERCE	UNLEAVENED

58. DAVID MARRIES MICHAL: 1 SAMUEL 18:17–28

As king of Israel, David had other wives besides Bathsheba. Some of them were remarkable, although not all had happy endings.

And Saul said to David, Behold my elder daughter Merab, her will I give you as a wife: only be you valiant for me, and fight the LORD's battles. For Saul said, Let not my hand be upon him, but let the hand of the Philistines be upon him. And David said to Saul, Who am I? and what is my life, or my father's family in Israel, that I should be son in law to the king? But it came to pass at the time when Merab Saul's daughter should have been given to David, that she was given to Adriel the Meholathite as a wife.

And Michal Saul's daughter loved David: and they told Saul, and the thing pleased him. And Saul said, I will give him her, that she may be a snare to him, and that the hand of the Philistines may be against him. Wherefore Saul said to David, You shall this day be my son in law in the one of the two. And Saul commanded his servants, saying, Commune with David secretly, and say, Behold, the king has delight in you, and all his servants love you: now therefore be the king's son in law. And Saul's servants spoke those words in the ears of David. And David said, Seems it to you a light thing to be a king's son in law, seeing that I am a poor man, and lightly esteemed? ...

And Saul said, Thus shall you say to David, The king desires not any dowry, but a hundred foreskins of the Philistines, to be avenged of the king's enemies. But Saul thought to make David fall by the hand of the Philistines. And when his servants told David these words, it pleased David well to be the king's son in law: and the days were not expired. Wherefore David arose and went, he and his men, and slew of the Philistines two hundred men; and David brought their foreskins, and they gave them in full tale to the king, that he might be the king's son in law. And Saul gave him Michal his daughter as a wife. And Saul saw and knew that the LORD was with David, and that Michal Saul's daughter loved him.

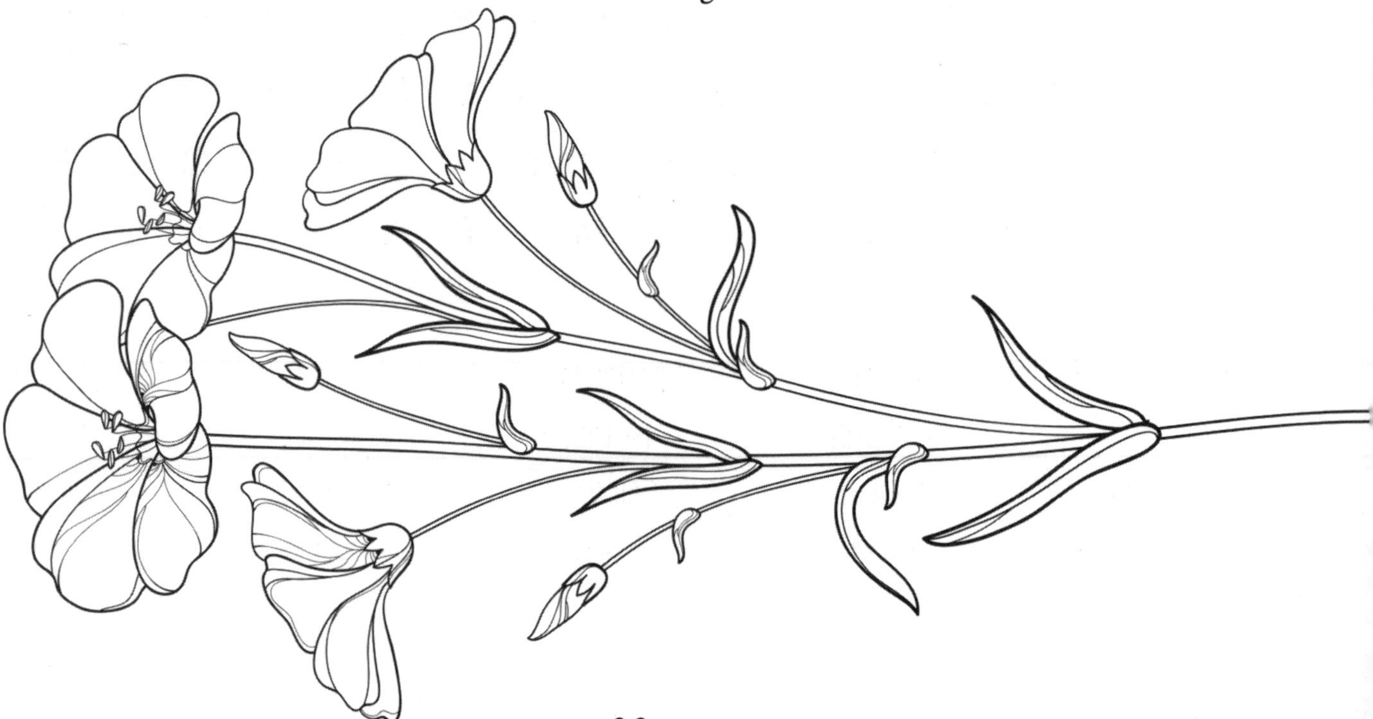

A	D	R	I	E	L	F	T	A	K	P	W	M	Q	Z	M	W	K	X	H
G	J	P	F	X	O	F	L	D	U	L	L	O	V	E	D	H	I	M	T
Z	M	B	C	O	A	K	J	K	Z	E	X	T	N	K	S	A	X	G	A
L	I	E	A	H	Y	Q	N	S	W	A	F	D	E	C	B	V	Y	C	C
J	P	D	R	T	U	G	I	S	O	S	M	V	L	H	K	E	W	H	F
M	D	Y	R	A	T	N	Z	D	V	E	M	P	S	O	U	N	R	A	S
R	O	V	E	X	B	L	D	I	X	E	X	T	S	K	N	G	T	E	P
I	W	L	G	I	L	C	E	R	W	D	E	X	P	I	R	E	D	K	H
C	R	U	G	U	U	K	V	S	E	A	E	S	F	U	B	D	R	L	I
R	Y	X	Y	U	E	V	W	W	E	D	R	O	V	K	Z	O	G	V	L
P	M	F	O	R	E	S	K	I	N	S	Y	N	V	I	R	U	L	B	I
C	M	Y	S	M	W	U	T	T	L	O	O	I	M	W	T	L	Y	Y	S
M	I	C	H	A	L	D	B	E	L	Z	O	N	E	P	Y	F	G	T	T
A	W	V	C	W	X	A	W	C	E	W	Q	L	B	U	G	X	H	H	I
H	U	W	T	T	Q	S	S	U	X	M	N	A	S	A	D	E	U	E	N
D	I	K	S	E	C	R	E	T	L	Y	E	W	Q	N	X	O	S	H	E
G	Y	O	C	O	M	M	U	N	E	G	H	D	R	W	A	J	K	A	S
A	M	N	P	B	J	M	D	X	G	K	C	N	F	Z	Y	R	U	N	R
R	H	D	L	I	G	H	T	T	H	I	N	G	R	N	K	E	E	D	W
U	P	C	E	W	C	T	P	W	J	A	Z	Y	T	X	S	L	E	W	M

MERAB	BATTLES	PHILISTINES	SON IN LAW	ADRIEL
MICHAL	PLEASED	SNARE	COMMUNE	SECRETLY
LIGHT THING	ESTEEMED	DOWRY	HUNDRED	FORESKINS
EXPIRED	LOVED HIM	AVENGED	BY THE HAND	SLEW

59. MICHAL PROTECTS DAVID: 1 SAMUEL 19:11–18

Saul also sent messengers to David's house, to watch him, and to slay him in the morning: and Michal David's wife told him, saying, If you save not your life to night, tomorrow you shall be slain. So Michal let David down through a window: and he went, and fled, and escaped. And Michal took an image, and laid it in the bed, and put a pillow of goats' hair for his bolster, and covered it with a cloth. And when Saul sent messengers to take David, she said, he is sick. And Saul sent the messengers again to see David, saying, Bring him up to me in the bed, that I may slay him. And when the messengers were come in, behold, there was an image in the bed, with a pillow of goats' hair for his bolster. And Saul said to Michal, Why have you deceived me so, and sent away my enemy, that he is escaped? And Michal answered Saul, He said to me, Let me go; why should I kill you? So David fled, and escaped.

MESSENGERS
HOUSE
WATCH
SLAY
SAVE YOUR LIFE
TOMORROW
WINDOW
ESCAPED
BEHOLD
IMAGE
GOATS HAIR
BOLSTER
CLOTH
SICK
DECEIVED
FLED
PROTECTS
SAMUEL
RAMAH
NAIOTH

H	S	S	G	B	I	T	O	L	O	L	E	S	C	A	P	E	D	I	H
P	S	A	O	O	E	O	G	T	N	Y	X	W	A	T	C	H	G	M	J
R	I	T	V	B	A	H	U	G	W	I	N	D	O	W	F	F	I	A	Y
D	K	M	D	E	P	T	O	D	C	A	B	H	F	B	O	K	U	G	E
D	E	J	E	E	Y	M	S	L	Z	Q	N	A	H	O	U	V	G	E	W
N	L	C	B	E	E	O	V	H	D	B	N	U	H	L	H	Q	Z	A	G
O	B	L	E	D	I	U	U	V	A	X	O	F	O	S	Z	T	W	E	M
T	R	X	S	I	R	T	W	R	S	I	R	S	U	T	H	V	Z	Q	U
M	O	P	G	U	V	S	I	I	L	L	R	S	S	E	A	T	Q	K	I
H	T	M	R	Q	T	E	H	S	H	I	H	P	E	R	T	G	R	X	K
K	N	K	O	O	P	W	D	L	M	O	F	H	Z	I	S	D	I	I	Y
U	B	A	B	R	T	Y	K	A	P	W	M	E	Y	R	I	Z	O	I	J
D	R	L	I	Y	R	E	S	Y	L	W	T	R	K	R	A	P	P	B	X
M	Y	O	M	O	J	O	C	Z	S	K	P	P	T	P	O	M	B	E	T
O	H	F	I	M	T	K	W	T	W	A	Z	M	E	I	A	N	A	B	M
O	V	G	L	I	N	H	N	X	S	V	M	D	H	M	D	S	F	H	L
H	K	S	P	E	A	U	A	H	A	F	F	U	O	W	A	R	Y	P	U
O	A	U	F	C	D	J	W	C	L	O	T	H	E	F	P	B	L	A	Q
H	M	E	S	S	E	N	G	E	R	S	J	X	J	L	Z	Y	H	P	C
Z	G	Y	Z	A	F	Q	Y	W	V	F	M	P	S	I	C	K	M	U	O

60. MICHAL DESPISES DAVID: 1 SAMUEL 25:44

But Saul had given Michal his daughter, David's wife, to Phalti the son of Laish, which was of Gallim.

2 SAMUEL 3:12–16

And Abner sent messengers to David on his behalf, saying,...Make your league with me, and, behold, my hand shall be with you, to bring about all Israel to you. And he said, Well; I will make a league with you: but one thing I require of you, that is, You shall not see my face, except you first bring Michal Saul's daughter, when you come to see my face. And David sent messengers to Ishbosheth Saul's son, saying, Deliver me my wife Michal, which I espoused to me for a hundred foreskins of the Philistines. And Ishbosheth sent, and took her from her husband, even from Phaltiel the son of Laish. And her husband went with her along weeping behind her to Bahurim. Then said Abner to him, Go, return. And he returned.

2 SAMUEL 6:12–23

David went and brought up the ark of God from the house of Obededom into the city of David with gladness.... And David danced before the LORD with all his might; and David was girded with a linen ephod. So David and all the house of Israel brought up the ark of the LORD with shouting, and with the sound of the trumpet. And as the ark of the LORD came into the city of David, Michal Saul's daughter looked through a window, and saw king David leaping and dancing before the LORD; and she despised him in her heart....

Then David returned to bless his household. And Michal the daughter of Saul came out to meet David, and said, How glorious was the king of Israel to day, who uncovered himself to day in the eyes of the handmaids of his servants, as one of the vain fellows shamelessly uncovers himself! And David said to Michal, It was before the LORD, which chose me before your father, and before all his house, to appoint me ruler over the people of the LORD, over Israel: therefore will I play before the LORD. And I will yet be more vile than thus, and will be base in my own sight: and of the maidservants which you have spoken of, of them shall I be had in honor. Therefore Michal the daughter of Saul had no child to the day of her death.

L	I	N	E	N	B	U	C	C	B	Z	F	T	L	T	M	Z	B	E	L
B	T	Y	D	F	C	X	U	R	F	S	L	D	S	W	G	F	I	W	F
Z	E	O	B	E	D	E	D	O	M	D	A	I	L	R	I	J	S	Q	E
I	G	Q	D	D	U	U	C	H	C	E	G	D	A	T	Z	P	M	K	P
U	N	Y	B	T	V	K	A	Z	S	S	O	E	F	I	Q	E	V	A	H
L	D	X	V	K	M	Y	K	Z	O	P	N	L	P	L	I	M	M	J	O
U	E	C	B	O	U	I	E	Q	S	I	K	I	B	I	T	M	G	I	D
G	R	A	F	A	O	H	O	Y	X	S	L	V	C	Q	M	Y	Z	N	D
L	J	Z	G	F	W	B	F	O	P	E	K	E	S	A	Y	F	X	R	G
A	R	E	T	U	R	N	B	F	T	D	L	R	U	L	W	A	A	D	A
D	N	Z	P	I	E	M	R	J	H	C	W	S	H	G	I	C	P	C	R
N	J	Z	R	E	U	R	E	G	F	N	H	J	X	F	F	E	H	Q	K
E	T	C	K	Z	L	L	A	E	C	Q	K	I	C	U	E	F	A	A	O
S	C	V	G	O	D	E	D	F	J	E	J	G	L	C	P	A	L	I	F
S	Q	G	U	D	A	P	M	H	I	W	X	I	Q	D	R	O	T	Q	G
E	S	P	O	U	S	E	D	G	C	Q	E	R	M	Q	L	E	I	X	O
C	R	S	A	C	R	I	F	I	C	E	D	D	T	C	O	E	I	L	D
F	Y	M	K	X	G	K	Z	W	N	G	A	E	L	R	Y	V	S	V	T
B	Z	M	W	D	A	N	C	E	D	P	E	D	K	C	A	U	S	S	Z
Y	W	E	E	P	I	N	G	A	G	G	J	E	S	B	L	Y	P	D	R

PHALTI
LEAGUE
MY FACE
DELIVER
MY WIFE
ESPOUSED
WEEPING
RETURN
ARK OF GOD
OBEDEDOM
GLADNESS
SACRIFICED
DANCED
GIRDED
LINEN
EPHOD
DESPISED
CAKE OF BREAD
FLAGON
CHILDLESS

61. ABIGAIL: 1 SAMUEL 25:2–22

Abigail is another wife of David, who earned her position through her noble actions.

And there was a man in Maon.... Now the name of the man was Nabal; and the name of his wife Abigail: and she was a woman of good understanding, and of a beautiful countenance: but the man was churlish and evil in his doings; and he was of the house of Caleb. And David heard in the wilderness that Nabal did shear his sheep. And David sent out ten young men, and David said to the young men, Get you up to Carmel, and go to Nabal, and greet him in my name: and thus shall you say to him that lives in prosperity, Peace be both to you, and peace be to your house, and peace be to all that you have. And now I have heard that you have shearers: now your shepherds which were with us, we hurt them not, neither was there anything missing to them, all the while they were in Carmel. Ask your young men, and they will show you. Wherefore let the young men find favor in your eyes: for we come in a good day: give, I pray you, whatsoever comes to your hand to your servants, and to your son David....

And Nabal answered David's servants, and said, Who is David? and who is the son of Jesse? there be many servants now a days that break away every man from his master. Shall I then take my bread, and my water, and my flesh that I have killed for my shearers, and give it to men, whom I know not where they be?...

And David said to his men, Gird you on every man his sword. And they girded on every man his sword; and David also girded on his sword: and there went up after David about four hundred men; and two hundred abode by the stuff. But one of the young men told Abigail, Nabal's wife, saying, Behold, David sent messengers out of the wilderness to salute our master; and he railed on them. But the men were very good to us, and we were not hurt, neither missed we any thing, as long as we were conversant with them, when we were in the fields: they were a wall to us both by night and day, all the while we were with them keeping the sheep. Now therefore know and consider what you will do; for evil is determined against our master, and against all his household: for he is such a son of Belial, that a man cannot speak to him.

Then Abigail made haste, and took two hundred loaves, and two bottles of wine, and five sheep ready dressed, and five measures of parched corn, and a hundred clusters of raisins, and two hundred cakes of figs, and laid them on asses. And she said to her servants, Go on before me; behold, I come after you. But she told not her husband Nabal. And it was so, as she rode on the ass, that she came down by the covert of the hill, and, behold, David and his men came down against her; and she met them.

S	W	G	X	Z	G	L	D	T	Y	P	G	E	K	V	C	U	G	C	C
I	K	D	S	S	S	F	D	X	O	R	O	F	H	D	H	U	V	O	O
R	A	I	Q	K	K	E	W	L	V	O	X	L	R	H	U	N	T	R	U
T	E	N	D	H	P	L	N	F	B	S	C	M	C	C	R	D	W	E	N
L	X	Q	L	R	H	L	A	C	W	P	I	W	Y	R	L	E	A	W	T
T	T	G	U	A	Y	O	B	K	D	E	L	X	O	J	I	R	F	W	E
K	S	P	F	I	F	W	O	F	P	R	U	O	U	F	S	S	W	P	N
Q	P	S	M	S	T	A	L	I	B	I	C	C	N	N	H	T	I	S	A
S	X	H	W	I	B	E	V	B	Q	T	P	O	G	W	C	A	L	Z	N
Z	T	Y	K	N	U	N	D	O	H	Y	D	K	M	B	D	N	D	F	C
S	K	H	R	S	L	T	K	D	R	Q	U	Y	E	R	L	D	E	T	E
F	H	F	W	L	C	M	Q	M	A	O	N	V	N	O	J	I	R	P	P
G	R	E	C	O	N	V	E	R	S	A	N	T	F	I	Z	N	N	Q	P
X	H	L	E	Q	I	C	U	U	A	P	G	X	S	Y	B	G	E	M	I
E	L	A	J	P	J	M	W	W	X	N	X	F	W	U	Z	Q	S	V	B
C	O	V	E	R	T	Y	P	T	S	O	N	O	F	J	E	S	S	E	N
A	B	I	G	A	I	L	D	U	N	V	F	G	C	X	S	J	R	Y	T
F	X	T	H	O	U	S	A	N	D	H	D	L	R	Z	I	W	P	W	P
U	T	O	Y	S	H	E	A	R	E	R	S	T	G	I	R	D	E	D	Y
V	H	P	N	H	Z	J	K	X	Z	Z	W	U	J	H	G	A	A	N	K

MAON
NABOL
THOUSAND
SHEEP
UNDERSTANDING
COUNTENANCE
CHURLISH
WILDERNESS
PROSPERITY
FAVOR
YOUNG MEN
SON OF JESSE
SHEARERS
GIRDED
CONVERSANT
ABIGAIL
RAISINS
COVERT
REQUITED
FELLOW

62. ABIGAIL'S ACTIONS SAVE HER HOUSEHOLD: 1 SAMUEL 25:23–42

And when Abigail saw David, she hasted, and lighted off the ass, and fell before David on her face, and bowed herself to the ground, and fell at his feet, and said, Upon me, my lord, upon me let this iniquity be: and let your handmaid, I pray you, speak in your audience, and hear the words of your handmaid. Let not my lord, I pray you, regard this man of Belial, even Nabal: for as his name is, so is he; Nabal [fool in Hebrew] is his name, and folly is with him: but I your handmaid saw not the young men of my lord, whom you did send. Now therefore, my lord, as the LORD lives, and as your soul lives, seeing the LORD has withheld you from coming to shed blood, and from avenging yourself with your own hand, now let your enemies, and they that seek evil to my lord, be as Nabal. And now this blessing which your handmaid has brought to my lord, let it even be given to the young men that follow my lord. I pray you, forgive the trespass of your handmaid: for the LORD will certainly make my lord a sure house; because my lord fights the battles of the LORD, and evil has not been found in you all your days.... When the LORD shall have dealt well with my lord, then remember your handmaid.

And David said to Abigail, Blessed be the LORD God of Israel, which sent you this day to meet me: and blessed be your advice, and blessed be you, which have kept me this day from coming to shed blood, and from avenging myself with my own hand.... So David received of her hand that which she had brought him, and said to her, Go up in peace to your house; see, I have hearkened to your voice, and have accepted your person. And Abigail came to Nabal; and, behold, he held a feast in his house, like the feast of a king; and Nabal's heart was merry within him, for he was very drunken: wherefore she told him nothing, less or more, until the morning light. But it came to pass in the morning, when the wine was gone out of Nabal, and his wife had told him these things, that his heart died within him, and he became as a stone. And it came to pass about ten days after, that the LORD smote Nabal, that he died.

And when David heard that Nabal was dead, he said, Blessed be the LORD, that has pleaded the cause of my reproach from the hand of Nabal, and has kept His servant from evil: for the LORD has returned the wickedness of Nabal upon his own head. And David sent and communed with Abigail, to take her to him as a wife....And Abigail hasted, and arose, and rode upon an ass..., and became his wife.

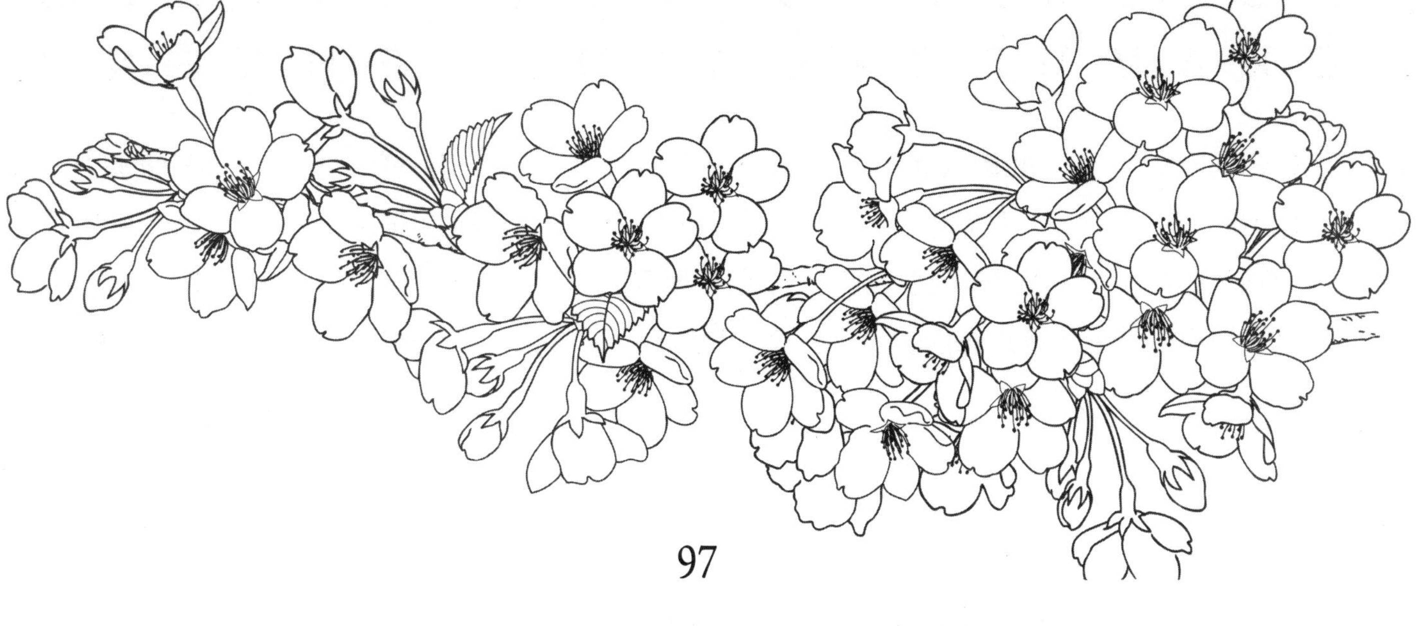

J	K	D	H	S	I	L	Z	U	P	E	A	C	E	B	X	P	A	M	B
O	X	Y	C	U	X	X	L	P	D	E	E	L	P	E	E	X	D	W	F
R	D	O	A	V	R	Q	H	C	R	J	N	G	I	L	L	N	V	S	G
Q	A	V	R	D	N	T	Q	R	R	W	L	Y	N	Y	S	A	S	W	L
O	M	Y	M	V	V	J	I	U	B	P	I	A	I	X	X	S	E	Z	J
T	S	Y	E	P	R	I	J	N	S	B	H	Y	Q	C	P	A	B	N	F
Y	E	U	L	B	Y	V	C	C	G	G	E	T	U	L	T	W	X	P	O
Q	L	G	X	S	A	F	T	E	E	Y	W	L	I	K	R	I	S	Q	L
S	S	N	K	H	A	S	T	E	D	U	S	K	T	O	E	F	B	Y	L
U	I	V	L	I	G	H	T	E	D	D	N	D	Y	L	S	E	S	Z	Y
R	B	O	W	E	D	B	I	D	O	D	I	E	C	F	P	Y	K	L	A
E	L	U	K	Z	Y	A	V	E	N	G	I	N	G	U	A	S	T	Z	E
H	G	Z	P	U	L	O	W	I	T	H	H	E	L	D	S	O	A	O	I
O	R	K	Y	I	O	J	F	F	G	O	O	G	Z	D	S	G	R	B	S
U	T	F	H	Z	J	Q	M	G	B	J	S	U	G	N	Y	H	W	Q	T
S	D	K	A	N	Z	M	N	B	D	R	E	G	K	F	D	L	I	F	A
E	Y	I	R	E	P	R	O	A	C	H	N	M	E	R	R	Y	Q	B	Y
O	E	W	L	P	Z	N	F	A	E	L	K	V	K	U	R	Y	G	P	E
F	G	E	E	Q	H	A	F	O	F	F	E	N	S	E	V	V	R	F	D
C	X	A	V	M	F	G	A	L	G	A	U	D	I	E	N	C	E	N	U

CARMEL	AUDIENCE	TRESPASS	STAYED	REPROACH
LIGHTED	FOLLY	SURE HOUSE	HURTING	HASTED
BOWED	WITHHELD	OFFENSE	PEACE	DAMSELS
INIQUITY	AVENGING	ADVICE	MERRY	AS A WIFE

63. ELIJAH AND THE WIDOW: 1 KINGS 17:8–11

And the word of the Lord came to [Elijah], saying, Arise, get you to Zarephath..., and dwell there: behold, I have commanded a widow woman there to sustain you.... When he came to the gate of the city, behold, the widow woman was there gathering of sticks: and he called to her, and said, Bring me, I pray you, a little water in a vessel, that I may drink. And as she was going to bring it, he called to her, and said, Bring me, I pray you, a morsel of bread in your hand.

And she said, As the Lord your God lives, I have not a cake, but a handful of meal in a barrel, and a little oil in a cruse: and, behold, I am gathering two sticks, that I may go in and dress it for me and my son, that we may eat it, and die. And Elijah said to her, Fear not; go and do as you have said: but make me thereof a little cake first, and bring it to me, and after make for you and for your son. For thus says the Lord God of Israel, The barrel of meal shall not waste, neither shall the cruse of oil fail, until the day that the Lord sends rain upon the earth. And she went and did according to the saying of Elijah: and she, and he, and her house, did eat many days. And the barrel of meal wasted not, neither did the cruse of oil fail, according to the word of the Lord.

ZAREPHATH
GATHERING
I PRAY YOU
VESSEL
HANDFUL OF MEAL
CRUSE OF OIL
DRESS IT
FAIL
MANY DAYS
ELIJAH
WIDOW WOMAN
STICKS
WATER
CAKE
BARREL
TWO STICKS
WORD OF THE LORD
RAIN
FEAR NOT
WASTE

F	W	M	I	F	E	A	R	N	O	T	P	V	I	W	C	J	H
E	X	O	Q	M	C	M	R	A	I	N	W	E	Z	G	Z	E	A
B	J	I	R	Z	A	F	S	X	K	X	W	S	J	Z	N	L	N
Q	Z	P	W	D	W	N	B	T	A	U	Y	S	L	S	N	I	D
B	A	R	T	D	O	I	Y	A	I	M	Y	E	U	G	W	J	F
D	R	A	F	W	R	F	D	D	R	C	O	L	E	O	A	A	U
R	E	Y	Z	I	O	J	T	O	A	R	K	F	R	Y	S	H	L
E	P	Y	I	O	Q	S	W	H	W	Y	E	S	A	M	T	J	O
S	H	O	T	J	U	W	T	S	E	W	S	L	I	I	E	P	F
S	A	U	M	S	V	P	W	I	Q	L	O	X	A	G	L	D	M
I	T	Y	I	W	A	T	E	R	C	O	O	M	N	A	R	W	E
T	H	Y	R	S	W	C	A	K	E	K	K	R	A	O	U	K	A
Q	X	G	A	T	H	E	R	I	N	G	S	W	D	N	J	J	L
C	R	U	S	E	O	F	O	I	L	I	D	B	Q	Z	K	N	D

64. ELIJAH REVIVES THE WIDOW'S SON: 1 KINGS 17:17–24

The son of the woman, the mistress of the house, fell sick; and his sickness was so sore, that there was no breath left in him. And she said to Elijah, What have I to do with you, O you man of God? are you come to me to call my sin to remembrance, and to slay my son? And he said to her, Give me your son. And he took him out of her bosom, and carried him up into a loft, where he abode, and laid him upon his own bed. And he cried to the LORD, and said, O LORD my God, have You also brought evil upon the widow with whom I sojourn, by slaying her son? And he stretched himself upon the child three times, and cried to the LORD, and said, O LORD my God, I pray You, let this child's soul come into him again. And the LORD heard the voice of Elijah; and the soul of the child came into him again, and he revived. And Elijah took the child, and brought him down out of the chamber into the house, and delivered him to his mother: and Elijah said, See, your son lives. And the woman said to Elijah, Now by this I know that you are a man of God, and that the word of the LORD in your mouth is truth.

B	T	S	F	C	C	O	M	E	A	G	A	I	N	I	S	I	R	L	S
Q	Z	D	R	Q	T	P	M	M	T	Q	F	B	O	S	O	M	W	J	I
K	E	S	U	T	W	O	M	A	N	S	S	O	N	S	R	S	A	I	C
L	F	B	A	O	C	P	Y	W	N	T	G	H	E	T	E	X	N	I	K
R	E	M	E	M	B	R	A	N	C	E	A	H	L	R	C	R	B	L	N
N	P	C	Q	R	U	G	J	T	G	G	N	F	O	E	N	D	F	T	E
C	S	M	I	S	T	R	E	S	S	J	R	O	G	T	P	H	N	B	S
I	J	F	O	M	Q	P	M	W	O	E	O	X	R	C	J	P	L	B	S
N	D	P	J	U	D	I	A	W	K	N	L	M	S	H	V	J	Q	R	G
B	P	P	W	O	T	E	N	W	K	T	I	V	C	E	M	M	Z	W	J
C	L	F	C	Z	B	H	O	R	Z	T	X	L	X	D	U	S	K	T	Z
W	C	M	Z	V	T	H	F	W	E	U	K	P	M	R	B	M	N	R	E
S	L	A	Y	I	N	G	G	X	H	V	C	Z	N	X	W	A	O	U	M
S	O	J	O	U	R	N	O	P	W	Z	I	L	T	Y	Z	I	B	T	F
Y	B	G	W	T	N	F	D	W	Z	O	N	V	L	O	K	R	R	H	W
W	X	C	M	Q	K	N	H	F	C	V	T	D	E	I	D	T	E	O	G
C	W	O	R	D	O	F	T	H	E	L	O	R	D	D	N	G	A	Z	J
C	H	A	M	B	E	R	D	J	M	F	J	O	T	G	I	A	T	W	H
M	V	J	I	N	T	H	R	E	E	T	I	M	E	S	Y	X	H	E	Y
L	P	C	R	L	O	F	T	C	H	I	L	D	S	S	O	U	L	B	R

WOMAN'S SON
REMEMBRANCE
SICKNESS
LOFT
STRETCHED
CHILD'S SOUL
REVIVED
MAN OF GOD
SOJOURN
WORD OF THE LORD
MISTRESS
SORE
BOSOM
NO BREATH
SLAYING
THREE TIMES
COME AGAIN
CHAMBER
MOUTH
TRUTH

65. JEZEBEL'S SCHEMING: 1 KINGS 21:1–16

When Ahab reigned over Israel, he married Jezebel, the daughter of Ethbaal, king of the Zidonians. She killed prophets of the Lord and schemed to ensure Ahab got a vineyard he wanted.

And it came to pass after these things, that Naboth the Jezreelite had a vineyard, which was in Jezreel, hard by the palace of Ahab king of Samaria. And Ahab spoke to Naboth, saying, Give me your vineyard, that I may have it for a garden of herbs, because it is near to my house: and I will give you for it a better vineyard than it; or, if it seem good to you, I will give you the worth of it in money. And Naboth said to Ahab, The Lord forbid it me, that I should give the inheritance of my fathers to you. And Ahab came into his house heavy and displeased.... And he laid him down upon his bed, and turned away his face, and would eat no bread.

But Jezebel his wife came to him, and said to him, Why is your spirit so sad, that you eat no bread? And he said to her, Because I spoke to Naboth the Jezreelite,... and he answered, I will not give you my vineyard. And Jezebel his wife said to him, Do you now govern the kingdom of Israel? arise, and eat bread, and let your heart be merry: I will give you the vineyard of Naboth the Jezreelite.

So she wrote letters in Ahab's name...saying, Proclaim a fast, and set Naboth on high among the people: and set two men, sons of Belial, before him, to bear witness against him, saying, You did blaspheme God and the king. And then carry him out, and stone him, that he may die. And the men of his city, even the elders and the nobles who were the inhabitants in his city, did as Jezebel had sent to them.... They proclaimed a fast, and set Naboth on high among the people. And there came in two men, children of Belial, and sat before him: and the men of Belial witnessed against him, even against Naboth, in the presence of the people, saying, Naboth did blaspheme God and the king. Then they carried him forth out of the city, and stoned him with stones, that he died. Then they sent to Jezebel, saying, Naboth is stoned, and is dead....

When Jezebel heard that Naboth was stoned, and was dead, that Jezebel said to Ahab, Arise, take possession of the vineyard of Naboth the Jezreelite, which he refused to give you for money: for Naboth is not alive, but dead. And...Ahab rose up to go down to the vineyard of Naboth the Jezreelite, to take possession of it.

U	I	Y	K	W	X	S	P	P	R	C	T	U	C	H	X	C	N	T	E
C	A	X	Q	O	W	Z	P	C	L	T	J	Y	P	Q	U	Y	U	A	K
C	Y	Y	Q	A	S	O	N	S	O	F	B	E	L	I	A	L	B	K	M
N	V	U	K	K	J	V	Z	I	O	H	J	Y	Z	K	Q	S	H	E	I
Q	D	I	S	P	L	E	A	S	E	D	O	A	N	E	Q	Q	J	P	L
V	I	N	H	E	R	I	T	A	N	C	E	N	N	C	B	Q	W	O	N
S	M	C	P	D	D	U	V	R	C	J	S	S	H	U	I	E	A	S	O
W	I	T	N	E	S	S	E	D	K	M	H	M	S	I	X	R	L	S	Z
X	X	A	G	W	S	S	N	M	O	G	K	Z	G	T	G	N	D	E	J
P	Y	G	N	O	E	P	F	S	J	O	A	Y	S	Y	Z	H	E	S	E
X	P	J	O	V	I	N	E	Y	A	R	D	G	M	X	Q	T	P	S	Z
B	R	P	B	Y	T	C	M	S	M	U	I	E	X	F	O	R	R	I	R
O	D	S	L	K	W	E	H	T	D	A	Y	P	L	I	B	D	E	O	E
L	I	U	E	O	P	W	A	E	L	O	S	G	Y	X	C	J	S	N	E
N	P	R	S	J	Y	B	H	H	R	X	S	Q	L	I	L	C	S	B	L
R	J	F	A	S	T	I	N	G	A	B	G	O	V	E	R	N	E	V	I
T	U	B	X	U	F	L	P	K	Y	B	S	U	Z	U	P	B	D	B	T
P	R	O	C	L	A	I	M	W	S	A	D	S	P	I	R	I	T	C	E
N	Q	V	G	B	T	T	N	P	P	N	A	B	O	T	H	U	O	W	R
G	A	R	D	E	N	Q	S	T	O	N	E	H	I	M	Y	O	B	X	N

NABOTH	JEZREELITE	VINEYARD	GARDEN	HERBS
INHERITANCE	NOBLES	AHAB	JEZEBEL	DISPLEASED
DEPRESSED	SAD SPIRIT	GOVERN	PROCLAIM	FASTING
SONS OF BELIAL	ON HIGH	STONE HIM	WITNESSED	TAKE POSSESSION

66. JEZEBEL'S VIOLENT DEATH: 2 KINGS 9:30–37

When Jehu was come to Jezreel, Jezebel heard of it; and she painted her face, and tired her head, and looked out at a window. And as Jehu entered in at the gate,... he lifted up his face to the window, and said, Who is on my side? who? And there looked out to him two or three eunuchs. And he said, Throw her down. So they threw her down: and some of her blood was sprinkled on the wall, and on the horses: and he trode her under foot. And when he was come in, he...said, Go, see now this cursed woman, and bury her: for she is a king's daughter. And they went to bury her: but they found no more of her than the skull, and the feet, and the palms of her hands. Wherefore they came again, and told him. And he said, This is the word of the LORD, which He spoke by His servant Elijah the Tishbite, saying, In the portion of Jezreel shall dogs eat the flesh of Jezebel: and the carcass of Jezebel shall be as dung upon the face of the field in the portion of Jezreel; so that they shall not say, This is Jezebel.

N	Q	P	M	S	F	T	U	W	V	R	H	A	T	W	Z	M	E	V	W
G	D	F	E	E	T	C	T	P	U	O	E	H	I	M	O	Q	Z	B	R
A	R	J	Y	O	P	A	L	M	S	W	L	Z	S	W	K	T	A	I	X
J	B	N	P	K	M	K	S	S	I	H	Z	B	H	I	K	R	C	F	Q
M	E	N	T	L	S	T	M	K	M	J	D	E	B	M	C	O	T	X	I
I	Q	H	X	H	A	S	C	B	U	X	U	U	I	U	A	D	C	V	G
A	V	A	U	R	R	I	Y	V	H	L	S	N	T	Z	R	E	U	A	H
Z	C	I	O	Q	C	O	F	H	X	S	L	U	E	K	C	S	F	Z	F
I	C	X	L	X	L	V	W	C	M	F	B	C	H	F	A	P	C	X	M
M	C	E	A	J	U	G	K	H	R	U	W	H	Z	J	S	R	Y	W	Q
R	U	C	E	H	B	S	H	K	E	F	X	S	J	P	S	I	H	Y	R
I	R	A	E	L	A	H	Z	O	I	R	Y	Q	T	D	P	N	V	U	K
U	S	S	B	J	C	N	B	T	R	N	D	S	H	P	Z	K	I	X	C
M	E	K	A	S	K	K	R	C	N	S	R	O	G	A	E	L	A	L	P
H	D	P	O	R	T	I	O	N	B	Q	E	C	W	I	E	E	H	D	J
Z	I	C	S	A	Q	J	O	Q	L	Q	V	S	K	N	C	D	A	E	O
K	B	B	S	L	F	W	C	E	O	U	R	K	V	T	L	X	L	H	O
R	Y	C	D	Y	E	I	D	I	O	Y	G	P	J	E	R	B	S	J	N
V	K	Z	O	X	U	W	L	P	D	O	M	J	R	D	B	A	F	J	M
B	D	U	N	G	W	I	N	D	O	W	C	P	D	O	G	S	Y	I	D

WINDOW
ZIMRI
EUNUCHS
BLOOD
HORSES
CURSED
FEET
DOGS
PORTION
TISHBITE
PAINTED
JEHU
SLEW
SPRINKLED
TRODE
SKULL
PALMS
DUNG
CARCASS
THROW HER DOWN

67. THE WOMAN WITH THE JAR OF OIL: 2 KINGS 4:1–7

Some of the women in the Bible remain unnamed. Although they may seem to be "lesser" characters, they are nonetheless important.

Now there cried a certain woman...to Elisha, saying, your servant my husband is dead; and you know that your servant did fear the Lord: and the creditor is come to take to him my two sons to be bondmen. And Elisha said to her, What shall I do for you? tell me, what have you in the house? And she said, your handmaid has not any thing in the house, save a pot of oil. Then he said, Go, borrow you vessels abroad of all your neighbors, even empty vessels; borrow not a few. And when you are come in, you shall shut the door upon you and upon your sons, and shall pour out into all those vessels, and you shall set aside that which is full.

So she went from him, and shut the door upon her and upon her sons, who brought the vessels to her; and she poured out. And it came to pass, when the vessels were full, that she said to her son, Bring me yet a vessel. And he said to her, There is not a vessel more. And the oil stayed. Then she came and told the man of God. And he said, Go, sell the oil, and pay your debt, and live you and your children of the rest.

O	P	S	N	E	O	G	D	K	I	L	U	N	N	S	B	B	L
S	V	I	E	N	O	T	A	F	E	W	E	B	N	E	O	U	C
H	E	M	I	L	J	S	E	L	N	U	M	O	O	R	R	P	C
U	S	C	G	P	L	J	C	R	O	M	P	N	T	V	R	O	Z
T	S	R	H	H	O	L	Z	A	U	D	T	D	H	A	O	T	H
T	E	E	B	W	X	U	V	J	T	J	Y	M	I	N	W	O	A
H	L	D	O	S	C	E	R	T	A	I	N	E	N	T	Q	F	N
E	S	I	R	R	T	U	L	O	J	W	J	N	G	Y	B	O	D
D	S	T	S	V	M	A	I	I	U	H	M	L	E	E	T	I	M
O	W	O	B	B	G	Z	Y	S	S	T	Z	Q	I	N	I	L	A
O	W	R	V	M	C	E	J	E	T	H	W	X	U	H	E	J	I
R	P	R	O	P	H	E	T	S	D	A	A	Y	F	U	L	L	D
B	I	D	E	B	T	Q	I	A	R	H	O	T	V	V	L	R	L

ELISHA
SERVANT
BONDMEN
HANDMAID
POT OF OIL
NOT A FEW
VESSELS
POUR OUT
STAYED
DEBT
EMPTY
FULL
SELL
CERTAIN
PROPHETS
CREDITOR
NOTHING
NEIGHBORS
BORROW
SHUT THE DOOR

68. AND 69. THE SHUNAMMITE WOMAN: 2 KINGS 4:8–37

And it fell on a day, that Elisha passed to Shunem, where was a great woman; and she constrained him to eat bread. And so it was, that as often as he passed by, he turned in there to eat bread. And she said to her husband, Behold now, I perceive that this is a holy man of God, which passes by us continually. Let us make a little chamber, I pray you, on the wall; and let us set for him there a bed, and a table, and a stool, and a candlestick: and it shall be, when he comes to us, that he shall turn in there. And it fell on a day, that he came there, and he turned into the chamber, and lay there.

And he said to Gehazi his servant, Call this Shunammite. And when he had called her, she stood before him. And he said to him, Say now to her, Behold, you have been careful for us with all this care; what is to be done for you? would you be spoken for to the king, or to the captain of the host? And she answered, I dwell among my own people. And he said, What then is to be done for her? And Gehazi answered, Verily she has no child, and her husband is old. And he said, Call her. And when he had called her, she stood in the door. And he said, About this season, according to the time of life, you shall embrace a son. And she said, Nay, my lord, you man of God, do not lie to your handmaid.

And the woman conceived, and bore a son at that season that Elisha had said to her, according to the time of life. And when the child was grown, it fell on a day, that he went out to his father to the reapers. And he said to his father, My head, my head. And he said to a lad, Carry him to his mother. And when he had taken him, and brought him to his mother, he sat on her knees till noon, and then died. And she went up, and laid him on the bed of the man of God, and shut the door upon him, and went out. And she called to her husband, and said, Send me, I pray you, one of the young men, and one of the asses, that I may run to the man of God, and come again. And he said, Wherefore will you go to him to day? it is neither new moon, nor sabbath. And she said, It shall be well.

Then she saddled an ass, and said to her servant, Drive, and go forward; slack not your riding for me, except I bid you. So she went and came to the man of God to mount Carmel. And it came to pass, when the man of God saw her afar off, that he said to Gehazi his servant, Behold yonder is that Shunammite: Run now, I pray you, to meet her, and say to her, Is it well with you? is it well with your husband? is it well with the child? And she answered, It is well. And when she came to the man of God to the hill, she caught him by the feet: but Gehazi came near to thrust her away. And the man of God said, Let her alone; for her soul is vexed within her: and the Lord has hidden it from me, and has not told me.

Then she said, Did I desire a son of my lord? did I not say, Do not deceive me?... And the mother of the child said, As the Lord lives, and as your soul lives, I will not leave you. And he arose, and followed her.... And when Elisha was come into the house, behold, the child was dead, and laid upon his bed. He went in therefore, and shut the door upon them two, and prayed to the Lord. And he went up, and lay upon the child, and put his mouth upon his mouth, and his eyes upon his eyes, and his hands upon his hands: and he stretched himself upon the child; and the flesh of the child waxed warm. Then he returned, and walked in the house to and fro; and went up, and stretched himself upon him: and the child sneezed seven times, and the child opened his eyes. And he called Gehazi, and said, Call this Shunammite. So he called her. And when she was come in to him, he said, Take up your son. Then she went in, and fell at his feet, and bowed herself to the ground, and took up her son, and went out.

C	S	C	L	G	C	A	P	T	A	I	N	R	B	C	I	C	U
M	A	F	H	F	D	R	A	G	L	R	C	U	H	Q	V	J	G
S	B	R	Y	A	R	J	H	D	F	N	O	C	T	T	E	V	L
S	H	X	E	O	M	N	B	W	G	M	N	A	I	P	R	H	H
H	E	U	R	F	K	B	Y	Z	E	Y	S	N	M	A	I	P	Y
U	K	A	N	N	U	R	E	G	H	H	T	D	E	S	L	N	N
N	E	R	T	A	I	L	K	R	A	E	R	L	O	S	Y	O	T
E	S	M	Z	B	M	R	F	R	Z	A	A	E	F	E	P	C	S
M	T	E	B	V	R	M	T	P	I	D	I	S	L	D	G	H	R
B	O	Z	H	R	K	E	I	A	P	Y	N	T	I	B	X	I	Y
T	O	P	I	P	A	M	A	T	B	W	E	I	F	Y	D	L	C
Y	L	Q	B	X	G	C	F	D	E	L	D	C	E	W	A	D	S
L	X	Q	G	R	U	B	E	D	F	C	E	K	D	G	O	Y	S
Z	D	H	O	L	Y	M	A	N	W	R	E	A	P	E	R	S	P

SHUNEM
PASSED BY
HOLY MAN
GEHAZI
VERILY
BED
STOOL
TIME OF LIFE
NO CHILD
REAPERS

CONSTRAINED
EAT BREAD
CHAMBER
SHUNAMMITE
CAPTAIN
TABLE
CANDLESTICK
CAREFUL
EMBRACE
MY HEAD

X	V	H	T	T	V	E	X	E	D	M	Q	J	S	T	T	J	W	C	C
L	L	I	I	D	K	W	U	O	H	A	N	D	A	C	J	W	B	Z	S
V	Z	W	X	N	A	E	N	K	A	S	A	R	B	W	W	H	M	T	T
W	N	O	W	E	I	J	Z	V	M	G	B	D	B	W	Q	A	R	W	A
H	T	A	K	E	U	P	S	J	Z	S	V	J	A	G	C	N	L	P	F
M	W	A	A	A	G	Y	N	H	M	U	A	H	T	N	T	D	A	Q	F
O	Z	R	Z	Z	W	J	K	X	C	H	M	N	H	C	T	S	L	R	H
U	G	O	F	W	L	A	T	Y	L	Z	E	Y	E	S	T	H	B	F	H
N	L	S	X	E	T	A	K	Y	V	N	I	F	K	Y	H	T	S	J	G
T	I	E	P	T	D	E	X	E	W	A	E	Y	S	C	Q	Y	T	V	S
C	P	N	E	W	M	O	O	N	N	X	B	Z	U	H	Q	E	R	R	F
A	N	J	L	O	W	G	S	H	L	E	X	Y	I	J	L	Y	E	L	F
R	D	F	L	Z	Z	Z	O	U	X	I	D	P	G	M	O	U	T	H	V
M	R	N	B	C	J	Z	C	Y	M	G	E	R	H	T	I	K	C	K	C
E	I	H	V	E	M	L	H	S	A	D	D	L	E	D	V	C	H	K	C
L	V	S	N	M	A	N	O	F	G	O	D	Q	V	G	L	H	E	X	A
B	E	B	N	B	C	R	V	R	Q	C	I	H	Y	F	Q	I	D	D	R
K	J	U	S	N	E	E	Z	E	D	W	D	X	O	Z	Y	L	D	G	R
H	O	D	A	K	G	D	M	I	T	I	S	W	E	L	L	D	P	C	Y
M	D	P	A	B	V	V	J	F	O	L	L	O	W	E	D	O	Z	R	W

CARRY
NEW MOON
IT IS WELL
DRIVE
VEXED
AROSE
AWAKENED
SNEEZED
CHILD
EYES

MAN OF GOD
SABBATH
SADDLED
MOUNT CARMEL
STAFF
FOLLOWED
STRETCHED
TAKE UP
MOUTH
HANDS

70. ONE INFANT AND TWO HARLOTS: 1 KINGS 3:16–28

Then came there two women, that were harlots, to the king [Solomon], and stood before him. And the one woman said, O my lord, I and this woman dwell in one house; and I was delivered of a child with her in the house. And it came to pass the third day after that I was delivered, that this woman was delivered also: and we were together; there was no stranger with us in the house, save we two in the house. And this woman's child died in the night; because she overlaid it. And she arose at midnight, and took my son from beside me, while your handmaid slept, and laid it in her bosom, and laid her dead child in my bosom. And when I rose in the morning to give my child suck, behold, it was dead: but when I had considered it in the morning, behold, it was not my son, which I did bear. And the other woman said, Nay; but the living is my son, and the dead is your son. And this said, No; but the dead is your son, and the living is my son. Thus they spoke before the king....

And the king said, Bring me a sword. And they brought a sword before the king. And the king said, Divide the living child in two, and give half to the one, and half to the other. Then spoke the woman whose the living child was to the king, for her bowels yearned upon her son, and she said, O my lord, give her the living child, and in no wise slay it. But the other said, Let it be neither mine nor yours, but divide it. Then the king answered and said, Give her the living child, and in no wise slay it: she is the mother thereof. And all Israel...feared the king: for they saw that the wisdom of God was in him, to do judgment.

V	M	B	O	W	E	L	S	K	P	W	E	S	O	K	Y	M	S
J	C	O	O	I	U	E	W	C	I	A	E	T	V	I	E	X	V
J	D	O	S	Q	A	Y	O	H	O	W	J	O	E	N	A	A	W
U	H	A	N	S	E	M	R	U	W	I	W	O	R	G	R	R	M
D	T	A	Z	S	T	D	D	P	Q	S	R	D	L	S	N	G	T
G	O	U	L	C	I	R	I	F	L	D	S	B	A	O	E	U	B
M	F	R	V	F	X	D	A	V	H	O	V	E	I	L	D	E	Q
E	C	H	I	L	D	L	E	N	I	M	R	F	D	O	Z	D	T
N	M	Y	S	O	N	S	Z	R	G	D	O	O	M	M	G	H	M
T	M	I	D	N	I	G	H	T	E	E	E	R	E	O	T	M	M
L	I	V	I	N	G	I	N	Q	H	D	R	E	H	N	D	R	S
K	W	M	Q	L	D	E	L	I	V	E	R	E	D	N	F	G	Q
U	B	O	S	O	M	M	O	T	H	E	R	Q	K	T	M	Q	N

KING SOLOMON
STRANGER
OVERLAID
MY SON
CONSIDERED
ARGUED
DIVIDE
BOWELS
WISDOM
MOTHER
STOOD BEFORE
DELIVERED
CHILD
MIDNIGHT
BOSOM
LIVING
SWORD
HALF
YEARNED
JUDGMENT

71. THE QUEEN OF SHEBA: 1 KINGS 10:1–13

When the queen of Sheba heard of the fame of Solomon concerning the name of the LORD, she came to prove him with hard questions. And she came to Jerusalem with a very great train, with camels that bore spices, and very much gold, and precious stones: and when she was come to Solomon, she communed with him of all that was in her heart. And Solomon told her all her questions: there was not any thing hidden from the king, which he told her not. And when the queen of Sheba had seen all Solomon's wisdom, and the house that he had built,... she said to the king, It was a true report that I heard in my own land of your acts and of your wisdom. However I believed not the words, until I came, and my eyes had seen it: and, behold, the half was not told me: your wisdom and prosperity exceeds the fame which I heard. Happy are your men, happy are these your servants, which stand continually before you, and that hear your wisdom. Blessed be the LORD your God, which delighted in you, to set you on the throne of Israel: because the LORD loved Israel for ever, therefore made He you king, to do judgment and justice. And she gave the king a hundred and twenty talents of gold, and of spices very great store, and precious stones: there came no more such abundance of spices as these which the queen of Sheba gave to king Solomon.... And king Solomon gave to the queen of Sheba all her desire, whatsoever she asked, beside that which Solomon gave her of his royal bounty. So she turned and went to her own country, she and her servants.

QUEEN OF SHEBA	FAME	SOLOMON	ASCENT	PROVE
HARD	QUESTIONS	GREAT TRAIN	CAMELS	BOUNTY
HIDDEN	MINISTERS	APPAREL	CUPBEARERS	
PROSPERITY	HAPPY	DELIGHTED	ABUNDANCE	

H	G	G	C	G	T	Z	X	E	Y	X	H	N	P	S	D	U	G	P	C	Q	I
U	G	A	Q	U	E	E	N	O	F	S	H	E	B	A	E	Z	R	T	U	P	M
J	J	Q	B	A	D	A	W	S	O	L	O	M	O	N	L	H	E	C	P	R	I
C	Z	Z	K	U	V	R	I	A	P	P	A	R	E	L	I	A	A	B	B	O	N
A	T	L	W	S	N	Q	U	E	S	T	I	O	N	S	G	R	T	K	E	E	I
M	O	B	E	V	C	D	W	C	I	A	Y	X	Q	X	H	D	T	Z	A	U	S
E	A	S	C	E	N	T	A	B	O	U	N	T	Y	T	T	L	R	F	R	F	T
L	H	I	D	D	E	N	Z	N	V	X	I	L	Z	P	E	P	A	A	E	X	E
S	E	N	W	M	U	Y	K	M	C	K	G	B	H	B	D	P	I	M	R	I	R
H	A	P	P	Y	O	W	G	K	L	E	A	U	M	L	C	F	N	E	S	B	S
C	M	W	R	L	H	N	P	R	O	S	P	E	R	I	T	Y	L	N	K	K	K

72. AND 73. DELILAH: JUDGES 16:1–22

It came to pass afterward, that [Samson] loved a woman in the valley of Sorek, whose name was Delilah. And the lords of the Philistines came up to her, and said to her, Entice him, and see wherein his great strength lies, and by what means we may prevail against him, that we may bind him to afflict him: and we will give you every one of us eleven hundred pieces of silver.

And Delilah said to Samson, Tell me, I pray you, wherein your great strength lies, and wherewith you might be bound to afflict you. And Samson said to her, If they bind me with seven green withes that were never dried, then shall I be weak, and be as another man. Then the lords of the Philistines brought up to her seven green withes which had not been dried, and she bound him with them. Now there were men lying in wait, abiding with her in the chamber. And she said to him, The Philistines be upon you, Samson. And he broke the withes, as a thread of tow is broken when it touches the fire. So his strength was not known.

And Delilah said to Samson, Behold, you have mocked me, and told me lies: now tell me, I pray you, wherewith you might be bound. And he said to her, If they bind me fast with new ropes that never were occupied, then shall I be weak, and be as another man. Delilah therefore took new ropes, and bound him therewith, and said to him, The Philistines be upon you, Samson. And there were liers in wait abiding in the chamber. And he broke them from off his arms like a thread.

And Delilah said to Samson, Until now you have mocked me, and told me lies: tell me wherewith you might be bound. And he said to her, If you weave the seven locks of my head with the web. And she fastened it with the pin, and said to him, The Philistines be upon you, Samson. And he awakened out of his sleep, and went away with the pin of the beam, and with the web. And she said to him, How can you say, I love you, when your heart is not with me? you have mocked me these three times, and have not told me wherein your great strength lies.

And it came to pass, when she pressed him daily with her words, and urged him, so that his soul was vexed to death; that he told her all his heart, and said to her, There has not come a razor upon my head; for I have been a Nazarite to God from my mother's womb: if I be shaved, then my strength will go from me, and I shall become weak, and be like any other man. And when Delilah saw that he had told her all his heart, she sent and called for the lords of the Philistines, saying, Come up this once, for he has showed me all his heart.... And she made him sleep upon her knees; and she called for a man, and she caused him to shave off the seven locks of his head; and she began to afflict him, and his strength went from him. And she said, The Philistines be upon you, Samson.... And he knew not that the Lord was departed from him. But the Philistines took him, and put out his eyes, and brought him down to Gaza, and bound him with fetters of brass; and he did grind in the prison house. However the hair of his head began to grow again after he was shaved.

U	E	H	M	D	Q	Y	U	W	X	B	S	Z	W	I	Z	R	L	S	S
S	S	D	M	E	X	Q	U	I	E	Z	I	J	O	F	J	J	I	H	A
E	A	C	G	X	C	O	A	G	P	A	V	N	G	H	P	Q	M	O	G
Y	M	T	I	P	J	L	F	A	R	O	K	G	D	G	E	L	C	U	B
G	S	D	V	T	P	C	F	T	E	N	C	Q	X	H	M	O	O	L	N
V	O	Z	R	E	Y	O	L	D	V	J	B	S	D	L	I	I	F	D	U
E	N	N	M	I	E	U	I	J	A	I	J	G	U	I	R	M	B	E	S
A	A	U	H	R	E	O	C	N	I	H	T	R	I	P	Q	F	X	R	I
D	T	C	C	S	R	D	T	W	L	I	R	E	P	A	J	R	T	S	L
D	E	L	I	L	A	H	C	H	X	D	A	E	K	E	S	R	W	B	V
O	T	X	S	K	D	D	V	O	V	G	Q	N	H	L	D	V	O	C	E
Y	P	I	A	S	O	U	F	B	E	C	S	W	S	G	R	P	P	T	R
H	E	B	R	O	N	N	N	T	R	T	L	I	E	A	H	J	O	X	J
H	N	X	V	U	F	L	E	S	P	O	E	T	P	T	J	Z	S	P	G
Y	T	E	G	T	D	W	L	E	H	R	K	H	H	E	Q	D	T	R	A
T	I	N	G	H	T	T	M	O	M	C	N	E	K	M	Z	P	G	W	Z
J	C	K	I	K	L	H	U	R	T	I	L	S	N	O	E	F	Y	H	A
Y	E	P	W	G	R	E	A	T	S	T	R	E	N	G	T	H	H	P	F
W	D	V	J	Q	R	F	P	H	I	L	I	S	T	I	N	E	S	A	J
B	O	U	N	D	I	G	P	N	D	G	C	Z	C	Z	B	J	S	X	Q

SAMSON	TWO POSTS	PHILISTINES	BIND HIM	DRIED
GAZA	SHOULDERS	ENTICE	AFFLICT	WEAK
CITY	HEBRON	GREAT STRENGTH	SILVER	BOUND
GATE	DELILAH	PREVAIL	GREEN WITHES	BROKEN

T	H	R	E	A	D	K	I	X	T	I	O	G	Q	S	S	I	N	U	U
G	V	Y	W	H	C	L	X	F	R	Q	S	K	D	W	E	P	A	N	Y
U	B	J	D	P	G	O	R	U	G	O	K	T	D	H	C	R	Z	B	A
C	S	O	E	R	C	C	W	S	E	V	E	N	O	D	K	E	A	L	Z
Y	J	W	P	I	E	K	S	K	W	F	A	H	B	I	S	S	R	P	T
L	E	Q	A	S	R	S	A	N	V	X	E	A	D	W	L	S	I	W	B
G	Z	R	R	O	E	A	S	G	D	X	Z	T	X	S	U	E	T	H	O
S	V	C	T	N	F	O	Z	I	T	U	T	K	T	P	X	D	E	U	C
M	E	O	E	H	A	D	N	O	K	S	U	H	T	E	L	K	F	R	R
O	X	J	D	O	X	A	F	B	R	H	P	N	X	B	R	D	Z	G	B
C	E	G	H	U	G	J	L	R	H	G	O	W	B	C	V	S	A	E	H
K	D	D	E	S	I	S	T	I	W	A	N	G	A	T	G	R	A	D	I
E	E	L	N	E	W	R	O	P	E	S	Y	Y	W	C	M	D	F	D	S
D	T	F	C	E	S	E	V	G	T	M	O	S	E	R	R	W	F	W	H
S	Z	F	Y	X	N	P	D	H	G	Y	U	Q	W	Y	B	E	L	Y	A
M	V	F	A	L	R	P	A	S	V	M	Y	A	M	T	R	A	I	X	V
N	O	L	I	E	R	S	I	N	W	A	I	T	J	L	A	V	C	U	E
V	E	Y	D	H	Z	K	H	U	S	G	P	F	F	N	S	E	T	Q	D
E	C	O	B	M	U	Y	O	U	Z	P	H	I	T	F	S	E	H	D	Z
P	I	N	O	F	T	H	E	B	E	A	M	J	M	I	D	E	W	S	D

NEW ROPES	LIERS IN WAIT	THREAD	SEVEN LOCKS	WEAVE
PIN OF THE BEAM	MOCKED	PRESSED	URGED	VEXED
RAZOR	NAZARITE	SHAVED	SEVEN LOCKS	AFFLICT
DEPARTED	FETTERS	BRASS	PRISON HOUSE	UPON YOU

74. RIZPAH: 2 SAMUEL 21:1–14

Then there was a famine in the days of David three years, year after year; and David inquired of the LORD. And the LORD answered, It is for Saul, and for his bloody house, because he slew the Gibeonites. And the king called the Gibeonites, and...said to the Gibeonites, What shall I do for you? and wherewith shall I make the atonement, that you may bless the inheritance of the LORD? And the Gibeonites said to him,...The man that consumed us, and that devised against us that we should be destroyed from remaining in any of the coasts of Israel, let seven men of his sons be delivered to us, and we will hang them up to the LORD in Gibeah of Saul, whom the LORD did choose.

And the king said, I will give them. But the king spared Mephibosheth, the son of Jonathan the son of Saul, because of the LORD's oath that was between them, between David and Jonathan the son of Saul. But the king took the two sons of Rizpah the daughter of Aiah, whom she bore to Saul, Armoni and Mephibosheth; and the five sons of Michal the daughter of Saul, whom she brought up for Adriel the son of Barzillai the Meholathite: and he delivered them into the hands of the Gibeonites, and they hanged them in the hill before the LORD: and they fell all seven together, and were put to death in the days of harvest, in the first days, in the beginning of barley harvest.

And Rizpah the daughter of Aiah took sackcloth, and spread it for her upon the rock, from the beginning of harvest until water dropped upon them out of heaven, and allowed neither the birds of the air to rest on them by day, nor the beasts of the field by night. And it was told David what Rizpah the daughter of Aiah, the concubine of Saul, had done. And David went and took the bones of Saul and the bones of Jonathan his son from the men of Jabeshgilead, which had stolen them from the street of Bethshan, where the Philistines had hanged them, when the Philistines had slain Saul in Gilboa: and he brought up from there the bones of Saul and the bones of Jonathan his son; and they gathered the bones of them that were hanged. And the bones of Saul and Jonathan his son buried they in the country of Benjamin in Zelah, in the sepulcher of Kish his father: and they performed all that the king commanded. And after that God was entreated for the land.

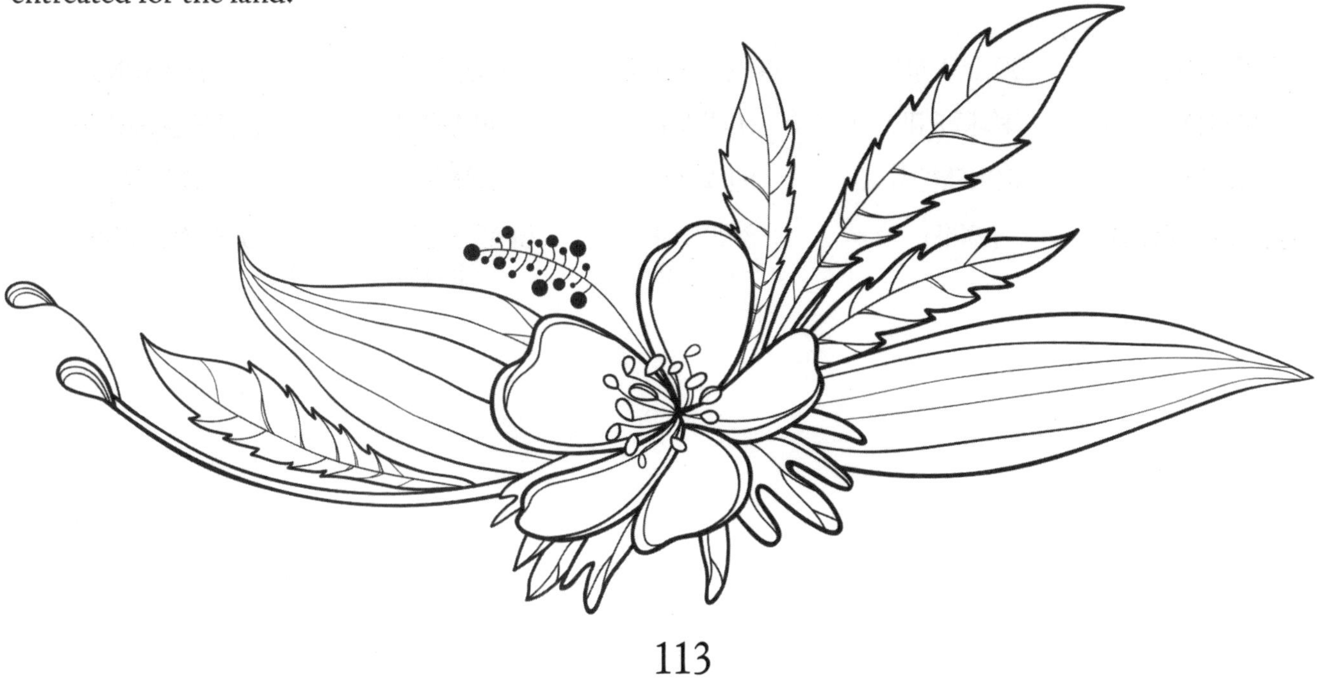

J	F	C	Z	P	G	I	B	E	O	N	I	T	E	S	N	Y	Z	W	X
W	C	A	W	G	M	D	S	H	E	J	R	R	A	O	X	B	H	X	T
S	Z	Y	Q	G	Z	K	B	P	P	M	S	Q	D	H	S	A	A	G	D
S	I	L	V	E	R	N	O	R	G	O	L	D	R	F	E	R	G	A	E
L	K	I	H	A	Z	K	S	I	X	Q	T	W	I	Z	V	L	I	V	L
H	A	R	V	E	S	T	O	Z	S	Y	F	M	E	A	E	E	H	B	I
H	R	J	S	R	V	K	M	P	M	U	Q	N	L	R	N	Y	Q	M	V
B	D	C	U	D	Z	I	H	A	D	N	K	O	W	M	S	F	G	S	E
I	U	O	I	T	W	C	M	H	C	Z	Q	H	Z	O	O	G	U	A	R
R	D	K	Y	R	X	W	W	X	G	I	T	K	Q	N	N	Z	M	C	E
D	F	I	N	H	E	R	I	T	A	N	C	E	W	I	S	F	R	K	D
O	S	X	F	Q	U	Y	L	A	Z	G	P	O	K	O	A	T	H	C	C
F	U	D	A	Y	A	N	D	N	I	G	H	T	N	R	P	O	Y	L	H
T	J	Z	H	R	G	W	O	M	K	S	C	H	J	Q	K	H	K	O	R
H	B	H	A	N	G	E	D	B	C	J	O	N	A	T	H	A	N	T	K
E	H	O	F	Y	A	T	O	N	E	M	E	N	T	F	P	C	X	H	U
A	Z	P	P	B	X	S	C	Y	D	C	K	Y	Z	A	H	V	X	Q	W
I	U	O	M	E	P	H	I	B	O	S	H	E	T	H	I	A	V	B	P
R	U	B	E	A	S	T	S	O	F	T	H	E	F	I	E	L	D	E	I
L	E	D	P	V	W	Z	I	M	I	C	H	A	L	W	K	U	Q	D	F

GIBEONITES	JONATHAN	INHERITANCE	SACKCLOTH	SEVEN SONS
MICHAL	HARVEST	RIZPAH	ARMONI	MEPHIBOSHETH
OATH	ATONEMENT	DELIVERED	HANGED	BARLEY
SILVER NOR GOLD	ADRIEL	BIRDS OF THE AIR	BEASTS OF THE FIELD	DAY AND NIGHT

75. HULDAH THE PROPHETESS: 2 KINGS 22:12–20

During the reign of King Josiah, the book of the law was found in the house of the Lord as it was being rebuilt. Huldah the prophetess was consulted so they could hear God's word on the matter.

And the king commanded Hilkiah the priest, and Ahikam the son of Shaphan, and Achbor the son of Michaiah, and Shaphan the scribe, and Asahiah a servant of the king's, saying, Go you, inquire of the Lord for me, and for the people, and for all Judah, concerning the words of this book that is found: for great is the wrath of the Lord that is kindled against us, because our fathers have not hearkened to the words of this book, to do according to all that which is written concerning us. So Hilkiah the priest, and Ahikam, and Achbor, and Shaphan, and Asahiah, went to Huldah the prophetess, the wife of Shallum the son of Tikvah, the son of Harhas, keeper of the wardrobe; (now she dwelled in Jerusalem in the college;) and they communed with her.

And she said to them, Thus says the Lord God of Israel, Tell the man that sent you to me, Thus says the Lord, Behold, I will bring evil upon this place, and upon the inhabitants thereof, even all the words of the book which the king of Judah has read: because they have forsaken Me, and have burned incense to other gods, that they might provoke Me to anger with all the works of their hands; therefore My wrath shall be kindled against this place, and shall not be quenched.

But to the king of Judah which sent you to inquire of the Lord, thus shall you say to him, Thus says the Lord God of Israel, As touching the words which you have heard; because your heart was tender, and you have humbled yourself before the Lord, when you heard what I spoke against this place, and against the inhabitants thereof, that they should become a desolation and a curse, and have rent your clothes, and wept before Me; I also have heard you, says the Lord. Behold therefore, I will gather you to your fathers, and you shall be gathered into your grave in peace; and your eyes shall not see all the evil which I will bring upon this place.

Y	D	P	C	C	N	P	G	P	Q	O	R	H	U	M	B	L	E	D	X
P	T	R	G	U	V	Y	E	I	I	Z	R	F	B	B	F	R	U	L	G
S	E	O	M	W	R	H	C	S	R	P	J	B	E	J	T	C	X	G	U
B	N	V	F	G	V	S	H	A	L	L	N	O	T	S	E	E	P	X	O
R	D	O	V	R	N	Y	E	E	K	L	X	B	T	F	L	L	Z	H	R
B	E	K	H	J	Q	P	R	B	D	E	S	O	L	A	T	I	O	N	Z
F	R	E	G	C	E	S	C	X	Q	S	V	I	C	Q	O	V	D	K	O
H	O	A	G	G	C	R	O	R	I	A	X	G	M	B	K	S	I	I	Q
E	P	R	P	R	B	D	G	W	N	R	N	C	B	O	N	S	T	N	V
A	N	Y	S	L	S	R	R	X	Q	I	A	J	W	O	D	E	P	D	H
R	T	C	O	A	Z	D	M	S	U	W	U	I	W	K	D	P	R	L	U
D	G	R	K	K	K	H	A	A	I	M	A	B	X	O	H	W	O	E	L
Y	H	O	F	T	H	E	L	O	R	D	G	L	O	F	Y	C	P	D	D
O	Q	D	V	Q	X	J	N	J	E	F	X	C	Y	T	S	O	H	V	A
U	V	L	I	P	A	J	H	O	W	R	A	T	H	H	H	L	E	E	H
C	B	H	F	O	R	T	H	E	P	E	O	P	L	E	I	L	T	O	T
W	R	I	T	T	E	N	Q	Y	L	Z	S	C	N	L	J	E	E	F	X
A	P	K	Q	M	Q	P	J	E	G	H	N	T	B	A	Z	G	S	V	H
I	M	I	E	I	T	L	I	N	C	E	N	S	E	W	Y	E	S	U	C
V	E	M	Q	U	E	N	C	H	E	D	S	U	F	B	V	M	J	F	Y

INQUIRE
KINDLED
FORSAKEN
HUMBLED
FOR THE PEOPLE
PROVOKE
BOOK OF THE LAW
QUENCHED
TENDER
CURSE
OF THE LORD
WRITTEN
INCENSE
HEARD YOU
HULDAH
SHALL NOT SEE
PROPHETESS
DESOLATION
WRATH
COLLEGE

76. ATHALIAH: 2 KINGS 9:26

Two and twenty years old was Ahaziah when he began to reign; and he reigned one year in Jerusalem. And his mother's name was Athaliah, the daughter of Omri king of Israel.

2 KINGS 11:1–3

And when Athaliah the mother of Ahaziah saw that her son was dead, she arose and destroyed all the seed royal. But Jehosheba, the daughter of king Joram, sister of Ahaziah, took Joash the son of Ahaziah, and stole him from among the king's sons which were slain; and they hid him, even him and his nurse, in the bedchamber from Athaliah, so that he was not slain. And he was with her hidden in the house of the Lord six years. And Athaliah did reign over the land.

E	N	U	R	S	E	C	Y	H	P	H	U	D	N	H	S	H	Q	A	O
Z	D	J	D	Z	S	Y	Q	C	V	D	D	S	N	J	P	S	D	J	Y
Y	B	D	F	V	S	I	J	D	B	Q	A	Y	W	R	J	F	W	E	A
J	I	U	V	T	U	A	D	O	S	P	B	V	M	A	J	D	V	R	T
H	H	Y	F	F	O	M	D	P	A	I	I	N	P	L	R	G	I	U	H
I	W	U	A	H	A	Z	I	A	H	S	X	N	N	P	G	O	J	S	A
D	A	K	E	V	V	M	S	Y	L	O	H	Y	D	H	N	F	V	A	L
D	H	I	N	R	H	Z	V	U	M	M	E	N	E	N	D	Z	W	L	I
E	Z	S	E	E	D	R	O	Y	A	L	R	X	B	A	M	Y	D	E	A
N	E	M	O	T	H	E	R	D	K	W	P	E	P	I	R	X	Q	M	H
C	Z	S	C	J	W	T	L	I	N	H	A	K	I	G	Q	S	M	V	P
U	V	R	N	Z	X	G	X	G	P	R	X	P	V	G	L	W	A	O	B
X	J	T	P	C	T	V	M	B	B	S	L	O	F	B	N	A	D	M	W
Q	T	W	A	I	Q	X	C	Z	P	W	D	I	A	Q	E	R	R	R	B
M	H	R	O	N	V	B	E	D	C	H	A	M	B	E	R	O	V	I	U
Q	W	M	W	N	Z	N	J	V	U	K	J	Y	G	F	F	S	D	H	F
O	P	J	H	X	Y	C	W	S	T	Q	J	W	E	V	R	E	P	Q	Y
S	H	J	E	H	O	S	H	E	B	A	U	X	I	X	L	K	Y	E	Q
B	C	O	P	N	A	Y	X	S	T	O	L	E	H	I	M	V	M	Y	L
S	J	R	F	Z	I	A	D	E	S	T	R	O	Y	E	D	I	S	N	A

REIGN
JERUSALEM
OMRI
ATHALIAH
MOTHER
AROSE
DESTROYED
SEED ROYAL
JEHOSHEBA
JOASH
STOLE HIM
HIDDEN
NURSE
BED CHAMBER
SIX YEARS

77. THE OTHER TAMAR: 2 SAMUEL 13:1–22

Absalom the son of David had a fair sister, whose name was Tamar; and Amnon the son of David loved her. And Amnon was so vexed, that he fell sick for his sister Tamar; for she was a virgin; and Amnon thought it hard for him to do any thing to her....

So Amnon lay down, and made himself sick: and when the king was come to see him, Amnon said to the king, I pray you, let Tamar my sister come, and make me a couple of cakes in my sight, that I may eat at her hand. Then David sent home to Tamar, saying, Go now to your brother Amnon's house, and dress him meat.

So Tamar went to her brother Amnon's house; and he was laid down. And she took flour, and kneaded it, and made cakes in his sight, and did bake the cakes. And she took a pan, and poured them out before him; but he refused to eat. And Amnon said, Have out all men from me. And they went out every man from him. And Amnon said to Tamar, Bring the meat into the chamber, that I may eat of your hand. And Tamar took the cakes which she had made, and brought them into the chamber to Amnon her brother. And when she had brought them to him to eat, he took hold of her, and said to her, Come lie with me, my sister. And she answered him, Nay, my brother, do not force me; for no such thing ought to be done in Israel: do not you this folly. And I, where shall I cause my shame to go? and as for you, you shall be as one of the fools in Israel. Now therefore, I pray you, speak to the king; for he will not withhold me from you.

However he would not hearken to her voice: but, being stronger than she, forced her, and lay with her. Then Amnon hated her exceedingly; so that the hatred wherewith he hated her was greater than the love wherewith he had loved her. And Amnon said to her, Arise, be gone. And she said to him, There is no cause: this evil in sending me away is greater than the other that you did to me. But he would not hearken to her. Then he called his servant that ministered to him, and said, Put now this woman out from me, and bolt the door after her. And she had a garment of divers colors upon her: for with such robes were the king's daughters that were virgins appareled. Then his servant brought her out, and bolted the door after her. And Tamar put ashes on her head, and rent her garment of divers colors that was on her, and laid her hand on her head, and went on crying. And Absalom her brother said to her, Has Amnon your brother been with you? but hold now your peace, my sister: he is your brother; regard not this thing. So Tamar remained desolate in her brother Absalom's house.

O	W	M	D	B	L	N	L	L	F	B	G	Q	N	H	A	O	G	M	T
A	N	E	V	F	C	U	I	B	I	L	A	Y	D	O	W	N	I	F	M
B	P	U	A	O	O	U	E	O	E	E	C	V	L	L	J	F	L	O	E
S	D	O	R	T	L	B	W	L	Q	A	U	W	I	D	B	A	F	R	X
A	K	Z	U	P	A	D	I	T	U	K	A	Q	A	Y	S	I	F	C	C
L	S	S	N	R	J	T	T	T	R	B	Q	A	F	O	B	R	F	E	E
O	O	U	D	Q	E	I	H	H	C	Q	A	P	B	U	Q	S	X	D	E
M	S	B	W	H	R	D	M	E	F	Z	P	K	O	R	I	I	H	S	D
J	Y	T	I	J	Y	H	E	D	R	O	N	S	Q	P	H	S	B	F	I
F	B	L	G	E	T	L	X	O	A	H	Q	F	W	E	A	T	S	I	N
J	C	E	M	I	L	A	D	O	H	A	A	C	K	A	M	E	B	E	G
P	I	A	H	P	L	P	M	R	R	M	L	N	Q	C	N	R	O	O	L
R	P	Y	K	N	L	Q	W	A	J	D	S	W	D	E	O	X	Q	V	Y
G	F	P	Y	E	X	J	W	T	R	M	Y	M	S	R	N	U	Z	Q	S
I	J	H	Z	S	S	N	Q	Y	S	H	A	M	E	D	E	K	F	W	T
J	J	A	W	H	A	T	E	D	K	D	E	S	O	L	A	T	E	M	C
N	D	K	Q	P	M	P	W	O	A	N	W	C	D	Z	C	T	Q	T	P
B	U	B	C	P	F	L	O	U	R	Y	K	N	E	A	D	E	D	S	X
K	W	M	M	D	D	O	V	B	E	B	J	F	O	L	L	Y	V	K	H
L	O	B	X	Q	S	L	K	E	U	M	W	C	F	L	P	U	B	P	H

ABSALOM	SUBTLE	FLOUR	FOLLY	BOLT THE DOOR
FAIR SISTER	LAY DOWN	KNEADED	SHAME	DESOLATE
TAMAR	EAT AT HER HAND	POURED	HATED	FORCED
AMNON	CAKES	LIE WITH ME	EXCEEDINGLY	HOLD YOUR PEACE

78. THE MESSIAH AND HIS BRIDE: PSALM 45:1–17

Your throne, O God, is for ever and ever: the scepter of Your kingdom is a right scepter. You love righteousness, and hate wickedness: therefore God, Your God, has anointed You with the oil of gladness above Your fellows. All Your garments smell of myrrh, and aloes, and cassia, out of the ivory palaces, whereby they have made You glad. Kings' daughters were among Your honorable women: upon Your right hand did stand the queen in gold of Ophir. Hearken, O daughter, and consider, and incline your ear; forget also your own people, and your father's house; so shall the king greatly desire your beauty: for He is your Lord; and worship you Him. And the daughter of Tyre shall be there with a gift; even the rich among the people shall entreat Your favor. The king's daughter is all glorious within: her clothing is of wrought gold. She shall be brought to the king in raiment of needlework: the virgins her companions that follow her shall be brought to you. With gladness and rejoicing shall they be brought: they shall enter into the king's palace. Instead of your fathers shall be your children, whom you may make princes in all the earth. I will make Your name to be remembered in all generations: therefore shall the people praise You for ever and ever.

H	K	A	L	O	E	S	W	K	V	L	G	I	R	D	P	P	N
W	O	I	X	I	P	F	A	V	O	R	D	F	G	Q	J	O	E
L	R	N	N	Q	V	R	R	F	I	T	A	D	R	T	M	P	B
Z	C	I	O	G	W	O	O	J	O	R	N	M	A	O	E	V	N
Y	B	E	T	R	S	G	R	S	I	M	A	L	C	U	E	M	E
T	R	L	Z	E	A	D	L	Y	P	N	T	W	E	C	K	T	E
L	G	P	E	O	R	B	A	O	P	E	P	D	P	H	N	P	D
R	B	K	E	S	C	Q	L	U	R	A	R	S	J	I	E	E	L
M	Y	R	R	H	S	A	Q	E	G	I	L	O	D	N	S	N	E
W	U	O	V	B	S	E	S	U	W	H	O	A	U	G	S	N	W
O	I	J	A	L	H	J	D	S	E	O	T	U	C	S	A	I	O
G	I	Z	U	R	Q	Q	G	X	I	E	M	E	S	E	L	J	R
I	N	D	I	T	I	N	G	A	W	A	N	E	R	I	S	Y	K
J	H	E	Q	R	F	A	I	R	E	R	Z	U	N	S	F	K	V

TOUCHING
WRITER
GRACE
GIRD
PROSPEROUSLY
ALOES
IVORY PALACES
HONORABLE WOMEN
FAVOR
NEEDLEWORK
INDITING
PEN
FAIRER
BLESSED
MEEKNESS
MYRRH
CASSIA
KINGS' DAUGHTERS
QUEEN
GLORIOUS

79. QUEEN VASHTI: ESTHER 1:1–22

Esther is one of the well-known heroines of the Bible. The story of how she delivered the Jewish people is celebrated every year on Purim—just as the book of Esther says it will be. The congregation dresses up and reads the story aloud, booing when Haman's name is mentioned.

Now it came to pass in the days of Ahasuerus,... he made a feast to all his princes and his servants; the power of Persia and Media, the nobles and princes of the provinces, being before him: when he showed the riches of his glorious kingdom and the honor of his excellent majesty many days....Also Vashti the queen made a feast for the women in the royal house which belonged to king Ahasuerus. On the seventh day, when the heart of the king was merry with wine, he commanded...the seven chamberlains that served in the presence of Ahasuerus the king, to bring Vashti the queen before the king with the crown royal, to show the people and the princes her beauty: for she was fair to look on. But the queen Vashti refused to come at the king's commandment by his chamberlains: therefore was the king very angry, and his anger burned in him. Then the king said to the wise men, which knew the times,...What shall we do to the queen Vashti according to law, because she has not performed the commandment of the king Ahasuerus by the chamberlains?

And Memucan answered..., Vashti the queen has not done wrong to the king only, but also to all the princes, and to all the people that are in all the provinces of the king Ahasuerus. For this deed of the queen shall come abroad to all women, so that they shall despise their husbands in their eyes, when it shall be reported, The king Ahasuerus commanded Vashti the queen to be brought in before him, but she came not. Likewise shall the ladies of Persia and Media say this day to all the king's princes, which have heard of the deed of the queen. Thus shall there arise too much contempt and wrath. If it please the king, let there go a royal commandment from him, and let it be written among the laws of the Persians and the Medes, that it be not altered, that Vashti come no more before king Ahasuerus; and let the king give her royal estate to another that is better than she. And when the king's decree which he shall make shall be published throughout all his empire, (for it is great,) all the wives shall give to their husbands honor, both to great and small. And the saying pleased the king and the princes..., that every man should bear rule in his own house, and that it should be published according to the language of every people.

L	Y	B	B	C	E	R	M	M	W	F	R	Q	M	M	D	D	M
A	F	E	A	S	T	T	E	E	H	I	C	R	E	B	R	S	H
N	V	A	S	H	T	I	X	P	D	T	M	D	N	N	R	P	E
G	A	K	R	G	N	P	Q	N	O	I	C	E	C	Z	A	R	S
U	V	P	C	I	I	G	U	O	K	R	A	C	H	M	E	O	K
A	E	Y	R	C	C	G	B	B	H	A	T	R	V	A	M	V	P
G	S	Y	D	I	H	H	B	L	P	R	B	E	C	J	P	I	H
E	S	F	D	I	N	B	E	E	H	E	S	E	D	E	I	N	O
Y	E	P	W	B	O	C	B	S	A	F	R	K	O	S	R	C	N
U	L	K	F	S	E	G	E	J	X	U	T	S	N	T	E	E	O
K	S	L	E	T	T	E	R	S	Q	L	T	Z	I	Y	Q	S	R
A	R	O	Y	A	L	E	S	T	A	T	E	Y	F	A	R	E	J
D	X	N	C	O	U	R	T	P	U	B	L	I	S	H	E	D	D

FEAST
PERSIA
MEDIA
NOBLES
PRINCES
PROVINCES
RICHES
MAJESTY
COURT
VESSELS
VASHTI
ROYAL ESTATE
DECREE
HONOR
LETTERS
PUBLISHED
LANGUAGE
EMPIRE
REPORTED
BEAUTY

80. ESTHER BECOMES QUEEN: ESTHER 2:1–17

After these things, when the wrath of king Ahasuerus was appeased, he remembered Vashti, and what she had done, and what was decreed against her. Then said the king's servants that ministered to him, Let there be fair young virgins sought for the king:... and let the maiden which pleases the king be queen instead of Vashti. And the thing pleased the king; and he did so.

Now in Shushan the palace there was a certain Jew, whose name was Mordecai.... And he brought up Hadassah, that is, Esther, his uncle's daughter: for she had neither father nor mother, and the maid was fair and beautiful; whom Mordecai, when her father and mother were dead, took for his own daughter.

So it came to pass, when the king's commandment and his decree was heard, and when many maidens were gathered together to Shushan the palace, to the custody of Hegai, that Esther was brought also to the king's house, to the custody of Hegai, keeper of the women. And the maiden pleased him, and she obtained kindness of him; and he speedily gave her her things for purification, with such things as belonged to her, and seven maidens, which were meet to be given her, out of the king's house: and he preferred her and her maids to the best place of the house of the women. Esther had not showed her people nor her kindred: for Mordecai had charged her that she should not show it. And Mordecai walked every day before the court of the women's house, to know how Esther did, and what should become of her.

Now when every maid's turn was come to go in to king Ahasuerus, after that she had been twelve months, according to the manner of the women, (for so were the days of their purifications accomplished, that is, six months with oil of myrrh, and six months with sweet odors, and with other things for the purifying of the women;) then thus came every maiden to the king; whatsoever she desired was given her to go with her out of the house of the women to the king's house. In the evening she went, and on the morrow she returned into the second house of the women...: she came in to the king no more, except the king delighted in her, and that she were called by name.

Now when the turn of Esther, the daughter of Abihail the uncle of Mordecai, who had taken her for his daughter, was come to go in to the king, she required nothing but what Hegai the king's chamberlain, the keeper of the women, appointed. And Esther obtained favor in the sight of all them that looked upon her. So Esther was taken to king Ahasuerus into his house royal in the tenth month, which is the month Tebeth, in the seventh year of his reign. And the king loved Esther above all the women, and she obtained grace and favor in his sight more than all the virgins; so that he set the royal crown upon her head, and made her queen instead of Vashti.

H	I	C	W	S	Q	M	D	P	R	M	S	L	H	M	W	M	B	P	M
A	O	A	V	P	B	R	Y	U	I	O	A	N	L	V	M	H	Z	S	O
O	P	P	Y	E	K	O	A	R	I	R	G	Z	B	J	G	I	S	K	B
B	U	T	V	E	I	Y	G	I	M	Z	Q	O	S	R	A	N	W	Y	T
F	N	I	W	D	N	A	I	F	D	G	C	Z	O	L	J	O	E	E	A
G	A	V	C	I	D	L	K	I	S	X	E	U	I	E	U	Y	E	F	I
G	N	I	A	L	R	C	E	C	T	P	Y	X	L	I	J	O	T	K	N
L	O	T	R	Y	E	R	E	A	G	S	I	L	O	G	C	U	O	I	E
I	H	Y	Z	E	D	O	P	T	L	I	J	A	F	N	B	N	D	N	D
E	Y	K	P	W	F	W	E	I	C	C	O	B	M	Z	H	G	O	D	F
L	F	G	O	P	Z	N	R	O	Y	X	E	O	Y	Y	A	W	R	N	A
S	C	U	S	T	O	D	Y	N	F	T	I	P	R	R	H	D	I	E	V
R	E	Q	U	I	R	E	D	M	C	Z	K	W	R	I	L	E	F	S	O
V	M	B	R	N	K	W	S	W	R	N	B	E	H	L	Q	M	X	S	R
X	Q	B	V	D	Y	Q	O	X	Q	Z	W	B	X	D	C	W	J	J	B
O	M	O	R	D	E	C	A	I	E	D	E	L	I	G	H	T	E	D	Y
E	C	A	T	B	O	G	W	C	O	N	C	U	B	I	N	E	S	R	M
H	I	W	D	D	W	E	S	T	H	E	R	K	Q	R	U	B	T	G	T
X	H	A	D	A	S	S	A	H	M	C	L	Y	K	E	R	V	L	H	E
L	H	E	R	C	B	Q	C	H	A	M	B	E	R	L	A	I	N	O	S

FAIR	KEEPER	OBTAINED FAVOR	KINDRED	HADASSAH
YOUNG	PURIFICATION	DELIGHTED	OIL OF MYRRH	ESTHER
CUSTODY	ROYAL CROWN	CONCUBINES	SPEEDILY	CAPTIVITY
CHAMBERLAIN	REQUIRED	SWEET ODOR	KINDNESS	MORDECAI

81. THE CONSPIRACY AGAINST THE JEWS: ESTHER 3:1–15

After these things did king Ahasuerus promote Haman the son of Hammedatha the Agagite, and advanced him, and set his seat above all the princes that were with him. And all the king's servants, that were in the king's gate, bowed, and reverenced Haman: for the king had so commanded concerning him. But Mordecai bowed not, nor did him reverence. Then the king's servants, which were in the king's gate, said to Mordecai, Why transgresses you the king's commandment?...

And when Haman saw that Mordecai bowed not, nor did him reverence, then was Haman full of wrath. And he thought scorn to lay hands on Mordecai alone; for they had showed him the people of Mordecai: wherefore Haman sought to destroy all the Jews that were throughout the whole kingdom of Ahasuerus, even the people of Mordecai....

And Haman said to king Ahasuerus, There is a certain people scattered abroad and dispersed among the people in all the provinces of your kingdom; and their laws are diverse from all people; neither keep they the king's laws: therefore it is not for the king's profit to allow them. If it please the king, let it be written that they may be destroyed: and I will pay ten thousand talents of silver to the hands of those that have the charge of the business, to bring it into the king's treasuries. And the king took his ring from his hand, and gave it to Haman the son of Hammedatha the Agagite, the Jews' enemy.

And the king said to Haman, The silver is given to you, the people also, to do with them as it seems good to you.... And the letters were sent by posts into all the king's provinces, to destroy, to kill, and to cause to perish, all Jews, both young and old, little children and women, in one day, even upon the thirteenth day of the twelfth month, which is the month Adar, and to take the spoil of them for a prey.

U	Y	W	H	D	D	S	J	Y	E	V	G	J	Y	O	A	S	O	K	S
F	A	V	W	I	E	X	N	U	B	S	L	Y	A	I	G	T	J	I	R
I	D	Y	C	B	D	S	M	C	D	K	U	X	M	B	A	Y	E	N	Z
Q	A	O	A	Z	C	N	T	K	Q	V	G	E	R	Z	G	U	G	G	S
M	R	B	S	S	J	W	S	O	E	K	D	M	E	E	I	N	A	S	Q
U	M	S	T	P	B	B	L	P	R	N	I	D	V	Z	T	S	D	G	T
K	Q	C	P	A	R	Z	H	R	N	Y	V	D	E	H	E	E	V	A	X
I	V	A	U	M	T	Y	X	E	I	F	E	G	R	C	A	A	A	T	C
C	W	T	R	Z	C	K	S	X	S	K	R	H	E	H	X	L	N	E	Y
O	Y	T	B	K	F	I	J	B	A	E	S	N	N	E	Q	E	C	M	Z
M	M	E	C	U	H	A	U	N	N	N	E	L	C	U	S	D	E	G	K
M	T	R	A	N	S	G	R	E	S	S	E	S	E	Z	I	P	D	F	U
A	C	E	C	Y	D	W	B	O	W	E	D	W	E	C	L	L	C	N	A
N	W	D	U	B	L	H	G	Q	I	A	F	R	W	I	V	U	S	T	W
D	G	U	W	S	V	R	A	Z	X	K	F	K	K	K	E	Y	O	X	R
M	N	C	H	F	H	H	V	M	N	B	P	I	W	G	R	Y	R	L	A
E	U	X	N	S	R	G	N	K	A	H	X	R	N	S	M	B	N	J	T
N	X	R	A	W	Z	D	T	W	F	N	X	W	V	P	V	N	M	R	H
T	D	Q	B	V	F	S	T	R	E	A	S	U	R	I	E	S	X	L	O
V	L	E	U	U	C	Y	W	Q	T	M	R	I	N	G	O	H	X	Z	R

HAMAN	AGAGITE	ADVANCED	BOWED	REVERENCE
KING'S GATE	TRANSGRESSES	NISAN	WRATH	SCORN
DESTROY	COMMANDMENT	CAST PUR	DIVERSE	ADAR
SCATTERED	SILVER	TREASURIES	RING	SEALED

82. ESTHER: FOR SUCH A TIME AS THIS: ESTHER 4:1–17

When Mordecai perceived all that was done, Mordecai rent his clothes, and put on sackcloth with ashes, and went out into the midst of the city, and cried with a loud and a bitter cry; and came even before the king's gate: for none might enter into the king's gate clothed with sackcloth. And in every province, wherever the king's commandment and his decree came, there was great mourning among the Jews, and fasting, and weeping, and wailing; and many lay in sackcloth and ashes. So Esther's maids and her chamberlains came and told it her. Then was the queen exceedingly grieved; and she sent raiment to clothe Mordecai, and to take away his sackcloth from him: but he received it not.

Then called Esther for Hatach, one of the king's chamberlains, whom he had appointed to attend upon her, and gave him a commandment to Mordecai, to know what it was, and why it was.... And Mordecai told him of all that had happened to him, and of the sum of the money that Haman had promised to pay to the king's treasuries for the Jews, to destroy them. Also he gave him the copy of the writing of the decree that was given at Shushan to destroy them, to show it to Esther, and to declare it to her, and to charge her that she should go in to the king, to make supplication to him, and to make request before him for her people....

Again Esther spoke to Hatach, and gave him commandment to Mordecai; all the king's servants, and the people of the king's provinces, do know, that whosoever, whether man or woman, shall come to the king into the inner court, who is not called, there is one law of his to put him to death, except such to whom the king shall hold out the golden scepter, that he may live: but I have not been called to come in to the king these thirty days. And they told to Mordecai Esther's words.

Then Mordecai commanded to answer Esther, Think not with yourself that you shall escape in the king's house, more than all the Jews. For if you altogether hold your peace at this time, then shall there enlargement and deliverance arise to the Jews from another place; but you and your father's house shall be destroyed: and who knows whether you are come to the kingdom for such a time as this? Then Esther bid them return Mordecai this answer, Go, gather together all the Jews that are present in Shushan, and fast you for me, and neither eat nor drink three days, night or day: I also and my maidens will fast likewise; and so will I go in to the king, which is not according to the law: and if I perish, I perish. .

G	Q	L	N	W	E	N	L	A	R	G	E	M	E	N	T	S	O	X	L
F	O	V	P	U	Y	G	Y	Q	C	T	U	U	N	T	D	U	X	W	T
A	G	I	R	M	E	F	S	J	S	S	D	D	S	U	M	P	J	W	O
S	F	W	N	K	I	N	G	D	O	M	E	A	V	E	A	P	Y	S	N
T	M	E	E	T	I	E	A	A	A	B	C	Y	A	S	L	L	W	A	B
I	I	E	X	S	O	K	U	D	U	S	R	P	L	V	W	I	A	C	Y
N	U	P	E	V	C	E	H	A	U	I	E	A	Q	X	U	C	I	K	J
G	H	I	Y	M	Y	A	C	N	J	Z	E	A	V	C	R	A	T	C	H
S	W	N	D	O	T	L	P	N	T	M	S	I	A	A	X	T	I	L	D
L	L	G	P	V	Z	R	T	E	T	A	I	V	P	W	I	I	N	O	E
Y	P	G	R	I	E	V	E	D	E	F	U	T	V	M	S	O	G	T	L
K	Z	E	X	G	E	R	C	Q	R	C	A	N	W	U	U	N	E	H	I
F	X	P	R	X	Y	K	L	F	U	Q	K	A	Q	L	C	U	X	Y	V
L	P	F	R	I	K	M	O	G	Q	E	E	K	P	P	H	R	E	U	E
D	X	I	N	E	S	M	T	T	Q	H	S	Q	D	X	A	J	D	E	R
C	M	B	Y	J	D	H	H	E	V	U	T	T	U	R	T	Z	N	K	A
C	D	I	Y	J	J	O	E	V	D	P	T	P	I	T	I	F	T	F	N
I	D	B	E	S	C	E	P	T	E	R	W	J	O	V	M	A	A	V	C
S	Q	A	L	U	D	T	H	R	E	E	D	A	Y	S	E	E	L	H	E
M	O	U	R	N	I	N	G	J	K	J	J	T	Q	A	S	H	E	S	T

SACKCLOTH	ASHES	MOURNING	FASTING	WEEPING
WAITING	GRIEVED	CLOTHE	DECREE	SUPPLICATION
REQUEST	SCEPTER	ESCAPE	ENLARGEMENT	DELIVERANCE
KINGDOM	SUCH A TIME	THREE DAYS	PERISH	GO IN TO

83. ESTHER'S BANQUET: ESTHER 5:1–14

Now it came to pass on the third day, that Esther put on her royal apparel, and stood in the inner court of the king's house, opposite the king's house: and the king sat upon his royal throne in the royal house, opposite the gate of the house. And it was so, when the king saw Esther the queen standing in the court, that she obtained favor in his sight: and the king held out to Esther the golden scepter that was in his hand. So Esther drew near, and touched the top of the scepter.

Then said the king to her, What will you, queen Esther? and what is your request? it shall be even given you to the half of the kingdom. And Esther answered, If it seem good to the king, let the king and Haman come this day to the banquet that I have prepared for him. Then the king said, Cause Haman to make haste, that he may do as Esther has said.

So the king and Haman came to the banquet that Esther had prepared. And the king said to Esther at the banquet of wine, What is your petition? and it shall be granted you: and what is your request? even to the half of the kingdom it shall be performed. Then answered Esther, and said, My petition and my request is; if I have found favor in the sight of the king, and if it please the king to grant my petition, and to perform my request, let the king and Haman come to the banquet that I shall prepare for them, and I will do tomorrow as the king has said.

Then went Haman forth that day joyful and with a glad heart: but when Haman saw Mordecai in the king's gate, that he stood not up, nor moved for him, he was full of indignation against Mordecai. Nevertheless Haman refrained himself: and when he came home, he sent and called for his friends, and Zeresh his wife. And Haman told them of the glory of his riches, and the multitude of his children, and all the things wherein the king had promoted him, and how he had advanced him above the princes and servants of the king. Haman said moreover, Yea, Esther the queen did let no man come in with the king to the banquet that she had prepared but myself; and tomorrow am I invited to her also with the king. Yet all this avails me nothing, so long as I see Mordecai the Jew sitting at the king's gate. Then said Zeresh his wife and all his friends to him, Let a gallows be made of fifty cubits high, and tomorrow speak you to the king that Mordecai may be hanged thereon: then go you in merrily with the king to the banquet. And the thing pleased Haman; and he caused the gallows to be made.

X	G	W	W	K	Y	E	T	O	M	O	R	R	O	W	B	B	E	P	N
E	G	O	L	D	E	N	S	C	E	P	T	E	R	J	G	C	P	P	I
S	F	T	D	K	R	Z	W	P	R	R	I	G	A	L	L	O	W	S	S
T	Y	C	I	Q	H	D	P	I	E	I	U	E	L	P	I	B	L	M	C
C	A	Q	N	O	T	F	Y	N	Z	K	C	W	C	A	X	E	V	O	R
K	P	Y	N	Y	Y	G	G	D	V	J	T	H	J	S	H	Z	B	R	O
B	P	T	E	A	E	S	N	I	B	L	K	D	E	N	K	S	W	D	Y
A	A	X	R	G	S	X	L	G	S	L	W	D	X	S	S	B	A	E	A
N	R	M	C	H	W	V	T	N	R	H	R	E	Q	U	E	S	T	C	L
Q	E	Q	O	V	E	Y	H	A	F	B	U	L	W	C	Z	C	B	A	H
U	L	X	U	M	Y	U	E	T	O	C	O	U	R	T	T	N	L	I	O
E	Z	S	R	V	G	S	L	I	H	L	C	L	J	O	R	D	D	U	U
T	G	B	T	C	Q	Z	J	O	S	P	E	T	I	T	I	O	N	T	S
E	E	T	E	W	P	C	L	N	J	Z	S	R	T	J	O	V	J	H	E
H	A	L	F	I	B	Y	B	U	C	R	U	O	N	A	M	A	T	R	E
C	E	R	R	D	R	E	W	N	E	A	R	J	F	A	V	O	R	O	J
M	U	L	T	I	T	U	D	E	B	P	Y	U	R	S	L	C	T	N	J
U	O	C	T	P	H	Z	P	Z	L	S	X	N	K	Y	J	A	U	E	V
Q	U	G	V	O	P	P	O	S	I	T	E	O	P	I	D	V	B	B	X
G	K	S	C	Z	U	X	T	V	N	P	R	E	P	A	R	E	B	T	V

ROYAL HOUSE	OPPOSITE
DREW NEAR	REQUEST
PETITION	TOMORROW
MULTITUDE	GALLOWS
THRONE	GOLDEN SCEPTER
PREPARE	RICHES
INNER COURT	FAVOR
BANQUET	MORDECAI
APPAREL	COURT
HALF	INDIGNATION

84. ESTHER SAVES THE JEWS: ESTHER 7:1–10

So the king and Haman came to banquet with Esther the queen. And the king said again to Esther on the second day at the banquet of wine, What is your petition, queen Esther? and it shall be granted you: and what is your request? and it shall be performed, even to the half of the kingdom. Then Esther the queen answered and said, If I have found favor in your sight, O king, and if it please the king, let my life be given me at my petition, and my people at my request: for we are sold, I and my people, to be destroyed, to be slain, and to perish. But if we had been sold for bondmen and bondwomen, I had held my tongue, although the enemy could not countervail the king's damage. Then the king Ahasuerus answered and said to Esther the queen, Who is he, and where is he, that dare presume in his heart to do so? And Esther said, The adversary and enemy is this wicked Haman. Then Haman was afraid before the king and the queen. And the king arising from the banquet of wine in his wrath went into the palace garden: and Haman stood up to make request for his life to Esther the queen; for he saw that there was evil determined against him by the king. Then the king returned out of the palace garden into the place of the banquet of wine; and Haman was fallen upon the bed whereon Esther was. Then said the king, Will he force the queen also before me in the house?... So they hanged Haman on the gallows that he had prepared for Mordecai.

B	E	I	G	C	G	D	D	Z	W	R	D	A	M	A	G	E	C
H	Y	S	P	A	U	L	S	L	A	I	N	E	C	Y	A	V	H
A	A	X	O	R	R	B	Z	M	O	O	O	C	O	D	U	S	A
A	D	N	E	I	L	D	I	C	B	B	U	P	U	E	W	E	M
R	M	V	G	N	D	S	E	T	B	U	F	A	N	S	I	C	B
E	S	Y	E	E	E	I	H	N	S	G	A	C	T	T	N	O	E
S	X	X	P	R	D	M	W	U	V	A	L	I	E	R	E	N	R
O	H	F	Z	E	S	M	Y	I	Q	G	L	F	R	O	R	D	L
L	X	I	V	R	O	A	J	R	C	G	E	I	V	Y	E	D	A
D	N	F	V	N	D	P	R	X	W	K	N	E	A	E	U	A	I
Q	K	T	J	R	D	Q	L	Y	R	R	E	D	I	D	T	Y	N
D	Z	Y	A	H	A	S	U	E	R	U	S	D	L	J	Z	M	S
J	S	W	O	P	X	Z	U	Y	W	R	A	T	H	I	H	J	R

WINE
ARE SOLD
SLAIN
COUNTERVAIL
AHASUERUS
WICKED
GARDEN
CHAMBERLAINS
CUBITS
PACIFIED
SECOND DAY
MY PEOPLE
DESTROYED
ENEMY
DAMAGE
ADVERSARY
WRATH
FALLEN
FIFTY
HANGED

85. THE FEAST OF PURIM: ESTHER 9:18–32

But the Jews that were at Shushan assembled together on the thirteenth day thereof; and on the fourteenth thereof; and on the fifteenth day of the same they rested, and made it a day of feasting and gladness. Therefore the Jews of the villages, that dwelled in the unwalled towns, made the fourteenth day of the month Adar a day of gladness and feasting, and a good day, and of sending portions one to another.

And Mordecai wrote these things, and sent letters to all the Jews that were in all the provinces of the king Ahasuerus, both near and far, to establish this among them, that they should keep the fourteenth day of the month Adar, and the fifteenth day of the same, yearly, as the days wherein the Jews rested from their enemies, and the month which was turned to them from sorrow to joy, and from mourning into a good day: that they should make them days of feasting and joy, and of sending portions one to another, and gifts to the poor. And the Jews undertook to do as they had begun, and as Mordecai had written to them; because Haman the son of Hammedatha, the Agagite, the enemy of all the Jews, had devised against the Jews to destroy them, and had cast Pur, that is, the lot, to consume them, and to destroy them; but when Esther came before the king, he commanded by letters that his wicked device, which he devised against the Jews, should return upon his own head, and that he and his sons should be hanged on the gallows. Wherefore they called these days Purim after the name of Pur.

Therefore for all the words of this letter, and of that which they had seen concerning this matter, and which had come to them, the Jews ordained, and took upon them, and upon their seed, and upon all such as joined themselves to them, so as it should not fail, that they would keep these two days according to their writing, and according to their appointed time every year; and that these days should be remembered and kept throughout every generation, every family, every province, and every city; and that these days of Purim should not fail from among the Jews, nor the memorial of them perish from their seed. Then Esther the queen, the daughter of Abihail, and Mordecai the Jew, wrote with all authority, to confirm this second letter of Purim. And he sent the letters to all the Jews, to the hundred twenty and seven provinces of the kingdom of Ahasuerus, with words of peace and truth, to confirm these days of Purim in their times appointed, according as Mordecai the Jew and Esther the queen had enjoined them, and as they had decreed for themselves and for their seed, the matters of the fastings and their cry. And the decree of Esther confirmed these matters of Purim; and it was written in the book.

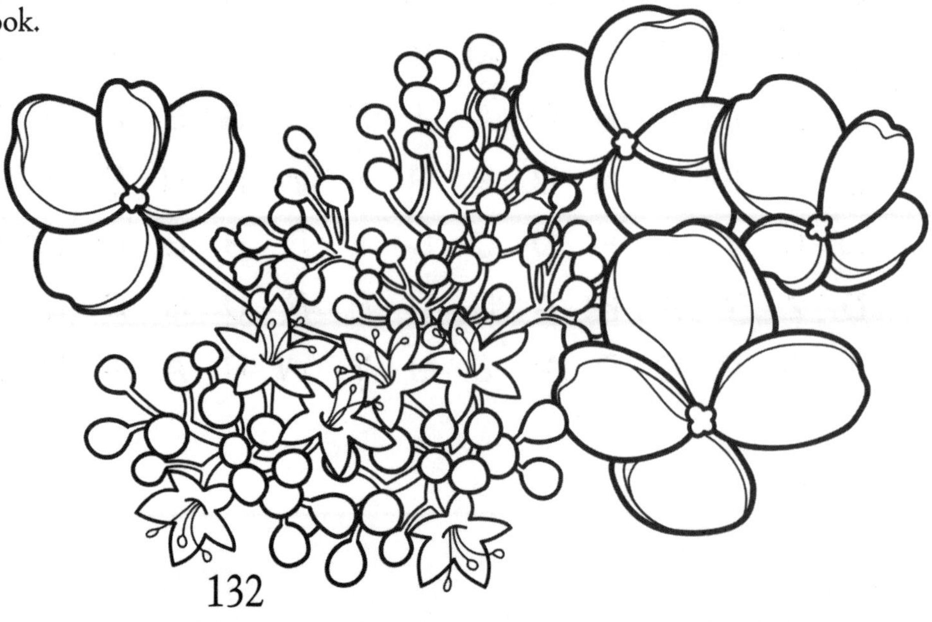

V	F	F	R	C	R	U	E	L	J	S	O	P	M	N	U	V	C	F	I
I	T	O	S	O	B	R	N	B	T	O	P	M	C	Q	V	I	E	G	U
L	W	G	U	A	W	S	J	Y	B	C	Y	D	H	K	C	L	V	I	T
P	K	D	P	R	T	Z	O	G	F	V	G	W	W	S	X	L	E	F	W
T	E	X	F	W	T	A	I	O	V	W	I	D	M	H	D	A	R	T	O
S	M	A	M	E	X	E	N	O	D	M	N	T	I	U	O	G	Y	S	D
Q	B	E	C	R	A	A	E	H	N	R	D	M	P	S	K	E	G	T	A
P	T	G	M	E	P	S	D	N	X	S	Y	W	L	H	W	S	E	O	Y
T	C	F	G	O	A	O	T	L	T	V	C	Z	J	A	G	V	N	T	S
C	J	N	N	O	R	N	R	I	J	H	V	L	H	N	E	S	E	H	F
V	V	M	F	F	V	I	D	T	N	L	O	Q	V	P	S	O	R	E	D
E	J	Y	W	A	V	V	A	T	I	G	H	J	I	V	T	R	A	P	N
Q	M	W	D	M	T	O	N	L	R	O	F	J	X	U	A	R	T	O	H
A	R	V	C	I	J	Z	G	G	D	U	N	R	R	T	B	O	I	O	Q
E	E	X	A	L	L	G	X	W	Y	Q	T	S	N	X	L	W	O	R	U
B	S	Z	W	Y	O	B	P	T	P	N	E	H	B	N	I	M	N	W	P
F	T	W	M	O	U	R	N	I	N	G	T	G	C	Z	S	Y	Y	R	P
E	E	K	U	W	W	G	L	A	D	N	E	S	S	X	H	R	S	Q	Q
Z	D	G	O	O	D	D	A	Y	L	Y	C	O	Y	M	O	E	T	Y	R
T	C	W	Q	P	H	D	N	U	N	W	A	L	L	E	D				U

SHUSHAN
FOURTEENTH
MOURNING
EVERY GENERATION
VILLAGES
GIFTS TO THE POOR
PEACE AND TRUTH
ENJOINED
PORTIONS
FEASTING
ESTABLISH
GOOD DAY
FAMILY
SORROW
UNWALLED
JOY
TWO DAYS
MEMORIAL
GLADNESS
RESTED

86. GOMER: HOSEA 1:2–11

The LORD said to Hosea, Go, take to you a wife of whoredoms and children of whoredoms: for the land has committed great whoredom, departing from the LORD. So he went and took Gomer...; which conceived, and bore him a son. And the LORD said to him, Call his name Jezreel; for yet a little while, and I will avenge the blood of Jezreel upon the house of Jehu, and will cause to cease the kingdom of the house of Israel. And it shall come to pass at that day, that I will break the bow of Israel in the valley of Jezreel.

And she conceived again, and bore a daughter. And God said to him, Call her name Loruhamah: for I will no more have mercy upon the house of Israel; but I will utterly take them away. But I will have mercy upon the house of Judah, and will save them by the LORD their God, and will not save them by bow, nor by sword, nor by battle, by horses, nor by horsemen.

Now when she had weaned Loruhamah, she conceived, and bore a son. Then said God, Call his name Loammi: for you are not My people, and I will not be your God. Yet the number of the children of Israel shall be as the sand of the sea, which cannot be measured nor numbered; and it shall come to pass, that in the place where it was said to them, You are not My people, there it shall be said to them, You are the sons of the living God. Then shall the children of Judah and the children of Israel be gathered together, and appoint themselves one head, and they shall come up out of the land.

W	W	B	I	A	H	O	S	E	A	I	K	E	B	F	H	Y	L
O	C	O	N	C	E	I	V	E	D	M	A	K	M	I	S	O	G
R	A	P	P	O	I	N	T	N	W	E	F	I	E	D	A	B	G
D	N	A	N	R	H	L	K	H	F	R	H	N	A	K	N	E	Z
O	O	B	A	N	D	I	D	L	K	C	B	G	S	Q	D	G	L
F	T	O	V	U	P	V	P	O	O	Y	Q	S	U	V	O	I	N
T	M	W	Z	M	W	I	D	R	H	X	W	O	R	M	F	N	V
H	Y	O	Q	B	F	N	W	U	O	Q	R	F	E	Y	T	N	P
E	P	F	H	E	T	G	N	H	N	P	W	J	D	S	H	I	H
L	E	I	L	R	K	G	O	A	C	P	L	U	J	Z	E	N	L
O	O	S	K	E	G	O	U	M	A	E	Y	D	X	L	S	G	O
R	P	R	A	D	B	D	B	A	E	R	T	A	A	A	E	X	A
D	L	A	T	W	Q	O	R	H	D	R	Q	H	W	B	A	R	M
R	E	E	S	A	T	J	E	Z	R	E	E	L	R	X	N	V	M
K	G	L	R	U	Z	U	Z	W	C	O	N	E	H	E	A	D	I
Z	Z	A	J	X	K	A	V	E	N	G	E	B	L	O	O	D	J

WORD OF THE LORD
CONCEIVED
HOSEA
JEZREEL
BOW OF ISRAEL
MERCY
NOT MY PEOPLE
MEASURED
LIVING GOD
ONE HEAD
BEGINNING
KINGS OF JUDAH
BLOOD
GOMER
AVENGE
LORUHAMAH
LOAMMI
NUMBERED
APPOINT
SAND OF THE SEA

87. GOMER RESTORED: HOSEA 3:1–5

Then said the Lord to me, Go yet, love a woman beloved of her friend, yet an adulteress, according to the love of the Lord toward the children of Israel, who look to other gods, and love flagons of wine. So I bought her to me for fifteen pieces of silver, and for a homer of barley, and a half homer of barley: and I said to her, You shall abide for me many days; you shall not play the harlot, and you shall not be for another man: so will I also be for you. For the children of Israel shall abide many days without a king, and without a prince, and without a sacrifice, and without an image, and without an ephod, and without teraphim: afterward shall the children of Israel return, and seek the Lord their God, and David their king; and shall fear the Lord and His goodness in the latter days.

J	I	K	S	E	E	K	T	H	E	L	O	R	D	J	Y	A	A	G	B
P	J	B	F	J	Z	O	G	N	I	B	E	L	O	V	E	D	T	S	A
M	U	G	P	I	Q	B	F	D	H	D	Q	E	U	F	H	D	H	P	D
Y	X	O	M	R	F	I	O	I	L	O	B	J	M	T	F	Z	E	J	U
G	S	O	Z	R	I	T	S	F	W	E	M	O	L	T	X	H	I	K	L
X	O	D	Y	D	I	P	E	S	V	A	L	E	H	E	Q	P	R	X	T
B	Y	N	D	J	V	W	F	E	U	X	K	U	R	R	E	F	K	K	E
P	J	E	I	E	J	Z	N	D	N	H	S	B	H	A	H	Q	I	Z	R
R	B	S	K	C	P	E	J	S	E	Q	A	Q	F	P	Q	H	N	L	E
I	Q	S	Z	J	H	U	S	K	A	Y	C	H	I	H	Z	H	G	C	S
N	D	S	T	H	A	M	F	B	Q	B	R	Z	F	I	C	U	I	O	S
C	Q	L	D	U	P	J	A	U	U	A	I	F	V	M	W	V	Q	G	N
E	W	O	M	A	N	K	W	Z	A	R	F	L	E	M	K	M	Q	O	E
A	G	U	E	K	E	P	H	O	D	L	I	A	F	M	L	M	D	K	H
B	G	S	I	L	V	E	R	K	P	E	C	G	N	I	M	A	G	E	A
P	J	H	K	M	M	F	L	E	Y	Y	E	O	V	N	Z	H	Q	R	R
J	M	R	J	O	E	X	L	J	M	Y	P	N	I	O	W	D	K	L	L
Q	H	E	R	F	R	I	E	N	D	G	C	S	X	F	A	P	T	E	O
M	V	X	R	T	H	E	K	T	L	A	T	T	E	R	D	A	Y	S	T
L	J	A	O	W	S	O	T	R	I	I	R	E	T	U	R	N	H	X	Z

WOMAN
BELOVED
HER FRIEND
ADULTERESS
FLAGONS
FIFTEEN
SILVER
HOMER
BARLEY
HARLOT
PRINCE
SACRIFICE
IMAGE
EPHOD
TERAPHIM
RETURN
SEEK THE LORD
GOODNESS
THEIR KING
LATTER DAYS

88. VISION OF THE WOMAN IN A BASKET:
ZECHARIAH 5:5–11

Then the angel that talked with me went forth, and said to me, Lift up now your eyes, and see what is this that goes forth. And I said, What is it? And he said, This is an ephah that goes forth. He said moreover, This is their resemblance through all the earth. And, behold, there was lifted up a talent of lead: and this is a woman that sits in the midst of the ephah. And he said, This is wickedness. And he cast it into the midst of the ephah; and he cast the weight of lead upon the mouth thereof. Then lifted I up my eyes, and looked, and, behold, there came out two women, and the wind was in their wings; for they had wings like the wings of a stork: and they lifted up the ephah between the earth and the heaven. Then said I to the angel that talked with me, Where do these bear the ephah? And he said to me, To build it a house in the land of Shinar: and it shall be established, and set there upon her own base.

ANGEL
WENT FORTH
LIFT UP
EPHAH
MOREOVER
BEHOLD
MIDST
WEIGHT
WICKEDNESS
RESEMBLENCE
LEAD
WOMAN
WIND
WINGS
STORK
EARTH
HEAVEN
HOUSE
SHINAR
ESTABLISHED

E	P	G	B	E	M	S	G	W	N	W	B	Z	C	S	G	W	L
D	V	U	F	P	X	O	Y	C	R	E	I	N	T	K	Q	R	I
U	C	O	E	H	P	B	R	L	A	L	E	N	R	H	F	E	F
C	N	F	S	A	J	K	M	E	G	Z	S	O	G	L	W	S	T
K	Q	H	T	H	O	N	T	O	O	V	M	T	N	S	I	E	U
O	C	H	A	I	T	V	H	W	I	V	V	E	G	Q	C	M	P
J	W	Y	B	W	W	V	S	E	S	W	E	F	F	D	K	B	H
E	E	O	L	V	O	C	T	I	Q	O	M	R	V	S	E	L	H
K	N	E	I	Z	C	Q	O	G	V	M	O	I	P	W	D	E	W
A	T	K	S	R	F	M	R	H	Q	A	C	K	M	B	N	N	O
O	F	H	H	K	A	B	K	T	D	N	Z	B	U	Y	E	C	G
E	O	E	E	S	S	N	M	U	M	I	Q	H	V	U	S	E	L
X	R	A	D	H	V	H	G	H	G	L	J	G	O	V	S	T	E
D	T	V	Y	I	W	Q	W	E	S	J	J	Z	F	A	K	W	A
Q	H	E	W	N	F	X	Y	N	L	W	I	N	D	Q	N	U	D
V	T	N	L	A	E	E	A	R	T	H	W	M	I	D	S	T	E
Y	T	H	Z	R	Z	L	Y	C	B	Y	G	P	U	J	N	Q	H
K	A	Q	H	O	U	S	E	E	B	E	H	O	L	D	A	U	W

89. THE WOMAN WITH THE ISSUE OF BLOOD:
MATTHEW 9:18–26

Behold, there came a certain ruler, and worshipped [Jesus], saying, My daughter is even now dead: but come and lay your hand upon her, and she shall live. And Jesus arose, and followed him, and so did His disciples. And, behold, a woman, which was diseased with an issue of blood twelve years, came behind Him, and touched the hem of His garment: for she said within herself, If I may but touch His garment, I shall be whole. But Jesus turned Him about, and when He saw her, He said, Daughter, be of good comfort; your faith has made you whole. And the woman was made whole from that hour. And when Jesus came into the ruler's house, and saw the minstrels and the people making a noise, He said to them, Give place: for the maid is not dead, but sleeps. And they laughed Him to scorn. But when the people were put forth, He went in, and took her by the hand, and the maid arose.

CERTAIN
RULER
WORSHIPED
DAUGHTER
DEAD
LAY YOUR HAND
JESUS
DISEASED
ISSUE OF BLOOD
TWELVE YEARS
HEM
GARMENT
COMFORT
BE WHOLE
MINSTRELS
NOISE
SLEEPS
LAUGHED
SCORN
FAME

W	J	K	H	U	K	O	E	B	T	B	T	L	R	O	T	R	M
M	N	I	G	R	B	Z	C	E	E	W	O	B	H	M	J	T	I
C	G	C	O	M	F	O	R	T	H	W	Z	O	R	X	P	L	N
J	V	T	L	I	M	U	S	A	D	A	H	J	K	D	R	I	S
C	U	B	Z	Z	U	S	J	U	N	J	D	O	O	Z	E	S	T
J	J	L	W	O	R	S	H	I	P	E	D	B	L	R	L	S	R
N	E	L	A	U	G	H	E	D	I	S	E	A	S	E	D	U	E
O	O	S	B	Y	U	F	A	M	E	M	N	N	H	Q	O	E	L
I	Q	G	U	U	S	V	V	U	Y	H	P	A	T	L	A	O	S
S	A	Q	W	S	S	Y	F	V	T	H	D	M	R	L	Y	F	S
E	M	W	E	M	S	C	U	D	S	R	E	Q	H	Q	C	B	G
E	T	S	W	N	X	G	O	C	K	Q	U	M	Z	G	E	L	A
G	E	X	H	J	J	A	Z	R	H	A	F	L	Z	C	R	O	R
L	A	Y	Y	O	U	R	H	A	N	D	D	M	E	P	T	O	M
P	W	H	D	G	Y	D	E	A	D	B	D	R	T	R	A	D	E
C	Q	G	O	U	B	G	Z	L	Y	G	O	B	S	R	I	L	N
P	A	Q	Q	T	W	E	L	V	E	Y	E	A	R	S	N	W	T
S	L	E	E	P	S	F	O	D	A	U	G	H	T	E	R	V	R

90. THE WIDOW WHO GAVE TWO MITES: MARK 12:38–44

Jesus sat opposite the treasury, and beheld how the people cast money into the treasury: and many that were rich cast in much. And there came a certain poor widow and she threw in two mites, which make a farthing. And He called to Him His disciples, and says to them, Verily I say to you, That this poor widow has cast more in, than all they which have cast into the treasury: for all they did cast in of their abundance; but she of her want did cast in all that she had, even all her living.

Z	L	P	G	K	X	D	E	W	Y	H	M	U	C	H	W	M	S	A	V
D	U	G	W	T	K	V	O	B	Y	R	L	I	V	I	N	G	G	B	P
I	U	I	M	P	B	T	Q	P	E	L	T	G	R	I	C	H	X	U	J
S	T	E	N	A	S	J	N	B	P	W	C	Q	S	B	Y	N	T	N	N
C	C	W	J	J	R	A	N	S	R	O	A	Y	W	X	W	F	X	D	V
I	J	H	O	A	E	K	L	A	P	I	S	R	F	X	S	P	P	A	A
P	P	R	I	M	N	K	E	U	U	R	J	I	E	K	C	O	V	N	L
L	F	U	M	S	I	I	K	T	T	G	Z	D	T	D	R	O	T	C	L
E	S	A	R	S	D	T	H	S	P	A	F	G	J	E	I	R	W	E	S
S	Y	E	R	V	J	O	E	O	V	L	T	U	G	I	B	W	E	B	H
H	C	Y	A	T	I	P	C	S	R	O	A	I	E	U	E	I	F	C	E
D	E	H	F	J	H	M	N	T	C	V	D	C	O	N	S	D	I	R	H
X	T	F	D	C	O	I	U	Z	R	O	E	Q	E	N	E	O	D	M	A
Y	Z	M	Z	V	R	R	N	W	M	I	C	R	H	S	S	W	L	U	D
O	F	O	E	O	O	Q	O	G	C	Q	N	T	I	L	Y	F	K	U	W
S	V	P	L	U	J	S	A	C	G	T	Y	E	U	L	R	F	F	M	A
D	J	W	H	D	X	W	Y	K	F	H	V	R	S	L	Y	S	S	X	G
B	J	M	Z	C	O	T	V	N	M	O	N	E	Y	P	E	S	V	S	C
L	C	A	S	T	I	N	T	O	P	P	X	J	U	R	Y	H	A	G	H
H	H	E	R	W	A	N	T	W	O	X	T	R	E	A	S	U	R	Y	G

HIS DOCTRINE
BEWARE
SCRIBES
SALUTATIONS
MARKETPLACE
OPPOSITE
TREASURY
MONEY
RICH
MUCH
POOR WIDOW
TWO MITES
FARTHING
DISCIPLES
VERILY
ABUNDANCE
CAST INTO
HER WANT
ALL SHE HAD
LIVING

91. MARTHA AND MARY: LUKE 10:38–42

He entered into a certain village: and a certain woman named Martha received Him into her house. And she had a sister called Mary, which also sat at Jesus' feet, and heard His word. But Martha was cumbered about much serving, and came to Him, and said, Lord, do You not care that my sister has left me to serve alone? bid her therefore that she help me. And Jesus answered and said to her, Martha, Martha, you are careful and troubled about many things: But one thing is needful: and Mary has chosen that good part, which shall not be taken away from her.

X	X	K	H	U	Y	W	A	D	Y	O	T	H	W	S	V	Y	J	Q	C
S	I	T	W	C	H	O	S	E	N	P	C	I	U	U	I	C	K	A	A
C	H	I	S	R	F	J	M	S	B	E	A	K	W	C	L	H	L	Z	R
J	F	J	S	Q	S	T	A	A	B	N	M	B	B	W	L	E	I	K	E
P	D	E	F	W	E	H	R	J	E	P	E	M	C	S	A	A	X	J	F
Q	A	S	J	B	O	E	T	F	B	J	T	N	P	I	G	R	S	T	U
A	Q	U	W	P	D	R	H	X	I	Q	O	Y	M	O	E	T	R	L	L
N	A	S	J	F	D	E	A	O	D	U	P	D	P	R	M	A	R	Y	J
Z	K	F	S	Y	I	F	L	K	H	H	A	F	N	C	G	F	X	Y	C
S	B	E	O	K	W	O	G	P	E	V	S	I	J	V	T	L	H	V	T
Y	L	E	N	I	D	R	W	G	R	G	S	U	O	L	X	J	G	M	Y
L	N	T	W	J	T	E	H	G	T	O	G	H	E	L	P	M	E	C	S
I	G	J	E	P	Z	M	A	I	S	R	N	Z	B	D	Y	V	E	K	A
X	X	A	T	R	M	G	B	G	L	F	O	E	D	M	Z	C	A	Y	T
H	M	H	I	S	W	O	R	D	C	P	C	U	E	J	A	N	M	V	K
W	I	I	I	J	S	E	R	V	I	N	G	N	B	D	M	V	H	C	V
G	O	O	D	P	A	R	T	D	P	R	M	I	J	L	F	Y	P	R	U
Q	L	O	O	W	T	N	C	U	M	B	E	R	E	D	E	U	Q	F	A
S	B	S	T	C	B	J	J	W	K	W	F	K	N	M	A	D	L	C	M
M	A	N	Y	T	H	I	N	G	S	N	C	E	R	T	A	I	N	R	M

CAME TO PASS	VILLAGE	CERTAIN	MARTHA	MARY
SAT	JESUS FEET	HEART	HIS WORD	CUMBERED
SERVING	BID HER	THEREFORE	HELP ME	CAREFUL
TROUBLED	MANY THINGS	NEEDFUL	CHOSEN	GOOD PART

92. AND 93. LAZARUS; THE REST OF THE STORY: JOHN 11:1–44

Now a certain man was sick, named Lazarus, of Bethany, the town of Mary and her sister Martha. (It was that Mary which anointed the Lord with ointment, and wiped His fee with her hair, whose brother Lazarus was sick.) Therefore his sisters sent to Him, saying, Lord, behold, he whom You love is sick. When Jesus heard that, He said, This sickness is not to death, but for the glory of God, that the Son of God might be glorified thereby. Now Jesus loved Martha, and her sister, and Lazarus. When He had heard therefore that he was sick, He abode two days still in the same place where He was.

Then after that said He to His disciples, Let us go into Judaea again. His disciples said to Him, Master, the Jews of late sought to stone You; and go You there again? Jesus answered, Are there not twelve hours in the day? If any man walk in the day, he stumbles not, because he sees the light of this world. But if a man walk in the night, he stumbles, because there is no light in him. These things said He: and after that He said to them, Our friend Lazarus sleeps; but I go, that I may awake him out of sleep. Then said His disciples, Lord, if he sleep, he shall do well. However Jesus spoke of his death: but they thought that He had spoken of taking of rest in sleep.

Then said Jesus to them plainly, Lazarus is dead. And I am glad for your sakes that I was not there, to the intent you may believe; nevertheless let us go to him. Then said Thomas, which is called Didymus, to his fellow disciples, Let us also go, that we may die with Him. Then when Jesus came, He found that he had lain in the grave four days already.

Now Bethany was near to Jerusalem, about fifteen furlongs off: and many of the Jews came to Martha and Mary, to comfort them concerning their brother. Then Martha, as soon as she heard that Jesus was coming, went and met Him: but Mary sat still in the house. Then said Martha to Jesus, Lord, if You had been here, my brother had not died. But I know, that even now, whatsoever You will ask of God, God will give it You. Jesus said to her, your brother shall rise again. Martha said to Him, I know that he shall rise again in the resurrection at the last day.

Jesus said to her, I am the resurrection, and the life: he that believes in Me, though he were dead, yet shall he live: and whosoever lives and believes in Me shall never die. Believe you this?

She said to him, Yea, Lord: I believe that You are the Christ, the Son of God, which should come into the world. And when she had so said, she went her way, and called Mary her sister secretly, saying, The Master is come, and calls for you. As soon as she heard that, she arose quickly, and came to Him. Now Jesus was not yet come into the town, but was in that place where Martha met Him. The Jews then which were with her in the house, and comforted her, when they saw Mary, that she rose up hastily and went out, followed her, saying, She goes to the grave to weep there.

Then when Mary was come where Jesus was, and saw Him, she fell down at His feet, saying to Him, Lord, if You had been here, my brother had not died. When Jesus therefore saw her weeping, and the Jews also weeping which came with her, He groaned in the spirit, and was troubled. And said, Where have you laid him? They said to Him, Lord, come and see.

Jesus wept. Then said the Jews, Behold how He loved him! And some of them said, Could not this man, which opened the eyes of the blind, have caused that even this man should not have died? Jesus therefore again groaning in Himself came to the grave. It was a cave, and a stone lay upon it. Jesus said, Take you away the stone. Martha, the sister of him that was dead, said to Him, Lord, by this time he stinks: for he has been dead four days. Jesus said to her, Said I not to you, that, if you would believe, you should see the glory of God? Then they took away the stone from the place where the dead was laid.

And Jesus lifted up His eyes, and said, Father, I thank You that You have heard Me. And I knew that You hear Me always: but because of the people which stand by I said it, that they may believe that You have sent Me. And when He thus had spoken, He cried with a loud voice, Lazarus, come forth. And he that was dead came forth, bound hand and foot with grave clothes: and his face was bound about with a napkin. Jesus says to them, Loose him, and let him go.

K	S	O	F	B	R	O	T	H	E	R	I	U	Q	S	T	P	P
R	R	E	S	U	R	R	E	C	T	I	O	N	R	O	D	O	P
I	O	I	T	E	K	H	Z	F	Y	A	P	J	T	N	Z	D	U
S	I	G	R	A	V	E	M	A	G	W	M	L	E	O	S	A	T
E	S	Z	C	H	R	I	S	T	A	A	T	P	S	F	I	N	B
A	X	T	L	A	Z	A	R	U	S	K	W	W	L	G	C	O	E
G	P	Y	T	H	E	L	I	F	E	E	O	Z	E	O	K	I	T
A	B	N	E	V	E	R	D	I	E	R	R	X	E	D	N	N	H
I	C	N	J	U	D	E	A	Y	N	W	L	J	P	K	E	T	A
N	E	W	S	T	U	M	B	L	E	S	D	V	S	J	S	E	N
S	B	E	L	I	E	V	E	W	V	N	D	Q	Q	D	S	D	Y
F	Q	P	G	L	O	R	Y	O	F	G	O	D	U	X	E	R	J
U	P	X	A	W	H	O	M	Y	O	U	L	O	V	E	S	M	L

LAZARUS	BETHANY	AWAKE	NEVER DIE	THE LIFE
ANOINTED	BROTHER	STUMBLES	SON OF GOD	RISE AGAIN
WHOM YOU LOVE	SICKNESS	RESURRECTION	SLEEPS	CHRIST
GLORY OF GOD	JUDEA	GRAVE	BELIEVE	WORLD

O	N	H	H	A	N	D	A	N	D	F	O	O	T	T	I	Q	D	P	U
G	E	A	O	Q	C	X	O	X	W	E	S	C	M	N	F	I	J	Q	N
L	M	X	T	Q	B	E	H	O	L	D	D	C	F	A	V	J	V	D	W
O	O	N	G	R	D	B	G	T	J	Q	A	O	O	N	S	C	E	D	N
R	U	N	L	M	O	T	I	R	V	E	L	M	N	R	M	T	Y	Y	P
Y	Y	M	M	H	V	U	Z	G	O	B	R	E	K	W	N	G	E	J	Q
R	Z	A	F	Y	Y	H	B	P	B	D	K	F	P	T	C	C	J	R	W
X	P	L	P	Y	Q	A	K	L	F	T	S	O	N	Z	A	S	S	W	G
W	E	E	P	I	N	G	A	A	E	B	S	R	N	Z	V	T	T	T	R
F	O	U	R	D	A	Y	S	B	M	D	J	T	E	A	E	I	O	A	O
V	Y	P	J	Y	V	U	O	C	F	K	U	H	M	D	P	N	N	D	A
N	Y	L	W	V	Y	W	I	I	L	D	Q	X	G	P	B	K	E	Y	N
L	E	T	H	I	M	G	O	X	D	O	Z	K	Q	R	P	S	I	X	E
C	O	M	F	O	R	T	E	D	Q	A	T	L	B	O	U	N	D	N	D
W	Z	E	R	G	U	X	V	R	K	N	L	H	M	Z	L	Z	U	K	W
E	V	U	C	B	L	O	O	S	E	H	I	M	E	K	L	N	Z	J	X
I	V	Z	E	C	L	T	M	S	N	V	S	D	K	S	D	A	R	J	J
F	A	T	H	E	R	M	I	W	N	W	V	O	O	H	E	A	R	D	D
Q	I	E	V	X	U	Q	E	F	J	M	W	V	U	G	J	B	H	G	L
Q	J	I	A	J	R	S	L	U	Y	J	D	L	L	L	Z	Y	X	M	G

MASTER	COMFORTED	GLORY	FATHER	HAND AND FOOT
WEEPING	GROANED	HEARD	LOOSE HIM	LET HIM GO
TROUBLED	BEHOLD	BOUND	COME FORTH	STINKS
CAVE	STONE	CLOTHES	NAPKIN	FOUR DAYS

94. MARY OF BETHANY ANOINTS JESUS: JOHN 12:1–8

Then Jesus six days before the passover came to Bethany, where Lazarus was which had been dead, whom He raised from the dead. There they made Him a supper; and Martha served: but Lazarus was one of them that sat at the table with Him. Then took Mary a pound of ointment of spikenard, very costly, and anointed the feet of Jesus, and wiped His feet with her hair: and the house was filled with the odor of the ointment. Then says one of His disciples, Judas Iscariot, Simon's son, which should betray Him, Why was not this ointment sold for three hundred pence, and given to the poor? This he said, not that he cared for the poor; but because he was a thief, and had the bag, and bore what was put therein. Then said Jesus, Let her alone: against the day of My burying has she kept this. For the poor always you have with you; but Me you have not always.

C	X	T	R	P	A	S	S	O	V	E	R	K	D	A	X	H	L	A	D
K	O	O	R	N	T	W	R	G	V	A	F	Q	G	Y	Y	F	W	P	J
G	S	T	D	E	O	S	A	T	A	T	T	A	B	L	E	E	X	E	K
X	I	J	D	O	K	S	T	P	M	S	U	Y	K	A	H	E	U	N	I
Q	S	W	S	P	R	P	U	I	V	U	O	H	L	B	F	T	H	C	D
W	H	H	V	M	Q	D	P	A	A	C	J	A	P	V	S	Y	X	E	Y
P	W	Z	G	D	G	K	V	P	O	Y	R	I	P	X	I	I	U	J	P
A	O	J	C	V	I	U	G	A	P	J	C	R	U	I	K	V	R	H	B
R	G	U	R	T	S	U	P	P	E	R	F	K	H	R	T	S	E	B	U
G	A	D	N	H	V	B	B	S	B	O	H	H	W	O	Q	X	L	S	R
A	O	I	A	D	P	G	L	B	F	M	V	F	T	K	L	U	G	E	Y
W	T	T	S	G	A	N	O	I	N	T	E	D	Z	H	J	N	C	R	I
J	I	T	H	E	P	O	O	R	D	Y	M	P	T	Z	U	F	B	E	N
Q	C	P	W	X	D	X	S	V	Y	D	W	S	E	G	D	J	E	D	G
O	O	M	E	M	N	R	U	A	X	A	V	F	W	S	A	O	T	X	U
N	S	N	H	D	H	Y	Q	T	L	O	Y	X	L	W	S	S	R	T	Z
H	T	X	S	P	I	K	E	N	A	R	D	N	I	T	K	K	A	D	W
A	L	S	X	T	W	G	U	X	I	G	R	R	B	I	D	O	Y	G	O
P	Y	W	Q	H	T	H	R	E	E	H	U	N	D	R	E	D	X	K	Q
O	I	N	T	M	E	N	T	Z	H	U	D	W	V	R	S	T	W	T	T

PASSOVER
SUPPER
RAISED
SERVED
SAT AT TABLE
POUND
OINTMENT
SPIKENARD
COSTLY
ANOINTED
FEET
WIPED
HAIR
ODOR
JUDAS
BETRAY
THREE HUNDRED
PENCE
BURYING
THE POOR

95. A WOMAN WASHES JESUS'S FEET: LUKE 7:36–50

One of the Pharisees desired...that [Jesus] would eat with him. And He went into the Pharisee's house, and sat down to meat. And, behold, a woman in the city, which was a sinner, when she knew that Jesus sat at meat in the Pharisee's house, brought an alabaster box of ointment, and stood at His feet behind Him weeping, and began to wash His feet with tears, and did wipe them with the hairs of her head, and kissed His feet, and anointed them with the ointment. Now when the Pharisee which had bidden Him saw it, he spoke within himself, saying, This man, if He were a prophet, would have known who and what manner of woman this is that touches Him: for she is a sinner.

And Jesus answering said to him, There was a certain creditor which had two debtors: the one owed five hundred pence, and the other fifty. And when they had nothing to pay, he frankly forgave them both. Tell me therefore, which of them will love him most? Simon answered and said, I suppose that he, to whom he forgave most. And He said to him, You have rightly judged. And He turned to the woman, and said to Simon, See you this woman? I entered into your house, you gave Me no water for My feet: but she has washed My feet with tears, and wiped them with the hairs of her head. You gave Me no kiss: but this woman since the time I came in has not ceased to kiss My feet. My head with oil you did not anoint: but this woman has anointed My feet with ointment. Wherefore I say to you, Her sins, which are many, are forgiven; for she loved much: but to whom little is forgiven, the same loves little. And He said to her, Your sins are forgiven.... And He said to the woman, Your faith has saved you; go in peace.

T	F	Z	V	A	T	H	I	S	F	E	E	T	U	H	R	C	D
E	M	A	N	N	E	R	O	F	W	O	M	A	N	A	I	P	N
A	J	Z	A	L	F	A	K	M	W	K	E	W	I	R	G	H	H
R	W	A	S	H	E	D	Q	Z	T	I	Z	Y	O	I	H	A	Y
S	U	W	D	A	N	O	I	N	T	E	D	V	V	S	T	R	G
I	O	D	P	A	L	A	B	A	S	T	E	R	F	O	L	I	O
N	I	C	E	K	F	X	L	W	E	U	O	P	O	F	Y	S	I
N	N	R	K	B	S	D	P	I	B	Q	K	R	R	H	J	E	N
E	T	N	I	C	T	B	A	P	I	W	K	O	G	E	U	E	P
R	M	W	S	W	I	O	S	E	D	E	N	P	A	R	D	S	E
S	E	A	S	P	U	R	R	D	D	D	F	H	V	H	G	O	A
C	N	X	E	E	N	E	C	S	E	M	L	E	E	E	E	U	C
N	T	Y	D	A	U	L	I	E	N	S	P	T	M	A	D	R	E
C	R	E	D	I	T	O	R	S	F	A	I	T	H	D	E	T	K

SINNER
OINTMENT
WASHED
WIPED
KISSED
BIDDEN
MANNER OF WOMAN
DEBTORS
RIGHTLY JUDGED
GO IN PEACE
PHARISEES
ALABASTER
AT HIS FEET
TEARS
HAIRS OF HER HEAD
ANOINTED
PROPHET
CREDITOR
FORGAVE
FAITH

96. MARY MAGDALENE AND THE WOMEN WHO MINISTERED TO JESUS: LUKE 8:1–3

It came to pass afterward, that He went throughout every city and village, preaching and showing the glad tidings of the kingdom of God: and the twelve were with Him, and certain women, which had been healed of evil spirits and infirmities, Mary called Magdalene, out of whom went seven devils, and Joanna the wife of Chuza Herod's steward, and Susanna, and many others, which ministered to Him of their substance.

AFTERWARD
THROUGHOUT
VILLAGE
PREACHING
SHOWING
GLAD
TIDINGS
KINGDOM
TWELVE
CERTAIN WOMEN
HEALED
EVIL SPIRITS
INFIRMITIES
MAGDALENE
SEVEN DEVILS
JOANNA
SUSANNA
HEROD
MINISTERED
SUBSTANCE

L	M	E	V	T	L	J	O	A	N	N	A	J	A	R	Z	E	B	K	N
H	E	R	O	D	P	X	Z	R	N	Y	T	I	D	I	N	G	S	S	B
Y	A	L	D	Y	J	Q	G	Z	C	H	E	A	L	E	D	S	G	C	S
G	M	C	S	U	B	S	T	A	N	C	E	F	V	N	R	S	B	E	C
R	B	R	S	E	W	K	L	F	J	J	F	W	Q	D	S	H	K	R	A
S	W	P	R	E	A	C	H	I	N	G	Z	P	W	Y	Y	C	I	T	A
L	P	Y	M	L	V	S	L	E	Z	F	W	Z	Y	C	V	P	N	A	C
C	C	B	B	X	O	H	P	X	W	V	U	B	R	I	Z	I	G	I	L
E	V	I	L	S	P	I	R	I	T	S	J	G	H	K	R	E	D	N	I
K	X	L	R	O	W	P	I	F	E	W	S	M	M	M	T	D	O	W	G
M	D	U	V	P	G	A	R	B	X	I	I	G	Q	F	S	M	M	O	N
T	H	R	O	U	G	H	O	U	T	Z	I	Y	E	S	M	A	T	M	D
L	U	G	A	J	I	V	I	L	L	A	G	E	J	T	A	B	T	E	M
X	T	J	G	J	A	F	T	E	R	W	A	R	D	D	G	J	W	N	M
S	H	O	W	I	N	G	E	N	Y	S	G	L	A	D	A	E	E	B	G
H	U	O	P	J	R	P	L	N	J	D	T	U	V	Z	L	Z	L	Z	H
N	J	I	N	F	I	R	M	I	T	I	E	S	J	E	E	Y	V	Z	O
S	S	U	S	A	N	N	A	E	W	U	J	G	V	P	N	E	E	M	W
P	L	C	H	D	W	X	P	S	M	I	N	I	S	T	E	R	E	D	O
B	D	G	T	G	P	E	S	E	V	E	N	D	E	V	I	L	S	V	D

97. AND 98. JESUS'S RESURRECTION: LUKE 23:50–24:12

It is remarkable that the first witnesses to Jesus's resurrection were a group of women.

There was a man named Joseph, a counselor; and he was a good man, and just: (the same had not consented to the counsel and deed of them;) he was of Arimathaea, a city of the Jews: who also himself waited for the kingdom of God. This man went to Pilate, and begged the body of Jesus. And he took it down, and wrapped it in linen, and laid it in a sepulcher that was hewn in stone, wherein never man before was laid. And that day was the preparation, and the sabbath drew on.

And the women also, which came with Him from Galilee, followed after, and beheld the sepulcher, and how His body was laid. And they returned, and prepared spices and ointments; and rested the sabbath day according to the commandment. Now upon the first day of the week, very early in the morning, they came to the sepulcher, bringing the spices which they had prepared, and certain others with them. And they found the stone rolled away from the sepulcher. And they entered in, and found not the body of the Lord Jesus.

And it came to pass, as they were much perplexed about this, behold, two men stood by them in shining garments: and as they were afraid, and bowed down their faces to the earth, they said to them, Why seek you the living among the dead? He is not here, but is risen: remember how He spoke to you when He was yet in Galilee, saying, The Son of Man must be delivered into the hands of sinful men, and be crucified, and the third day rise again. And they remembered His words, and returned from the sepulcher, and told all these things to the eleven, and to all the rest.

It was Mary Magdalene, and Joanna, and Mary the mother of James, and other women that were with them, which told these things to the apostles. And their words seemed to them as idle tales, and they believed them not.

G	C	O	U	N	S	E	L	Y	N	T	A	C	C	C	B	J	H
K	Z	U	R	E	O	V	B	A	Q	N	Z	S	Z	O	O	Q	E
S	P	R	E	P	A	R	A	T	I	O	N	P	J	N	D	F	W
X	M	G	C	O	U	N	S	E	L	O	R	G	U	S	Y	N	N
N	W	R	A	P	P	E	D	H	Y	T	D	A	S	E	O	P	D
W	A	I	T	E	D	H	N	W	B	U	M	C	T	N	F	S	L
W	P	I	L	A	T	E	G	O	O	D	M	A	N	T	J	T	I
P	H	O	A	R	I	M	A	T	H	A	E	A	M	E	E	O	N
M	H	Y	B	F	W	O	M	E	N	Q	T	M	O	D	S	N	E
I	M	U	K	I	N	G	D	O	M	O	F	G	O	D	U	E	N
O	S	A	B	B	A	T	H	K	T	H	W	O	H	P	S	G	V
S	K	G	A	L	I	L	E	E	J	O	S	E	P	H	Y	R	V
T	R	H	S	E	P	U	L	C	H	E	R	D	A	U	Q	R	C

JOSEPH
GOOD MAN
JUST
COUNSEL
KINGDOM OF GOD
BODY OF JESUS
LINEN
HEWN
PILATE
WOMEN
COUNSELOR
CONSENTED
ARIMATHAEA
WAITED
PREPARATION
WRAPPED
SEPULCHER
STONE
SABBATH
GALILEE

P	L	L			A	Y	S	O	N	O	F	M	A	N	E	E	R
E	F	T	D	P	B	P	W	S	Y	B	Z	Z	P	W	A	N	O
H	I	B	B	P	Y	P	O	V	T	Y	S	E	Y	E	R	T	L
I	R	E	O	S	A	R	E	S	J	O	T	Y	B	O	L	E	L
S	S	H	W	I	H	M	I	R	T	H	O	X	U	A	Y	R	E
B	T	E	R	P	N	I	O	S	P	L	N	P	Q	P	M	E	D
O	D	L	S	E	H	T	N	R	E	L	E	L	I	N	H	D	A
D	A	D	Q	J	S	U	M	G	N	A	E	S	J	N	T	I	W
Y	Y	C	U	R	F	T	N	E	I	I	G	X	I	D	G	N	A
P	O	F	S	P	I	C	E	S	N	N	N	A	E	F	F	T	Y
C	R	U	C	I	F	I	E	D	F	T	G	G	I	D	N	A	A
I	D	L	E	T	A	L	E	S	Q	H	S	X	P	N	V	M	U
S	N	F	N	A	H	C	O	M	M	A	N	D	M	E	N	T	Y

BEHELD
CRUCIFIED
RESTED
FIRST DAY
COMMANDMENT
OINTMENTS
PERPLEXED
SON OF MAN
RISE AGAIN
IDLE TALES
HIS BODY
ROLLED AWAY
MORNNG
EARLY
STONE
ENTERED IN
SHINING
SPICES
APOSTLES
STOOPING

99. PETER'S MOTHER-IN-LAW: MATTHEW 8:14–15

When Jesus was come into Peter's house, He saw his wife's mother laid, and sick of a fever. And He touched her hand, and the fever left her: and she arose, and ministered to them. When the evening was come, they brought to Him many that were possessed with devils: and He cast out the spirits with His word, and healed all that were sick: that it might be fulfilled which was spoken by Isaiah the prophet, saying, Himself took our infirmities, and bore our sicknesses. Now when Jesus saw great multitudes about Him, He gave commandment to depart to the other side.

Y	T	M	U	J	S	S	G	T	I	H	N	D	L	G	H	W	N	F	I
K	C	A	O	E	I	Q	R	P	O	S	M	Y	X	T	B	X	J	C	H
A	S	T	U	T	M	Z	G	S	O	U	A	Y	F	K	C	B	R	Y	L
X	M	C	J	I	H	I	M	T	I	F	C	I	K	Q	O	Y	L	I	S
G	J	E	S	U	S	E	N	M	K	I	A	H	A	M	M	F	Z	E	I
R	U	V	U	F	P	J	R	I	R	C	A	M	E	H	M	B	S	H	C
Z	R	E	D	I	W	O	N	I	S	G	D	G	J	D	A	T	W	A	K
S	L	N	W	E	O	E	S	M	N	T	Z	U	Y	X	N	L	X	A	W
Z	S	I	Y	A	H	O	U	S	E	L	E	N	X	U	D	E	C	I	S
H	Z	N	F	Y	O	S	Y	L	E	E	A	R	B	R	M	W	A	C	Y
H	R	G	R	D	Y	I	Z	R	J	S	G	W	E	A	E	H	S	M	E
A	S	X	E	H	E	L	G	N	A	R	S	F	O	D	N	I	T	G	G
W	G	O	G	B	W	V	E	O	T	Q	T	E	A	K	T	S	O	T	N
L	P	Q	J	O	N	H	I	F	M	U	X	E	D	X	F	W	U	J	E
V	L	E	A	K	A	V	A	L	T	R	T	N	B	A	T	O	T	Y	K
I	W	Y	T	F	E	E	P	N	S	H	P	Z	K	U	Z	R	D	B	U
W	B	X	I	E	O	E	K	V	D	T	E	K	O	S	E	D	Y	W	B
G	P	I	Z	K	R	Q	R	C	I	A	A	R	O	S	E	E	U	J	S
I	N	F	I	R	M	I	T	I	E	S	D	L	I	F	E	V	E	R	I
L	Q	S	P	I	R	I	T	S	A	U	K	G	N	W	Q	S	C	G	T

JESUS	PETER	HOUSE	MOTHER-IN-LAW	SICK
FEVER	EVENING	TOUCHED	HAND	LEFT HER
AROSE	MINISTERED	POSSESSED	DEVILS	CAST OUT
SPIRTS	HIS WORD	ISAIAH	INFIRMITIES	COMMANDMENT

100. THE DAUGHTER OF JAIRUS: LUKE 8:41–56

There came a man named Jairus, and he was a ruler of the synagogue: and he fell down at Jesus' feet, and besought Him that He would come into his house: for he had one only daughter, about twelve years of age, and she lay a dying. But as He went the people thronged Him. And a woman having an issue of blood twelve years, which had spent all her living upon physicians, neither could be healed of any, came behind Him, and touched the border of His garment: and immediately her issue of blood stanched. And Jesus said, Who touched Me? When all denied, Peter and they that were with Him said, Master, the multitude throng You and press You, and say You, Who touched Me? And Jesus said, Somebody has touched Me: for I perceive that virtue is gone out of Me. And when the woman saw that she was not hidden, she came trembling, and falling down before Him, she declared to Him before all the people for what cause she had touched Him, and how she was healed immediately. And He said to her, Daughter, be of good comfort: your faith has made you whole; go in peace.

While He yet spoke, there comes one from the ruler of the synagogue's house, saying to him, Your daughter is dead; trouble not the Master. But when Jesus heard it, He answered him, saying, Fear not: believe only, and she shall be made whole. And when He came into the house, He permitted no man to go in, save Peter, and James, and John, and the father and the mother of the maiden. And all wept, and bewailed her: but He said, Weep not; she is not dead, but sleeps. And they laughed Him to scorn, knowing that she was dead. And He put them all out, and took her by the hand, and called, saying, Maid, arise. And her spirit came again, and she arose immediately: and He commanded to give her meat. And her parents were astonished: but He charged them that they should tell no man what was done.

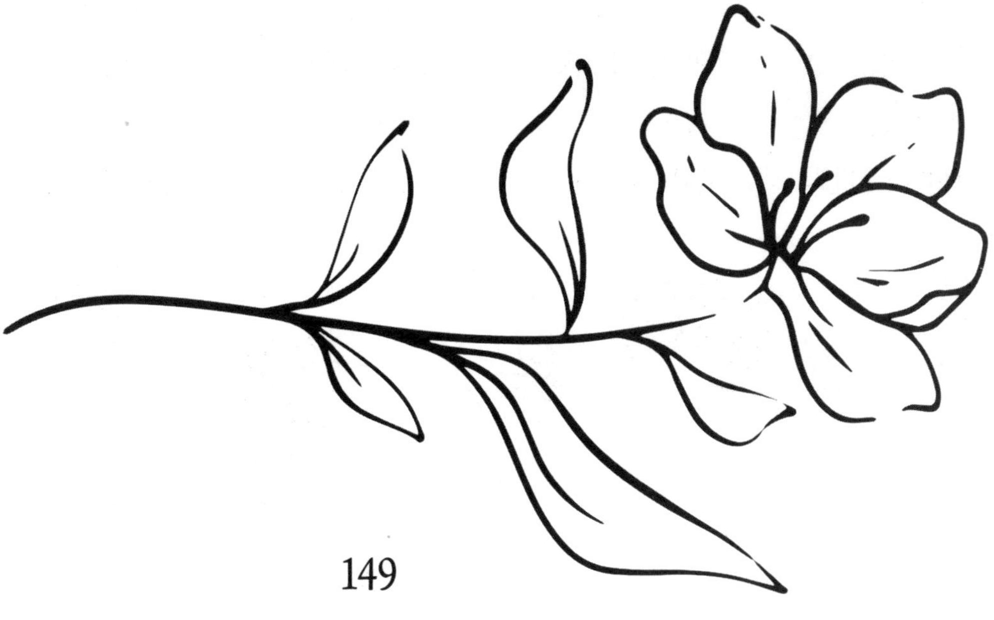

Y	T	B	M	A	D	V	P	T	D	T	C	O	Z	K	T	Y	Z	R	B
X	I	S	Y	V	X	U	I	I	U	R	G	X	R	I	W	M	E	V	O
F	K	F	Y	H	U	F	S	I	N	E	Q	X	G	M	E	A	D	L	C
M	R	N	Q	Q	H	Y	F	T	J	P	C	X	E	M	L	I	O	T	Q
R	K	S	J	W	C	N	F	O	S	G	N	I	J	E	V	D	L	R	U
G	S	Y	N	A	G	O	G	U	E	B	N	B	J	D	E	Z	D	E	L
S	R	L	P	H	Y	S	I	C	I	A	N	S	E	I	T	M	F	M	B
F	L	U	D	R	W	A	L	H	W	U	Q	R	C	A	Z	U	C	B	F
K	A	E	L	Y	S	E	W	E	Y	U	Q	J	P	T	B	U	F	L	U
U	Z	K	E	E	I	Y	W	D	W	N	S	I	N	E	O	B	E	I	D
L	R	X	G	P	R	N	G	X	A	H	X	J	B	L	A	M	A	N	A
R	R	F	N	M	S	F	G	G	X	W	O	S	Q	Y	P	A	R	G	U
J	F	H	B	K	A	C	V	U	X	E	V	L	E	B	W	F	N	F	G
G	F	Z	T	I	S	C	U	J	G	E	I	R	E	A	L	I	O	V	H
I	G	Y	D	H	Y	U	J	S	I	P	H	K	B	L	R	D	T	F	T
W	M	C	K	W	C	F	Z	F	I	N	M	R	A	L	Z	I	E	I	E
B	E	L	I	E	V	E	N	Q	K	O	H	G	T	U	J	Q	S	Z	R
E	Q	Q	Z	P	B	Y	S	U	O	T	X	R	L	N	X	G	U	E	N
V	O	J	A	I	R	U	S	A	S	T	O	N	I	S	H	E	D	U	U
B	E	W	A	I	L	E	D	F	A	V	I	R	T	U	E	N	Q	E	D

JAIRUS	RULER	SYNAGOGUE	DAUGHTER	TWELVE
DYING	PHYSICIANS	FEAR NOT	BELIEVE	WHOLE
BEWAILED	WEEP NOT	SLEEPS	MAID	ARISE
IMMEDIATELY	ASTONISHED	VIRTUE	TREMBLING	TOUCHED

101. HERODIAS: MATTHEW 14:1–11

At that time Herod the tetrarch heard of the fame of Jesus, and said to his servants, This is John the Baptist; he is risen from the dead; and therefore mighty works do show forth themselves in him. For Herod had laid hold on John, and bound him, and put him in prison for Herodias' sake, his brother Philip's wife. For John said to him, It is not lawful for you to have her. And when he would have put him to death, he feared the multitude, because they counted him as a prophet. But when Herod's birthday was kept, the daughter of Herodias danced before them, and pleased Herod. Whereupon he promised with an oath to give her whatsoever she would ask. And she, being before instructed of her mother, said, Give me here John Baptist's head in a charger [platter]. And the king was sorry: nevertheless for the oath's sake, and them which sat with him at meat, he commanded it to be given her. And he sent, and beheaded John in the prison. And his head was brought in a charger, and given to the damsel: and she brought it to her mother.

L	A	H	S	O	P	F	F	X	D	H	C	Z	H	P	V	G	W
S	J	D	O	F	M	B	X	A	U	W	Y	P	E	E	D	G	S
R	B	O	U	N	D	H	I	M	M	L	D	L	R	G	A	G	N
V	B	U	H	P	R	O	M	I	S	E	D	E	O	C	M	A	O
O	E	S	T	N	M	J	E	Z	N	M	W	A	D	H	S	M	L
B	J	S	O	Z	T	O	H	Y	L	E	B	S	I	A	E	U	Q
Q	K	W	V	Q	M	H	R	E	D	A	M	E	A	R	L	L	I
B	V	Q	F	X	Q	J	E	A	R	A	W	D	S	G	Y	T	B
I	Y	E	C	J	U	C	G	B	P	O	U	F	K	E	S	I	M
R	T	E	T	R	A	R	C	H	A	G	D	G	U	R	D	T	X
T	T	K	D	M	D	Z	K	L	Q	P	X	U	H	L	F	U	W
H	C	M	P	R	O	P	H	E	T	D	T	S	D	T	U	D	W
D	C	O	M	M	A	N	D	E	D	Z	B	I	R	L	E	E	H
A	F	C	Z	G	C	P	H	I	L	I	P	E	S	U	R	R	R
Y	I	Z	Z	C	G	M	G	N	O	G	Z	G	S	T	Q	A	U
J	N	Z	X	E	N	I	K	T	Y	L	D	A	N	C	E	D	K
O	B	U	C	Q	H	I	L	U	Q	T	V	V	J	V	L	O	Z
P	R	I	S	O	N	I	M	Q	B	E	H	E	A	D	E	D	W

HEROD
TETRARCH
FAME
JOHN THE BAPTIST
BOUND HIM
PRISON
PHILIP
LAWFUL
MULTITIUDE
PROPHET
BIRTHDAY
HERODIAS
DAUGHTER
DANCED
PLEASED
PROMISED
CHARGER
COMMANDED
BEHEADED
DAMSEL

102. THE WOMAN OF CANAAN: MATTHEW 15:21–28

Then Jesus went from there, and departed into the coasts of Tyre and Sidon. And, behold, a woman of Canaan came out of the same coasts, and cried to Him, saying, Have mercy on me, O Lord, You Son of David; my daughter is grievously vexed with a devil. But He answered her not a word. And His disciples came and besought Him, saying, Send her away; for she cries after us. But He answered and said, I am not sent but to the lost sheep of the house of Israel. Then came she and worshipped Him, saying, Lord, help me. But He answered and said, It is not meet to take the children's bread, and to cast it to dogs. And she said, Truth, Lord: yet the dogs eat of the crumbs which fall from their masters' table. Then Jesus answered and said to her, O woman, great is your faith: be it to you even as you will. And her daughter was made whole from that very hour.

Q	L	K	E	H	D	W	G	Y	R	T	O	G	D	Q	Y	S	O	Z	C
C	Z	O	G	T	E	B	K	C	O	P	W	R	O	Z	N	O	K	S	F
I	O	Y	A	L	O	L	M	W	U	I	W	W	G	H	J	N	Y	D	G
D	M	A	C	G	U	S	P	H	G	O	H	O	S	N	F	O	Y	J	N
E	C	M	S	Z	I	M	G	M	R	N	V	M	H	Q	E	F	Y	A	L
T	H	A	R	T	P	E	I	M	E	A	A	B	D	K	T	D	K	N	O
F	X	D	J	W	S	R	V	S	I	D	O	N	H	O	G	A	N	S	S
S	R	E	S	Q	V	C	K	A	D	V	Y	F	K	I	O	V	V	W	T
F	B	W	X	T	A	Y	P	G	H	B	Y	U	Q	N	I	I	S	E	S
L	T	H	P	R	B	T	U	O	K	W	I	W	C	E	F	D	E	R	H
L	S	O	C	U	P	H	L	V	N	W	J	J	C	Y	V	Q	J	E	E
B	N	L	V	T	M	Q	U	U	L	K	K	K	W	R	S	Y	W	D	E
T	Y	E	K	H	E	N	Q	S	S	S	Y	R	K	D	U	Z	J	N	P
C	A	N	A	A	N	P	F	N	Y	E	V	E	X	E	D	M	L	O	L
P	F	J	H	O	U	S	E	O	F	I	S	R	A	E	L	T	B	T	P
M	A	G	R	E	A	T	F	A	I	T	H	B	D	K	T	E	U	S	J
H	U	A	T	C	W	K	V	G	Q	D	B	E	S	O	U	G	H	T	Q
B	Y	I	C	H	I	L	D	R	E	N	S	B	R	E	A	D	Q	P	T
N	Z	I	Q	J	X	N	K	D	O	H	D	N	T	A	B	L	E	D	K
O	S	T	Y	R	E	Z	N	O	T	M	E	E	T	K	U	M	H	N	W

TYRE
SIDON
CANAAN
COASTS
MERCY
SON OF DAVID
VEXED
ANSWERED NOT
BESOUGHT
LOST SHEEP
HOUSE OF ISRAEL
HELP ME
NOT MEET
CHILDREN'S BREAD
DOGS
TRUTH
CRUMBS
TABLE
GREAT FAITH
MADE WHOLE

103. THE WIDOW OF NAIN: LUKE 7:11–17

It came to pass the day after, that He went into a city called Nain; and many of His disciples went with Him, and many people. Now when He came near to the gate of the city, behold, there was a dead man carried out, the only son of his mother, and she was a widow: and many people of the city were with her. And when the Lord saw her, He had compassion on her, and said to her, Weep not. And He came and touched the bier: and they that bore him stood still. And He said, Young man, I say to you, Arise. And he that was dead sat up, and began to speak. And He delivered him to his mother. And there came a fear on all: and they glorified God, saying, That a great prophet is risen up among us; and, That God has visited His people.

F	O	Z	D	B	B	B	J	V	X	W	X	S	N	Z	X	V	W	O	D
H	K	F	R	I	J	I	K	Y	L	E	S	J	D	M	H	I	B	Q	R
T	D	L	Q	U	S	H	E	Y	V	J	R	P	O	C	C	S	A	A	L
O	I	R	E	X	K	C	E	R	Z	C	W	G	E	H	H	I	B	U	S
U	H	U	I	D	D	R	I	C	K	P	P	I	F	A	K	T	W	M	T
C	A	M	A	H	Y	O	K	P	L	S	D	I	D	U	K	E	M	P	O
H	C	O	F	Y	K	G	F	K	L	M	K	U	I	O	D	D	O	O	O
E	U	R	H	R	O	V	A	R	O	E	D	K	L	J	W	M	Q	I	D
D	W	E	E	P	N	O	T	P	I	M	S	T	A	R	L	Z	K	Q	S
H	B	P	Z	Z	N	B	E	C	O	M	P	A	S	S	I	O	N	A	T
D	E	L	I	V	E	R	E	D	L	Z	X	M	N	N	V	H	P	T	I
I	O	L	T	U	N	E	Y	S	J	E	N	I	X	A	Y	N	I	R	L
T	E	L	U	E	G	L	O	R	I	F	I	E	D	D	I	D	J	I	L
S	A	T	U	P	D	K	U	W	R	Q	Z	H	D	D	X	N	O	W	A
F	H	I	H	L	T	K	N	O	J	J	U	D	A	E	A	P	U	C	R
D	X	J	N	C	U	O	G	J	O	N	L	Y	S	O	N	R	K	J	I
X	M	B	D	O	D	W	M	Y	A	F	R	X	J	I	T	G	B	I	S
F	J	W	D	P	A	J	A	I	F	W	A	X	S	X	K	Z	E	F	E
M	J	X	P	T	L	V	N	B	T	Z	V	R	E	G	I	O	N	T	S
I	H	D	E	A	D	M	A	N	N	I	F	T	R	R	B	D	G	J	O

NAIN
DISCIPLES
DEAD MAN
ONLY SON
WIDOW
COMPASSION
WEEP NOT
TOUCHED
BIER
STOOD STILL
YOUNG MAN
ARISE
SAT UP
SPEAK
DELIVERED
VISISTED
RUMOR
JUDAEA
REGION
GLORIFIED

104. THE WOMAN WITH A SPIRIT OF INFIRMITY

LUKE 13:10–16

He was teaching in one of the synagogues on the sabbath. And, behold, there was a woman which had a spirit of infirmity eighteen years, and was bowed together, and could in no wise lift up herself. And when Jesus saw her, He called her to Him, and said to her, Woman, you are loosed from your infirmity. And He laid His hands on her: and immediately she was made straight, and glorified God. And the ruler of the synagogue answered with indignation, because that Jesus had healed on the sabbath day, and said to the people, There are six days in which men ought to work: in them therefore come and be healed, and not on the sabbath day. The Lord then answered him, and said, You hypocrite, does not each one of you on the sabbath loose his ox or his ass from the stall, and lead him away to watering? And ought not this woman, being a daughter of Abraham, whom Satan has bound, lo, these eighteen years, be loosed from this bond on the sabbath day?

V	B	U	L	X	Q	T	L	Y	M	G	R	D	M	E	D	K	P	S	A
O	Q	B	Y	U	L	B	G	L	F	L	K	T	A	T	G	S	W	I	I
Y	A	K	G	P	J	T	H	L	Z	O	E	D	D	X	P	A	Q	W	G
B	E	H	E	A	L	E	D	O	D	R	M	T	E	T	J	B	L	A	X
H	Y	E	A	R	S	O	E	R	Z	I	R	F	S	Q	M	B	Z	T	C
B	C	Q	R	W	A	I	B	S	A	F	H	H	T	D	I	A	R	E	S
W	A	J	D	I	W	T	Z	G	B	I	T	S	R	R	L	T	B	R	P
O	L	N	C	A	C	O	I	S	R	E	Q	P	A	X	T	H	Q	I	Z
M	L	N	V	P	Q	G	A	I	A	D	D	D	I	V	Y	L	F	N	C
A	E	F	N	F	O	E	X	J	H	K	S	F	G	K	J	O	T	G	V
N	D	G	S	M	I	T	H	Q	A	L	N	U	H	F	M	D	Y	F	B
J	T	W	J	F	P	H	R	E	M	B	W	C	T	I	N	W	U	H	O
U	O	J	Q	T	V	E	H	K	P	E	I	G	H	T	E	E	N	H	U
L	H	P	F	L	C	R	H	D	U	A	N	B	O	N	D	M	I	Q	N
F	E	I	N	D	I	G	N	A	T	I	O	N	Y	T	N	Z	I	N	D
M	R	K	V	W	Z	L	J	S	M	O	C	V	X	T	A	B	M	O	S
J	H	T	V	S	P	H	Y	P	O	C	R	I	T	E	F	J	S	K	V
T	S	P	I	R	I	T	O	F	I	N	F	I	R	M	I	T	Y	T	Y
S	Y	N	A	G	O	G	U	E	P	Q	L	O	O	S	E	D	A	J	V
Y	S	P	L	I	F	T	U	P	B	O	W	E	D	M	C	M	Q	Q	V

SYNAGOGUE
SPIRIT OF INFIRMITY
EIGHTEEN
BOWED
TOGETHER
LIFT UP
CALLED TO HER
WOMAN
LOOSED
MADE STRAIGHT
GLORIFIED
INDIGNATION
SABBATH
HYPOCRITE
WATERING
ABRAHAM
BOUND
YEARS
BOND
BE HEALED

105. AND 106. THE SAMARITAN WOMAN AT THE WELL
JOHN 4:7–42

There came a woman of Samaria to draw water: Jesus said to her, Give Me to drink. (For His disciples were gone away to the city to buy meat.) Then said the woman of Samaria to Him, How is it that You, being a Jew, ask drink of me, which am a woman of Samaria? for the Jews have no dealings with the Samaritans. Jesus answered and said to her, If you knew the gift of God, and who it is that says to you, Give Me to drink; you would have asked of Him, and He would have given you living water. The woman said to Him, Sir, You have nothing to draw with, and the well is deep: from where then have You that living water? Are You greater than our father Jacob, which gave us the well, and drank thereof himself, and his children, and his cattle?

Jesus answered and said to her, Whosoever drinks of this water shall thirst again: but whosoever drinks of the water that I shall give him shall never thirst; but the water that I shall give him shall be in him a well of water springing up into everlasting life. The woman said to Him, Sir, give me this water, that I thirst not, neither come here to draw. Jesus said to her, Go, call your husband, and come here. The woman answered and said, I have no husband. Jesus said to her, You have well said, I have no husband: for you have had five husbands; and he whom you now have is not your husband: in that said you truly. The woman said to Him, Sir, I perceive that You are a prophet. Our fathers worshipped in this mountain; and you say, that in Jerusalem is the place where men ought to worship.

Jesus said to her, Woman, believe Me, the hour comes, when you shall neither in this mountain, nor yet at Jerusalem, worship the Father. You worship you know not what: we know what we worship: for salvation is of the Jews. But the hour comes, and now is, when the true worshippers shall worship the Father in spirit and in truth: for the Father seeks such to worship him. God is a Spirit: and they that worship Him must worship Him in spirit and in truth.

The woman said to Him, I know that Messiah comes, which is called Christ: when He is come, He will tell us all things. Jesus said to her, I that speak to you am He. And upon this came His disciples, and marveled that He talked with the woman: yet no man said, What seek You?, or, Why talk You with her? The woman then left her water pot, and went her way into the city, and said to the men, Come, see a man, which told me all things that ever I did: is not this the Christ? Then they went out of the city, and came to Him.... And many of the Samaritans of that city believed on Him for the saying of the woman, which testified, He told me all that ever I did. So when the Samaritans were come to Him, they besought Him that He would tarry with them: and He abode there two days. And many more believed because of His own word; and said to the woman, Now we believe, not because of your saying: for we have heard Him ourselves, and know that this is indeed the Christ, the Savior of the world.

H	O	Y	Z	M	B	K	G	A	A	I	J	Y	C	B	X	N	X	L	H
G	I	F	T	O	F	G	O	D	S	E	B	B	W	F	G	S	G	I	B
M	S	F	E	J	C	S	P	E	H	R	L	O	O	M	I	D	W	V	L
X	F	A	T	H	E	R	J	A	C	O	B	Z	R	F	L	V	U	I	Y
G	P	Z	H	P	J	A	C	L	C	H	G	F	S	K	C	D	E	N	M
R	P	X	I	D	E	A	L	I	N	G	S	M	H	Z	I	R	C	G	D
E	Q	Z	R	I	R	R	M	O	U	N	T	A	I	N	X	A	H	W	N
A	H	Z	S	I	U	O	P	D	C	N	V	W	P	J	M	W	Q	A	Y
T	S	B	T	K	S	E	M	R	D	D	O	U	E	D	A	F	O	T	A
E	Y	B	W	F	A	M	B	I	U	N	T	P	D	R	H	R	J	E	Z
R	L	U	V	B	L	Q	J	N	S	O	G	C	C	U	U	O	P	R	M
Z	E	Y	U	C	E	O	S	K	H	Z	T	P	C	F	S	M	T	S	B
B	J	C	Y	E	M	C	H	J	E	L	G	D	H	J	B	T	A	C	Y
K	E	V	E	R	L	A	S	T	I	N	G	P	L	G	A	H	V	M	N
N	S	P	R	I	N	G	I	N	G	H	P	H	V	I	N	E	R	Q	T
V	W	W	V	Y	G	Q	Z	X	X	C	E	B	J	S	D	W	D	P	Q
N	U	B	Q	U	Z	O	P	R	O	P	H	E	T	U	S	E	E	T	W
M	H	R	B	S	A	I	D	T	R	U	L	Y	L	M	E	L	E	A	X
P	H	D	G	N	Y	E	A	V	T	E	O	X	P	O	Q	L	P	N	P
W	F	S	A	M	A	R	I	A	P	E	R	C	E	I	V	E	Q	Z	Z

SAMARIA	DEALINGS	LIVING WATER	DEEP	FATHER JACOB
SPRINGING	DRINK	GIFT OF GOD	SAID TRULY	EVERLASTING
GREATER	THIRST	JERUSALEM	HUSBAND	FIVE
DRAW FROM THE WELL	PERCEIVE	PROPHET	WORSHIPED	MOUNTAIN

V	H	T	R	U	T	H	U	L	G	U	Z	H	Y	R	J	H	K	U	Z
G	Q	F	Y	D	A	A	T	N	K	E	W	M	V	P	U	A	W	N	O
Z	W	I	W	S	A	L	V	A	T	I	O	N	F	C	V	L	U	M	D
B	T	M	A	R	V	E	L	E	D	T	D	S	Z	K	P	L	H	F	W
C	O	M	E	Q	J	T	Q	N	P	V	D	F	S	R	N	T	F	I	I
L	F	G	P	V	S	Z	K	A	L	A	V	C	P	B	U	H	Q	N	L
X	P	S	H	R	C	P	G	H	N	Y	R	E	K	L	E	I	N	I	L
H	O	U	R	V	A	N	I	J	F	M	Y	C	C	D	A	N	S	S	O
Y	J	I	C	Q	M	Y	J	R	K	L	J	G	E	K	W	G	W	H	F
H	D	G	Y	O	Q	B	E	X	I	N	L	W	Q	L	A	S	G	N	H
Z	S	X	C	C	A	X	X	D	C	T	B	E	Z	L	S	E	N	T	I
I	C	H	R	I	S	T	A	D	B	E	I	A	H	B	A	W	T	F	M
E	I	I	O	H	X	C	W	A	G	E	S	O	I	G	P	J	M	U	G
N	H	I	V	M	O	W	F	Y	W	X	T	M	H	U	J	B	E	J	A
H	T	Y	S	W	O	R	S	H	I	P	P	E	R	S	I	Y	S	O	P
M	E	A	T	T	O	E	A	T	M	P	W	O	P	X	A	Q	S	X	V
R	P	R	M	G	K	L	Y	D	A	Z	C	H	Y	T	M	Q	I	J	U
H	A	R	V	E	S	T	O	M	K	H	L	X	A	X	H	Y	A	T	B
Y	M	B	O	L	I	F	G	O	C	Q	P	W	D	E	E	O	H	T	Q
Q	L	D	Q	S	E	E	A	M	A	N	P	N	W	B	Q	K	L	U	Q

HOUR	WAGES	PARCEL	WORSHIPPERS	SPIRIT
TRUTH	SALVATION	MESSIAH	I AM HE	CHRIST
MARVELED	COME	SEE A MAN	ALL THINGS	MEAT TO EAT
PRAYED		SENT		HARVEST
WILL OF HIM				FINISH

107. THE WOMAN CAUGHT IN ADULTERY: JOHN 8:1–11

The scribes and Pharisees brought to [Jesus] a woman taken in adultery; and when they had set her in the midst, they say to Him, Master, this woman was taken in adultery, in the very act. Now Moses in the law commanded us, that such should be stoned: but what say You? This they said, tempting Him, that they might have to accuse Him. But Jesus stooped down, and with His finger wrote on the ground, as though he heard them not. So when they continued asking Him, He lifted up Himself, and said to them, He that is without sin among you, let him first cast a stone at her. And again He stooped down, and wrote on the ground. And they which heard it, being convicted by their own conscience, went out one by one, beginning at the eldest, even to the last: and Jesus was left alone, and the woman standing in the midst. When Jesus had lifted up Himself, and saw none but the woman, He said to her, Woman, where are those your accusers? has no man condemned you? She said, No man, Lord. And Jesus said to her, Neither do I condemn you: go, and sin no more. Then spoke Jesus again to them, saying, I am the light of the world: he that follows Me shall not walk in darkness, but shall have the light of life.

T	R	G	W	X	S	T	O	N	E	D	P	O	O	M	C	D	Q
I	M	C	I	L	D	A	V	B	B	V	H	W	L	O	B	I	U
N	O	O	T	J	B	U	F	U	M	E	A	H	F	U	L	X	H
T	R	N	H	N	E	G	I	O	S	R	R	A	T	N	I	U	F
H	N	D	O	U	K	H	N	D	C	Y	I	Q	F	T	G	A	I
E	I	E	U	V	M	T	G	T	R	A	S	C	E	O	H	C	R
M	N	M	T	A	Y	A	E	E	I	C	E	A	J	F	T	C	S
I	G	N	S	R	P	W	R	M	B	T	E	S	W	O	O	U	T
D	X	E	I	S	O	W	X	P	E	E	S	T	A	L	F	S	S
S	R	D	N	D	H	K	K	L	S	B	K	B	K	I	L	E	T
T	I	S	C	Y	I	I	A	E	I	U	W	Y	A	V	I	R	O
U	S	I	N	N	O	M	O	R	E	Y	A	T	T	E	F	S	N
V	N	V	C	D	P	T	E	M	P	T	I	N	G	S	E	T	E
N	Z	S	T	O	O	P	E	D	A	D	U	L	T	E	R	Y	M

MORNING
TAUGHT
PHARISEES
IN THE MIDST
STONED
STOOPED
WITHOUT SIN
FIRST STONE
CONDEMNED
LIGHT OF LIFE
SIN NO MORE
TEMPLE
SCRIBES
ADULTERY
VERY ACT
TEMPTING
FINGER
CAST
ACCUSERS
MOUNT OF OLIVES

108. THE PARABLE OF THE PERSISTENT WIDOW: LUKE 18:1–8

He spoke a parable to them to this end, that men ought always to pray, and not to faint; saying, There was in a city a judge, which feared not God, neither regarded man: and there was a widow in that city; and she came to him, saying, Avenge me of mine adversary. And he would not for a while: but afterward he said within himself, Though I fear not God, nor regard man; yet because this widow troubles me, I will avenge her, lest by her continual coming she weary me. And the Lord said, Hear what the unjust judge says. And shall not God avenge His own elect, which cry day and night to Him, though He bear long with them? I tell you that He will avenge them speedily. Nevertheless when the Son of Man comes, shall He find faith on the earth?

A	X	V	D	R	E	G	A	R	D	E	D	K	V	K	E	O	D	Z	Z
G	F	W	B	O	I	Y	N	I	J	Y	P	A	J	H	C	W	A	Y	L
Z	I	E	X	U	E	B	U	K	N	V	X	K	Q	F	O	A	Y	R	G
H	Y	N	A	X	N	Q	T	F	R	S	B	D	N	Z	N	H	A	R	Q
N	L	B	G	R	D	N	F	A	R	O	D	Z	O	O	T	Y	N	D	O
L	E	A	E	T	E	V	Y	I	U	N	A	O	T	J	I	A	D	Q	N
U	W	S	L	A	T	D	V	T	S	O	V	T	G	B	N	O	N	X	T
S	K	E	U	W	R	R	N	H	W	F	E	E	D	I	U	K	I	H	H
T	Z	V	M	R	A	L	O	O	G	M	N	X	X	Q	A	M	G	U	E
O	S	V	B	V	M	Y	O	U	T	A	G	P	E	G	L	I	H	L	E
C	K	K	H	J	R	H	S	N	B	N	E	A	L	K	U	Z	T	W	A
N	O	T	F	A	I	N	T	P	G	L	M	P	E	R	U	C	G	I	R
C	U	K	V	A	A	Z	J	W	R	W	E	Y	C	P	O	L	W	D	T
U	N	J	U	S	T	D	X	H	N	A	Z	S	T	A	D	H	E	O	H
R	W	E	A	R	Y	D	G	I	M	F	Y	F	G	R	C	D	P	W	K
Y	G	W	U	T	Q	M	Z	H	Y	M	N	J	Q	A	S	R	M	V	M
D	C	Q	G	F	K	A	P	M	K	O	A	G	G	B	S	O	M	Q	N
Z	K	D	J	U	D	G	E	A	T	D	I	R	G	L	F	I	Z	Z	Z
S	Y	T	P	K	S	P	E	E	D	I	L	Y	P	E	B	J	D	Q	C
Q	A	D	V	E	R	S	A	R	Y	Z	J	I	N	O	B	A	E	Z	L

PARABLE
ALWAYS PRAY
NOT FAINT
JUDGE
FEARED NOT
REGARDED
WIDOW
AVENGE ME
ADVERSARY
TROUBLES
CONTINUAL
WEARY
UNJUST
ELECT
DAY AND NIGHT
BEAR LONG
SPEEDILY
SON OF MAN
FAITH
ON THE EARTH

109. ANANIAS AND SAPPHIRA: ACTS 5:1–11

A certain man named Ananias, with Sapphira his wife, sold a possession, and kept back part of the price, his wife also being privy to it, and brought a certain part, and laid it at the apostles' feet. But Peter said, Ananias, why has Satan filled your heart to lie to the Holy Ghost, and to keep back part of the price of the land?...you have not lied to men, but to God. And Ananias hearing these words fell down, and gave up the ghost: and great fear came on all them that heard these things. And the young men arose, wound him up, and carried him out, and buried him.

And it was about the space of three hours after, when his wife, not knowing what was done, came in. And Peter answered to her, Tell me whether you sold the land for so much? And she said, Yea, for so much. Then Peter said to her, How is it that you have agreed together to tempt the Spirit of the Lord? behold, the feet of them which have buried your husband are at the door, and shall carry you out. Then fell she down immediately at his feet, and yielded up the ghost: and the young men came in, and found her dead, and, carrying her forth, buried her by her husband. And great fear came upon all the church, and upon as many as heard these things.

O	T	M	A	J	C	V	L	I	E	D	I	O	Z	Z	R	P	Q
P	U	H	P	G	K	G	L	O	F	S	M	H	X	F	H	C	D
D	G	F	R	T	R	I	S	N	P	F	M	Y	B	Z	Z	Z	B
B	F	N	B	E	A	E	N	W	R	O	E	H	I	T	P	D	S
C	J	E	C	U	E	S	E	Y	I	W	D	O	L	S	O	L	O
O	S	K	A	A	R	H	X	D	V	W	I	L	K	A	S	M	L
N	A	O	E	R	R	I	O	R	Y	R	A	Y	X	T	S	H	D
C	P	H	V	P	G	R	E	U	K	O	T	G	U	A	E	X	T
E	P	P	I	T	T	H	I	D	R	A	E	H	H	N	S	H	H
I	H	S	Q	W	P	B	G	E	R	S	L	O	N	A	S	H	E
V	I	P	O	W	E	R	A	R	D	Q	Y	S	A	F	I	Y	L
E	R	E	N	R	N	F	G	C	D	O	E	T	D	X	O	L	A
D	A	A	N	A	N	I	A	S	K	H	U	L	M	B	N	M	N
F	N	J	M	C	E	R	T	A	I	N	U	T	U	U	M	A	D
I	P	R	I	C	E	T	E	M	P	T	T	M	S	D	O	O	X

SAPPHIRA
KEPT BACK
PRIVY
SATAN
HOLY GHOST
CONCEIVED
BURIED
SOLD THE LAND
TEMPT
FEAR
ANANIAS
POSSESSION
PRICE
CERTAIN
LIED
POWER
CARRIED OUT
THREE HOURS
AGREED
IMMEDIATELY

110. THE DISCIPLE TABITHA/DORCAS: ACTS 9:36–42

There was at Joppa a certain disciple named Tabitha, which by interpretation is called Dorcas: this woman was full of good works and almsdeeds [acts of charity] which she did. And it came to pass in those days, that she was sick, and died: whom when they had washed, they laid her in an upper chamber. And forasmuch as Lydda was near to Joppa, and the disciples had heard that Peter was there, they sent to him two men, desiring him that he would not delay to come to them. Then Peter arose and went with them. When he was come, they brought him into the upper chamber: and all the widows stood by him weeping, and showing the coats and garments which Dorcas made, while she was with them. But Peter put them all forth, and kneeled down, and prayed; and turning him to the body said, Tabitha, arise. And she opened her eyes: and when she saw Peter, she sat up. And he gave her his hand, and lifted her up, and when he had called the saints and widows, presented her alive. And it was known throughout all Joppa; and many believed in the Lord.

G	R	J	B	Z	C	Y	C	R	I	B	V	L	Y	A	T	H	M	V	D
M	X	O	J	U	N	J	J	O	K	E	G	J	P	Z	L	A	N	E	T
L	S	P	K	V	O	C	T	M	O	L	N	A	V	X	R	I	Y	Y	T
I	T	P	O	C	T	U	Q	T	N	I	E	S	M	D	L	M	V	U	A
V	G	A	C	D	C	O	A	T	S	E	Q	W	U	W	F	O	L	E	B
A	L	L	F	O	R	T	H	K	B	V	R	U	F	I	C	Z	P	B	I
U	X	F	R	C	T	Y	G	B	A	E	U	Z	E	D	I	K	T	U	T
I	X	S	P	R	A	Y	E	D	U	D	G	G	Q	O	T	P	O	P	H
O	D	C	F	A	S	A	I	N	T	S	N	A	Q	W	V	H	T	P	A
G	O	O	D	W	O	R	K	S	T	Z	Y	R	T	S	N	K	V	E	A
P	C	M	R	J	X	L	W	Y	Z	K	L	I	T	X	B	S	C	R	L
C	X	V	U	C	K	P	I	F	I	H	P	S	P	C	P	V	D	C	M
D	D	U	E	O	A	U	Y	K	Q	D	T	E	O	E	T	R	Y	H	S
Y	T	O	Y	J	T	S	X	E	A	Y	H	L	Y	W	T	Q	C	A	D
U	H	J	E	L	V	G	A	R	M	E	N	T	S	A	D	E	K	M	E
N	D	K	K	S	L	C	N	I	H	A	K	H	K	S	Z	G	R	B	E
T	V	K	N	E	E	L	E	D	Z	I	L	A	K	H	E	O	A	E	D
Q	D	I	S	C	I	P	L	E	X	Z	H	T	D	E	M	D	U	R	S
I	N	T	E	R	P	R	E	T	A	T	I	O	N	D	V	L	W	X	O
W	I	F	V	H	K	X	D	X	V	Y	P	L	F	U	Z	I	W	K	R

TABITHA
DORCAS
PETER
WASHED
JOPPA
WIDOWS
COATS
KNEELED
ARISE
ALIVE
DISCIPLE
INTERPRETATION
GOOD WORKS
BELIEVED
UPPER CHAMBER
ALMSDEEDS
GARMENTS
ALL FORTH
PRAYED
SAINTS

111. AND 112. RHODA: ACTS 12:5–19

Peter therefore was kept in prison: but prayer was made without ceasing of the church to God for him. And when Herod would have brought him forth, the same night Peter was sleeping between two soldiers, bound with two chains: and the keepers before the door kept the prison. And, behold, the angel of the Lord came upon him, and a light shined in the prison: and he smote Peter on the side, and raised him up, saying, Arise up quickly. And his chains fell off from his hands. And the angel said to him, Gird yourself, and bind on your sandals. And so he did. And he said to him, Cast your garment about you, and follow me. And he went out, and followed him; and knew not that it was true which was done by the angel; but thought he saw a vision. When they were past the first and the second ward, they came to the iron gate that leads to the city; which opened to them of its own accord: and they went out, and passed on through one street; and immediately the angel departed from him.

And when Peter was come to himself, he said, Now I know of a surety, that the Lord has sent His angel, and has delivered me out of the hand of Herod, and from all the expectation of the people of the Jews. And when he had considered the thing, he came to the house of Mary the mother of John, whose surname was Mark; where many were gathered together praying. And as Peter knocked at the door of the gate, a damsel came to hearken, named Rhoda and when she knew Peter's voice, she opened not the gate for gladness, but ran in, and told how Peter stood before the gate. And they said to her, You are mad. But she constantly affirmed that it was even so. Then said they, It is his angel.

But Peter continued knocking: and when they had opened the door, and saw him, they were astonished. But he, beckoning to them with the hand to hold their peace, declared to them how the Lord had brought him out of the prison. And he said, Go show these things to James, and to the brethren. And he departed, and went into another place. Now as soon as it was day, there was no small stir among the soldiers, what was become of Peter. And when Herod had sought for him, and found him not, he examined the keepers, and commanded that they should be put to death. And he went down from Judaea to Caesarea, and there abode.

X	K	W	F	F	R	S	W	W	M	E	G	S	I	D	G	I	K
T	S	I	J	O	D	M	A	T	O	F	P	U	U	R	A	K	L
F	G	T	L	S	E	O	I	N	E	Y	G	R	S	R	R	K	D
O	D	H	S	N	P	P	R	K	D	R	B	E	O	A	M	B	E
L	G	O	E	F	A	R	O	D	D	A	Q	T	L	I	E	B	L
L	S	U	C	V	R	A	N	Z	G	O	L	Y	D	S	N	M	I
O	L	T	O	I	T	Y	G	G	Z	T	S	S	I	E	T	K	V
W	E	C	N	S	E	E	A	E	Z	M	M	U	E	D	Q	S	E
M	E	E	D	I	D	R	T	B	P	N	O	T	R	U	B	H	R
E	P	A	W	O	J	T	E	O	M	K	T	T	S	P	J	I	E
S	I	S	A	N	A	N	G	E	L	J	E	G	O	C	R	N	D
A	N	I	R	I	N	H	B	G	L	I	G	H	T	D	Y	E	D
W	G	N	D	Q	E	P	M	V	Y	E	A	C	C	O	R	D	G
T	S	G	J	Q	E	N	Y	J	G	C	H	A	I	N	S	C	H

PRAYER
WITHOUT CEASING
SLEEPING
SOLDIERS
CHAINS
LIGHT
SHINED
SMOTE
RAISED UP
SANDALS
GARMENT
FOLLOW ME
VISION
SECOND WARD
IRON GATE
ACCORD
DEPARTED
SURETY
ANGEL
DELIVERED

F	H	R	S	V	A	F	F	I	R	M	E	D	W	D	M	E	D
A	O	A	J	A	M	E	S	J	Y	R	Y	E	K	I	O	Q	K
S	U	N	E	L	E	X	A	M	I	N	E	D	U	K	T	L	N
T	S	I	O	B	R	A	A	F	A	H	O	I	N	Q	H	S	O
O	E	N	P	D	M	A	D	H	E	R	O	D	J	J	E	P	C
N	O	J	E	V	H	E	G	L	A	D	N	E	S	S	R	R	K
I	F	U	N	U	W	F	O	U	N	D	N	O	T	F	O	H	E
S	M	B	E	C	K	O	N	I	N	G	A	J	X	W	F	O	D
H	A	J	D	Q	W	D	O	O	R	T	B	S	G	P	J	D	R
E	R	K	N	J	S	O	U	G	H	T	O	U	X	Z	O	A	J
D	Y	R	I	D	R	H	J	D	Z	P	D	M	L	A	H	G	W
Q	H	O	L	D	T	H	E	I	R	P	E	A	C	E	N	S	W
Z	F	C	R	B	R	O	U	G	H	T	H	I	M	O	U	T	T

HOUSE OF MARY
MOTHER OF JOHN
KNOCKED
DOOR
RHODA
GLADNESS
RAN IN
MAD
AFFIRMED
HEROD
OPENED
ASTONISHED
BECKONING
HOLD THEIR PEACE
BROUGHT HIM OUT
JAMES
SOUGHT
FOUND NOT
EXAMINED
ABODE

113. LYDIA: ACTS 16:11–15, 40

On the sabbath we went out of the city by a river side, where prayer was wont to be made; and we sat down, and spoke to the women which resorted there. And a certain woman named Lydia, a seller of purple, of the city of Thyatira, which worshipped God, heard us: whose heart the Lord opened, that she attended to the things which were spoken of Paul. And when she was baptized, and her household, she besought us, saying, If you have judged me to be faithful to the Lord, come into my house, and abide there. And she constrained us…And they went out of the prison, and entered into the house of Lydia: and when they had seen the brethren, they comforted them, and departed.

E	D	V	P	T	H	W	C	O	M	F	O	R	T	E	D	E	C
I	J	J	M	E	B	O	R	I	V	E	R	S	I	D	E	F	O
P	U	H	U	W	R	A	N	D	A	T	T	E	N	D	E	D	N
G	H	U	O	D	E	S	P	O	F	T	G	N	U	W	T	S	S
L	F	G	G	U	G	N	E	T	R	J	C	I	X	B	H	E	T
U	U	Z	W	Y	S	E	K	C	I	A	M	O	N	G	L	L	R
D	E	V	O	U	T	E	D	Q	U	Z	B	N	L	E	C	L	A
E	H	P	P	Z	P	H	H	K	V	T	E	L	P	O	K	E	I
F	A	I	T	H	F	U	L	O	L	C	I	D	E	A	N	R	N
V	Y	L	H	T	R	E	J	C	L	W	P	O	Y	C	U	Y	E
X	G	E	X	P	E	L	L	E	D	D	V	C	N	M	V	L	D
W	O	R	S	H	I	P	P	E	D	J	L	Y	D	I	A	F	P
P	U	R	P	L	E	T	O	T	C	O	A	S	T	S	J	M	X
B	G	G	J	G	I	Q	E	C	H	I	E	F	M	E	N	U	M

HONORABLE
PERSECUTION
COASTS
RIVERSIDE
SELLER
WORSHIPPED
PAUL
HOUSEHOLD
FAITHFUL
COMFORTED
DEVOUT
CHIEF MEN
EXPELLED
COLONY
LYDIA
PURPLE
ATTENDED
BAPTIZED
JUDGED
CONSTRAINED

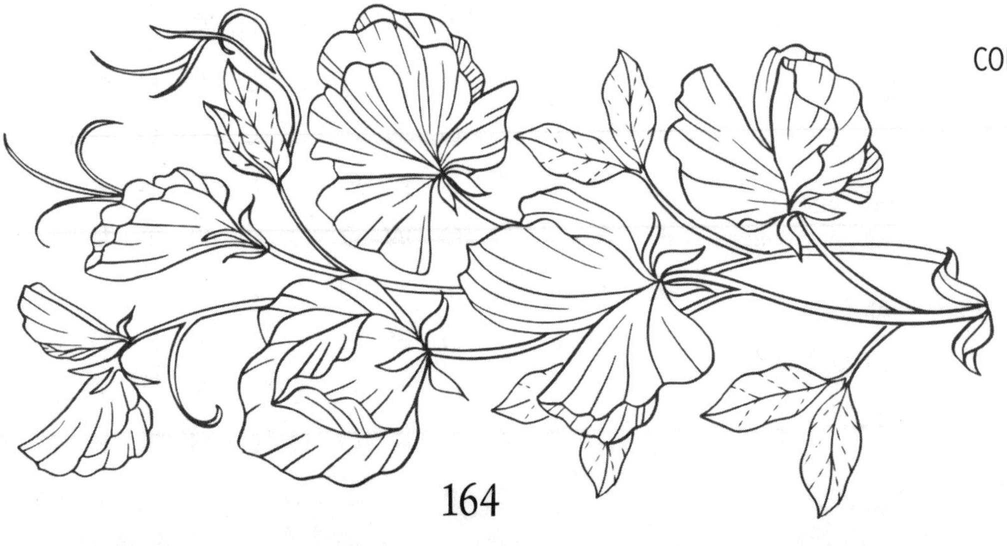

114. THE DAMSEL POSSESSED WITH A SPIRIT OF DIVINATION: ACTS 16:16–22

A certain damsel possessed with a spirit of divination met us, which brought her masters much gain by soothsaying: the same followed Paul and us, and cried, saying, These men are the servants of the Most High God, which show to us the way of salvation. And this did she many days. But Paul, being grieved, turned and said to the spirit, I command you in the name of Jesus Christ to come out of her. And he came out the same hour. And when her masters saw that the hope of their gains was gone, they caught Paul and Silas, and drew them into the marketplace to the rulers, and brought them to the magistrates, saying, These men, being Jews, do exceedingly trouble our city, and teach customs, which are not lawful for us to receive, neither to observe, being Romans. And the multitude rose up together against them: and the magistrates rent off their clothes, and commanded to beat them.

DAMSEL
SPIRIT
DIVINATION
MET US
MASTERS
MUCH GAIN
SOOTHSAYING
FOLLOWING
SERVANT
MOST HIGH GOD
SALVATION
MANY DAYS
COMMAND
JESUS CHRIST
COME OUT
SAME HOUR
PAUL
SILAS
MARKETPLACE
MULTITUDE

D	F	H	B	O	V	K	E	F	Q	U	Y	O	A	R	Z	S	J	J	A
N	A	P	A	Y	S	R	V	M	S	A	M	E	H	O	U	R	S	W	K
N	U	M	U	S	W	A	O	O	U	A	L	P	I	S	B	A	E	I	B
V	I	J	S	I	L	A	S	M	U	L	T	I	T	U	D	E	R	Z	W
J	P	R	E	E	S	L	I	I	R	H	I	X	N	M	M	X	V	L	Z
M	O	A	Q	S	L	Y	Z	L	Q	Q	Q	U	G	V	O	K	A	M	H
A	V	Y	U	F	U	B	M	T	L	L	E	M	C	K	S	H	N	E	F
S	K	Q	W	L	M	S	V	A	V	L	M	M	R	R	T	K	T	T	P
T	P	I	L	P	I	D	C	K	N	C	G	V	V	M	H	K	F	U	S
E	N	U	C	C	M	N	B	H	C	Y	T	I	S	X	I	J	K	S	P
R	M	L	T	S	J	R	V	C	R	O	D	U	U	H	G	S	C	O	I
S	X	C	O	M	E	O	U	T	I	I	M	A	Q	K	H	A	T	F	R
P	P	P	I	T	V	L	O	Y	Y	I	S	M	Y	O	G	L	Z	K	I
Y	I	E	F	A	G	R	E	C	B	C	K	T	A	S	O	V	N	U	T
M	A	S	O	O	T	H	S	A	Y	I	N	G	U	N	D	A	X	J	H
S	V	Q	R	H	O	B	K	K	J	S	B	V	T	E	D	T	K	N	Y
U	M	U	C	H	G	A	I	N	W	Z	S	K	F	D	C	I	G	Q	C
A	M	A	R	K	E	T	P	L	A	C	E	J	T	U	B	O	H	K	I
U	K	D	I	V	I	N	A	T	I	O	N	G	W	H	W	N	F	A	Q
T	E	R	L	H	S	T	U	F	O	L	L	O	W	I	N	G	P	H	A

115. HONORABLE WOMEN OF GREECE AND DAMARIS

ACTS 17:1–4, 12

Now when they had passed through Amphipolis and Apollonia, they came to Thessalonica, where was a synagogue of the Jews: and Paul, as his manner was, went in to them, and three sabbath days reasoned with them out of the scriptures, opening and alleging, that Christ must needs have suffered, and risen again from the dead; and that this Jesus, whom I preach to you, is Christ. And some of them believed, and consorted with Paul and Silas; and of the devout Greeks a great multitude, and of the chief women not a few...Therefore many of them believed; also of honorable women which were Greeks, and of men, not a few.

ACTS 17:32–34

And when they heard of the resurrection of the dead, some mocked: and others said, We will hear you again of this matter. So Paul departed from among them. However certain men clung to him, and believed: among the which was Dionysius the Areopagite, and a woman named Damaris, and others with them.

T	T	L	G	R	E	E	K	S	C	M	Q	R	D	T	Q	I	H
P	P	V	E	S	X	Z	S	D	H	V	N	E	I	D	N	R	O
L	R	Y	C	X	O	G	C	A	I	R	U	S	O	Q	Y	D	P
M	A	U	D	B	V	Y	R	M	E	T	O	U	N	X	B	T	E
Z	A	B	T	E	H	P	I	A	F	N	Q	R	Y	W	P	H	N
X	G	T	U	L	Q	D	P	R	W	H	D	R	S	K	M	E	I
P	L	C	T	I	G	E	T	I	O	M	S	E	I	Z	U	S	N
C	O	A	C	E	I	V	U	S	M	E	L	C	U	A	L	S	G
P	W	H	C	V	R	O	R	J	E	I	S	T	S	M	T	A	H
R	U	E	E	E	N	U	E	F	N	M	Z	I	R	P	I	L	O
W	Q	A	K	D	R	T	S	G	U	G	C	O	J	H	T	O	N
M	M	R	B	G	Y	N	J	X	V	Q	Z	N	W	I	U	N	O
B	P	Y	Y	V	Y	Y	T	M	Q	M	A	D	O	P	D	I	R
X	P	O	U	G	A	P	O	L	L	O	N	I	A	O	E	C	A
L	S	U	A	C	O	N	S	O	R	T	E	D	E	L	E	A	B
D	M	O	C	K	E	D	B	U	C	D	N	Y	E	I	V	P	L
V	J	L	C	B	U	M	I	M	G	E	A	H	Y	S	X	L	E
Z	D	E	A	D	Y	L	N	O	T	A	F	E	W	T	A	R	B

APOLLONIA
SCRIPTURES
BELIEVED
DEVOUT
MULTITUDE
HONORABLE
DEAD
MOCKED
MATTER
DAMARIS
AMPHIPOLIS
THESSALONICA
OPENING
CONSORTED
GREEKS
CHIEF WOMEN
NOT A FEW
RESURRECTION
HEAR YOU
DIONYSIUS

116. PRISCILLA: ACTS 18:1–3, 18–21, 24–26

After these things Paul departed from Athens, and came to Corinth; and found a certain Jew named Aquila, born in Pontus, lately come from Italy, with his wife Priscilla;...and came to them. And because he was of the same craft, he abode with them, and wrought: for by their occupation they were tentmakers…Paul after this tarried there yet a good while, and then took his leave of the brethren, and sailed from there into Syria, and with him Priscilla and Aquila.... And he came to Ephesus, and left them there: but he himself entered into the synagogue, and reasoned with the Jews. When they desired him to tarry longer time with them, he consented not; but bid them farewell, saying, I must by all means keep this feast that comes in Jerusalem: but I will return again to you, if God will. And he sailed from Ephesus…And a certain Jew named Apollos, born at Alexandria, an eloquent man, and mighty in the scriptures, came to Ephesus. This man was instructed in the way of the Lord; and being fervent in the spirit, he spoke and taught diligently the things of the Lord, knowing only the baptism of John. And he began to speak boldly in the synagogue: whom when Aquila and Priscilla had heard, they took him to them, and expounded to him the way of God more perfectly.

M	D	B	A	P	T	I	S	M	O	F	J	O	H	N	P	U	K
M	S	Q	M	N	J	S	O	Y	E	H	Z	S	P	O	K	E	A
G	F	M	H	H	T	H	R	Q	C	Y	V	Y	L	F	X	M	T
I	E	R	Q	A	T	A	M	D	U	Q	C	R	M	A	T	Q	H
D	R	G	P	G	R	D	U	Q	Y	H	T	I	I	H	Q	M	E
V	V	P	T	K	B	P	O	G	Y	V	D	A	G	E	U	O	N
T	E	U	C	O	R	I	N	T	H	G	I	L	H	L	F	R	S
T	N	D	O	W	G	Y	G	E	A	T	Q	R	T	O	W	E	F
H	T	P	R	I	S	C	I	L	L	A	W	N	Y	Q	I	P	K
E	Y	E	V	D	G	F	E	R	Y	R	W	M	Q	U	F	E	N
L	Z	Y	I	N	S	T	R	U	C	T	E	D	D	E	U	R	T
O	E	X	P	O	U	N	D	E	D	H	N	F	Z	N	U	F	A
R	Q	E	Y	T	E	N	T	M	A	K	E	R	S	T	W	E	R
D	I	L	I	G	E	N	T	L	Y	A	X	A	N	I	H	C	R
G	G	V	M	S	C	R	I	P	T	U	R	E	S	G	L	T	I
Y	F	S	A	M	E	C	R	A	F	T	D	H	U	Z	E	L	E
T	L	T	F	Q	R	R	A	Q	U	I	L	A	P	M	J	Y	D
H	K	X	U	R	Q	Q	I	M	Q	O	Q	F	O	F	H	F	A

CORINTH
PRISCILLA
TENTMAKERS
SYRIA
MIGHTY
INSTRUCTED
SPOKE
DILIGENTLY
BAPTISM OF JOHN
MORE PERFECTLY
ATHENS
AQUILA
SAME CRAFT
TARRIED
ELOQUENT
SCRIPTURES
FERVENT
TAUGHT
THE LORD
EXPOUNDED

117. THE WIVES IN TYRE; PHILIP'S DAUGHTERS: ACTS 21:3–6, 8–9

Now when we had discovered Cyprus, we left it on the left hand, and sailed into Syria, and landed at Tyre: for there the ship was to unlade her burden. And finding disciples, we tarried there seven days: who said to Paul through the Spirit, that he should not go up to Jerusalem. And when we had accomplished those days, we departed and went our way; and they all brought us on our way, with wives and children, till we were out of the city: and we kneeled down on the shore, and prayed. And when we had taken our leave one of another, we took ship; and they returned home again…And the next day we that were of Paul's company departed, and came to Caesarea: and we entered into the house of Philip the evangelist, which was one of the seven; and abode with him. And the same man had four daughters, virgins, which did prophesy.

M	N	M	S	H	U	W	G	V	I	R	G	I	N	S	I	D	W	C	R
E	C	C	Q	N	P	S	E	N	Y	T	U	U	I	F	V	C	K	A	V
K	J	U	R	K	Y	R	J	Q	O	A	O	X	G	T	B	T	T	E	C
U	I	W	D	E	Z	S	A	T	Y	R	E	U	B	X	T	E	E	S	P
P	N	Z	U	P	T	W	S	Y	J	V	W	G	T	E	A	B	J	A	G
Q	E	L	D	C	J	U	D	U	E	D	I	R	A	N	K	W	E	R	D
V	X	Q	A	C	E	W	R	U	Y	D	G	E	R	U	E	L	R	E	F
I	B	Y	S	D	V	S	I	N	J	E	K	O	R	D	N	R	U	A	O
M	J	B	E	B	E	U	Y	N	E	C	D	V	I	Q	L	R	S	H	U
B	N	D	V	L	K	N	L	R	Q	D	O	C	E	T	E	F	A	E	R
X	U	L	E	A	I	W	V	P	I	H	H	M	D	P	A	G	L	W	D
E	O	M	N	O	W	U	K	O	C	A	J	O	P	I	V	H	E	P	A
V	D	Y	D	V	R	R	C	P	H	Z	V	N	M	A	E	D	M	R	U
T	I	P	A	L	A	R	F	T	G	F	X	E	Y	E	N	C	V	O	G
B	A	Z	Y	Q	O	R	S	H	I	P	W	X	O	W	C	Y	F	P	H
I	K	D	S	C	F	W	A	F	V	K	C	N	S	P	P	E	A	H	T
K	L	E	F	T	H	A	N	D	S	N	W	T	E	Y	H	M	Q	E	E
U	C	L	K	N	E	V	A	N	G	E	L	I	S	T	D	H	H	S	R
O	R	K	C	H	A	S	K	C	P	H	I	L	I	P	N	N	K	Y	S
H	W	C	Y	P	R	U	S	R	Z	C	K	N	E	E	L	E	D	C	J

CYPRUS
LEFT HAND
SYRIA
TYRE
UNLADE
TARRIED
SEVEN DAYS
JERUSALEM
KNEELED
PRAYED
TAKEN LEAVE
SHIP
RETURNED HOME
COMPANY
CAESAREA
PHILIP
EVANGELIST
FOUR DAUGHTERS
VIRGINS
PROPHESY

118. DRUSILLA: ACTS 24:22–27

When Felix heard these things, having more perfect knowledge of that way, he deferred them, and said, When Lysias the chief captain shall come down, I will know the uttermost of your matter. And he commanded a centurion to keep Paul, and to let him have liberty, and that he should forbid none of his acquaintance to minister or come to him. And after certain days, when Felix came with his wife Drusilla, which was a Jewess, he sent for Paul, and heard him concerning the faith in Christ. And as he reasoned of righteousness, temperance, and judgment to come, Felix trembled, and answered, Go your way for this time; when I have a convenient season, I will call for you. He hoped also that money should have been given him of Paul, that he might loose him: wherefore he sent for him the oftener, and communed with him. But after two years... Felix, willing to show the Jews a pleasure, left Paul bound

M	C	Y	O	X	Z	J	K	M	T	P	T	S	I	Y	O	J	F	H	D
R	K	F	F	J	A	U	E	N	R	E	A	S	O	N	E	D	V	C	R
H	L	Q	A	E	E	T	X	Y	O	O	E	O	A	M	T	M	V	W	U
Z	I	N	I	H	J	W	T	Y	M	W	H	F	Q	T	M	I	F	M	S
A	B	W	T	E	K	F	E	W	N	F	L	T	M	K	O	N	E	M	I
Q	E	H	H	W	L	Q	C	S	N	K	S	E	I	N	M	I	L	I	L
B	R	Z	I	V	Z	B	Y	Y	S	T	Z	N	D	G	O	S	I	A	L
E	T	O	N	Z	L	Y	S	I	A	S	C	E	Z	G	N	T	X	K	A
B	Y	X	C	A	R	W	C	Q	I	I	V	R	J	C	E	E	S	P	K
Q	G	L	H	A	A	J	R	E	D	O	D	L	Y	M	Y	R	M	H	M
E	N	L	R	S	A	C	Q	U	A	I	N	T	A	N	C	E	B	M	V
F	B	U	I	G	O	C	C	A	R	P	E	O	X	U	E	D	C	D	H
Q	J	N	S	U	J	P	A	F	D	E	F	E	R	R	E	D	G	M	F
I	M	G	T	K	Q	V	T	E	C	O	N	V	E	N	I	E	N	T	I
O	U	T	T	E	R	M	O	S	T	B	J	Q	N	G	B	H	K	W	Q
C	F	Y	J	U	D	G	M	E	N	T	X	K	I	Z	N	H	D	I	O
T	E	M	P	E	R	A	N	C	E	S	J	R	B	G	V	V	G	O	N
K	P	R	I	G	H	T	E	O	U	S	N	E	S	S	B	W	F	C	W
C	E	N	T	U	R	I	O	N	O	J	C	Y	R	U	L	P	M	A	D
P	M	S	G	I	B	L	Z	O	T	R	E	M	B	L	E	D	P	U	Q

FELIX
KNOWLEDGE
DEFERRED
LYSIAS
UTTERMOST
CENTURION
LIBERTY
ACQUAINTANCE
MINISTER
DRUSILLA
JEWESS
FAITH IN CHRIST
REASONED
RIGHTEOUSNESS
TEMPERANCE
JUDGMENT
TREMBLED
CONVENIENT
MONEY
OFTENER

119. WOMEN IN THE BOOK OF ROMANS: ROMANS 16:1–16

I commend to you Phebe our sister, which is a servant of the church which is at Cenchrea: that you receive her in the Lord, as becomes saints, and that you assist her in whatsoever business she has need of you: for she has been a succorer [helper] of many, and of myself also. Greet Priscilla and Aquila my helpers in Christ Jesus: who have for my life laid down their own necks: to whom not only I give thanks, but also all the churches of the Gentiles. Likewise greet the church that is in their house. Salute my well-beloved Epaenetus, who is the first-fruits of Achaia to Christ. Greet Mary, who bestowed much labor on us. Salute Andronicus and Junia, my kinsmen, and my fellow-prisoners, who are of note among the apostles, who also were in Christ before me. Greet Amplias my beloved in the Lord. Salute Urbane, our helper in Christ, and Stachys my beloved. Salute Apelles approved in Christ. Salute them which are of Aristobulus' household. Salute Herodion my kinsman. Greet them that be of the household of Narcissus, which are in the Lord. Salute Tryphena and Tryphosa, who labor in the Lord. Salute the beloved Persis, which labored much in the Lord. Salute Rufus chosen in the Lord, and his mother and mine. Salute Asyncritus, Phlegon, Hermas, Patrobas, Hermes, and the brethren which are with them. Salute Philologus, and Julia, Nereus, and his sister, and Olympas, and all the saints which are with them. Salute one another with a holy kiss. The churches of Christ salute you.

H	A	I	X	N	U	K	T	R	Y	P	H	O	S	A	P	E	A
F	E	L	L	O	W	P	R	I	S	O	N	E	R	S	E	M	Q
L	F	S	T	F	I	M	F	H	I	O	B	D	O	T	R	O	G
A	H	U	H	R	N	N	M	A	S	Y	F	X	M	V	S	T	A
Q	O	C	T	G	Z	Z	S	H	T	L	I	T	A	M	I	H	C
W	D	C	L	P	H	E	B	E	E	A	R	J	N	A	S	E	O
D	C	O	S	O	Q	H	Z	D	R	I	S	U	S	R	T	R	M
R	F	R	F	P	K	G	I	J	O	D	T	N	A	Y	R	O	M
B	E	L	O	V	E	D	P	K	F	D	F	I	I	O	Y	F	E
D	A	P	J	U	L	I	A	M	N	O	R	A	N	F	P	R	N
H	O	L	Y	K	I	S	S	P	E	W	U	W	T	R	H	U	D
P	R	I	S	C	I	L	L	A	R	N	I	H	S	O	E	F	N
R	O	G	B	C	A	K	Q	W	U	K	T	G	B	M	N	U	W
V	S	A	L	U	T	E	M	R	S	E	B	W	T	E	A	S	N
X	C	H	U	R	C	H	E	S	O	F	C	H	R	I	S	T	F

PRISCILLA
JUNIA
TRYPHOSA
MOTHER OF RUFUS
JULIA
HOLY KISS
SALUTE
SUCCOR
LAID DOWN
BELOVED
PHEBE
MARY OF ROME
TRYPHENA
PERSIS
SISTER OF NERUS
ROMAN SAINTS
CHURCHES OF CHRIST
COMMEND
FIRST FRUIT
FELLOW PRISONERS

120. EUNICE AND LOIS: 2 TIMOTHY 1:3–7

Women were important in the establishment of the early church. Formerly, worshippers in the synagogue were divided by gender, but now they were part of the worship, as they were able to ask their husbands questions during the service. (See 1 Corinthians 14:34.)

I thank God, whom I serve from my forefathers with pure conscience, that without ceasing I have remembrance of you in my prayers night and day; greatly desiring to see you, being mindful of your tears, that I may be filled with joy; when I call to remembrance the unfeigned faith that is in you, which dwelled first in your grandmother Lois, and your mother Eunice; and I am persuaded that in you also. Wherefore I put you in remembrance that you stir up the gift of God, which is in you by the putting on of my hands. For God has not given us the spirit of fear; but of power, and of love, and of a sound mind.

FOREFATHERS
PURE
CONSCIENCE
WITHOUT CEASING
REMEMBRANCE
NIGHT AND DAY
DESIRING
MINDFUL
JOY
UNFEIGNED FAITH
DWELLED
GRANDMOTHER
LOIS
EUNICE
PERSUADED
GIFT OF GOD
SPIRIT OF FEAR
POWER
LOVE
SOUND MIND

D	K	I	P	U	F	T	Q	N	H	O	N	A	H	L	O	I	S	Q	V
D	L	E	H	U	N	T	X	X	G	W	B	P	M	A	N	Y	P	Q	J
I	J	T	S	R	R	Z	P	B	S	A	V	O	I	D	L	Z	E	B	T
T	I	H	A	U	G	E	D	P	D	H	O	W	N	T	M	K	R	G	F
G	R	A	N	D	M	O	T	H	E	R	A	E	D	L	E	R	S	I	Y
O	I	S	O	U	N	D	M	I	N	D	O	R	F	S	U	D	U	G	U
Q	C	F	D	E	S	I	R	I	N	G	W	B	U	H	N	Z	A	G	N
C	C	W	T	M	L	O	V	E	S	D	Z	S	L	Z	I	R	D	K	F
O	D	Y	F	O	F	Q	J	Z	K	I	W	U	C	X	C	Z	E	D	E
N	C	U	S	U	F	I	Q	T	T	D	T	E	O	I	E	S	D	N	I
S	G	K	U	H	X	G	P	D	E	E	M	Z	L	P	M	Z	U	R	G
C	Z	O	X	Y	J	D	O	C	O	Q	Q	T	G	L	R	G	K	Y	N
I	N	I	G	H	T	A	N	D	D	A	Y	M	A	V	E	B	F	M	E
E	E	U	Z	W	J	O	G	I	O	Z	K	N	U	J	X	D	D	Y	D
N	E	V	B	Z	S	F	O	R	E	F	A	T	H	E	R	S	B	B	F
C	V	R	E	M	E	M	B	R	A	N	C	E	L	K	T	N	B	U	A
E	O	K	X	V	L	D	P	C	W	T	K	J	J	Y	J	N	Z	H	I
P	V	M	P	N	B	H	Y	I	B	L	H	I	H	L	O	Q	R	S	T
A	Y	S	P	I	R	I	T	O	F	F	E	A	R	X	Y	B	P	M	H
D	I	M	U	W	I	T	H	O	U	T	C	E	A	S	I	N	G	N	G

121. EUODIAS AND SYNTYCHE: PHILIPPIANS 4:2–7

I beseech Euodias, and beseech Syntyche, that they be of the same mind in the Lord. And I entreat you also, true yoke-fellow, help those women which labored with me in the gospel, with Clement also, and with other my fellow-laborers, whose names are in the book of life. Rejoice in the Lord always: and again I say, Rejoice. Let your moderation be known to all men. The Lord is at hand. Be careful for nothing; but in every thing by prayer and supplication with thanksgiving let your requests be made known to God. And the peace of God, which passes all understanding, shall keep your hearts and minds through Christ Jesus.

E	G	Z	F	S	B	D	E	Y	F	F	Y	Y	V	H	B	G	Q	O	V
R	T	Q	B	W	U	A	G	T	I	D	L	U	F	J	K	S	J	M	N
L	D	H	H	P	D	P	T	O	V	N	A	U	G	Z	R	A	P	I	O
E	H	V	A	E	F	F	P	H	S	U	O	G	D	V	J	M	U	P	T
O	M	V	Z	N	A	K	J	L	A	P	N	A	N	V	O	E	B	E	H
C	E	O	T	L	K	R	V	A	I	N	E	Z	J	M	D	M	O	A	I
S	R	N	D	J	P	S	T	V	M	C	D	L	P	B	Q	I	O	C	N
L	Y	E	T	E	Z	B	G	S	V	W	A	J	T	V	Q	N	K	E	G
Y	Y	N	J	R	R	S	G	I	A	C	T	T	I	Q	A	D	O	O	O
U	W	G	T	O	E	A	Z	Q	V	N	U	I	I	B	V	Q	F	F	K
Z	E	S	O	Y	I	A	T	Y	M	I	D	Q	K	O	S	A	L	G	C
P	S	S	P	V	C	C	T	I	O	L	N	M	A	I	N	E	I	O	A
Z	M	F	A	Y	O	H	E	N	O	K	T	G	I	H	L	S	F	D	L
J	I	E	L	Y	N	M	E	A	M	N	E	L	A	N	F	Z	E	T	W
N	W	N	B	X	C	L	C	A	R	E	F	U	L	Q	D	Q	I	W	A
C	O	J	F	H	S	Z	M	A	D	E	K	N	O	W	N	S	F	E	Y
Q	C	A	L	L	U	N	D	E	R	S	T	A	N	D	I	N	G	C	S
J	E	U	O	D	I	A	S	Q	B	S	S	I	M	L	Z	D	Q	Y	I
I	X	K	S	F	E	L	L	O	W	L	A	B	O	R	E	R	S	F	R
B	Z	C	E	E	B	E	Y	B	M	U	U	H	W	O	B	L	E	J	T

EUODIAS
SYNTYCHE
SAME MIND
ENTREAT
YOKE
FELLOW LABORERS
GOSPEL
BOOK OF LIFE
REJOICE
ALWAYS
MODERATION
AT HAND
CAREFUL
NOTHING
SUPPLICATION
THANKSGIVING
MADE KNOWN
PEACE OF GOD
ALL UNDERSTANDING
HEARTS AND MINDS

122. CLAUDIA AND APPHIA: 2 TIMOTHY 4:17–21

Notwithstanding the Lord stood with me, and strengthened me; that by me the preaching might be fully known, and that all the Gentiles might hear: and I was delivered out of the mouth of the lion. And the Lord shall deliver me from every evil work, and will preserve me to His heavenly kingdom: to whom be glory for ever and ever. Amen. Salute Prisca and Aquila, and the household of Onesiphorus. Erastus abode at Corinth: but Trophimus have I left at Miletum sick. Do your diligence to come before winter. Eubulus greets you, and Pudens, and Linus, and Claudia, and all the brethren.

PHILEMON 1:2–3

And to our beloved Apphia, and Archippus our fellow-soldier, and to the church in your house: grace to you and peace, from God our Father and the Lord Jesus Christ.

L	O	R	D	J	E	S	U	S	C	H	R	I	S	T	Y	E	G
U	W	S	T	R	E	N	G	T	H	E	N	E	D	M	E	F	Y
U	I	W	Q	P	A	T	I	V	L	F	V	O	I	J	T	U	G
T	N	C	B	U	F	I	S	P	Y	Z	N	W	E	Z	H	L	O
E	T	F	E	L	L	O	W	S	O	L	D	I	E	R	U	L	D
V	E	X	V	S	H	P	R	I	S	C	A	E	Z	L	B	Y	O
E	R	B	E	L	O	V	E	D	M	G	L	C	B	H	Q	K	U
R	V	C	G	R	E	E	T	S	Y	O	U	Z	R	P	D	N	R
Y	G	R	A	C	E	A	N	D	P	E	A	C	E	Y	I	O	F
E	M	E	B	P	A	O	G	W	H	T	S	Q	T	A	L	W	A
V	G	U	M	J	A	P	P	H	I	A	L	H	H	Q	I	N	T
I	Y	I	V	P	A	G	M	E	E	J	D	Y	R	U	G	V	H
L	S	W	A	Q	Z	Q	U	C	K	J	B	C	E	I	E	R	E
W	V	R	Y	Q	X	O	I	M	Q	Y	E	U	N	L	N	P	R
O	M	R	H	E	H	O	U	S	E	H	O	L	D	A	C	P	K
R	D	P	R	E	A	C	H	I	N	G	M	G	Y	J	E	T	C
K	C	L	A	U	D	I	A	L	I	N	U	S	J	I	K	B	F
T	M	O	U	T	H	O	F	T	H	E	L	I	O	N	Z	T	T

STRENGTHENED ME
PREACHING
FULLY KNOWN
MOUTH OF THE LION
EVERY EVIL WORK
PRISCA
AQUILA
HOUSEHOLD
DILIGENCE
WINTER
GREETS YOU
BRETHREN
CLAUDIA
LINUS
BELOVED
APPHIA
FELLOW SOLDER
GRACE AND PEACE
GOD OUR FATHER
LORD JESUS CHRIST

123., 124., 125. THE VIRTUOUS WOMAN IN PROVERBS 31
PROVERBS 31:10–31

Who can find a virtuous woman? for her price is far above rubies. The heart of her husband does safely trust in her, so that he shall have no need of spoil. She will do him good and not evil all the days of her life. She seeks wool, and flax, and works willingly with her hands. She is like the merchants' ships; she brings her food from afar. She rises also while it is yet night, and gives meat to her household, and a portion to her maidens. She considers a field, and buys it: with the fruit of her hands she plants a vineyard. She girds her loins with strength, and strengthens her arms. She perceives that her merchandise is good: her candle goes not out by night. She lays her hands to the spindle, and her hands hold the distaff. She stretches out her hand to the poor; yea, she reaches forth her hands to the needy. She is not afraid of the snow for her household: for all her household are clothed with scarlet. She makes herself coverings of tapestry; her clothing is silk and purple. Her husband is known in the gates, when he sits among the elders of the land. She makes fine linen, and sells it; and delivers girdles to the merchant. Strength and honor are her clothing; and she shall rejoice in time to come. She opens her mouth with wisdom; and in her tongue is the law of kindness. She looks well to the ways of her household, and eats not the bread of idleness. Her children arise up, and call her blessed; her husband also, and he praises her. Many daughters have done virtuously, but you excel them all. Favor is deceitful, and beauty is vain: but a woman that fears the Lord, she shall be praised. Give her of the fruit of her hands; and let her own works praise her in the gates.

S	P	O	I	L	E	L	O	T	G	J	D	W	O	O	L	D	W
V	A	H	O	U	S	E	H	O	L	D	N	S	W	P	Q	K	R
I	A	F	L	M	A	I	D	E	N	S	U	T	I	O	D	Z	D
W	F	V	E	N	O	T	E	V	I	L	C	X	L	R	G	R	O
F	A	M	J	L	H	E	A	L	Z	Y	O	V	L	T	I	I	H
L	R	P	M	V	Y	Y	H	N	R	M	N	I	I	I	V	S	I
A	U	N	I	G	H	T	C	K	P	T	S	R	N	O	E	E	M
X	V	K	N	M	F	S	R	B	X	J	I	T	G	N	S	S	G
K	P	F	U	S	V	R	X	U	I	D	D	U	L	L	M	F	O
M	E	R	C	H	A	N	T	R	S	T	E	O	Y	F	E	E	O
W	S	S	H	I	P	U	I	D	E	T	R	U	C	Z	A	B	D
V	V	M	A	A	I	M	G	J	H	I	S	S	N	G	T	I	Z
K	P	R	I	C	E	G	R	U	B	I	E	S	S	J	J	I	Z

PRICE
SAFELY TRUST
DO HIM GOOD
WOOL
WILLINGLY
SHIP
RISES
GIVES MEAT
PORTION
CONSIDERS
VIRTUOUS
RUBIES
SPOIL
NOT EVIL
FLAX
MERCHANT
AFAR
NIGHT
HOUSEHOLD
MAIDENS

Y N F L X V N E E D Y B A U U M S T
Q I I O Q O C B X V V K F E D E A P
S L E I F Z F L Z W O W S Z I R S O
T V L N Z Q Q S O C S C X L S C P O
R E D S Z E T C C T M Y E X T H C R
E L Z L T M S O A A H V Q X A A C R
N K Z X D Y K N U N R I M L F N O I
G E S X X E W U O C D L N V F D V D
T T A P E S T R Y W C L E G V I E W
H E S T R E T C H E S S E T K S R K
E Y H E R H A N D S P I N D L E A S
N R E A C H E S F O R T H B W K G X
S P A U R G K N U N A F R A I D E K
A V I N E Y A R D C C L O T H E D J

FIELD	HER HANDS
VINEYARD	LOINS
STRENGTHENS	MERCHANDISE
CANDLE	SPINDLE
DISTAFF	STRETCHES
POOR	REACHES FORTH
NEEDY	UNAFRAID
SNOW	CLOTHED
SCARLET	COVERAGE
TAPESTRY	CLOTHING

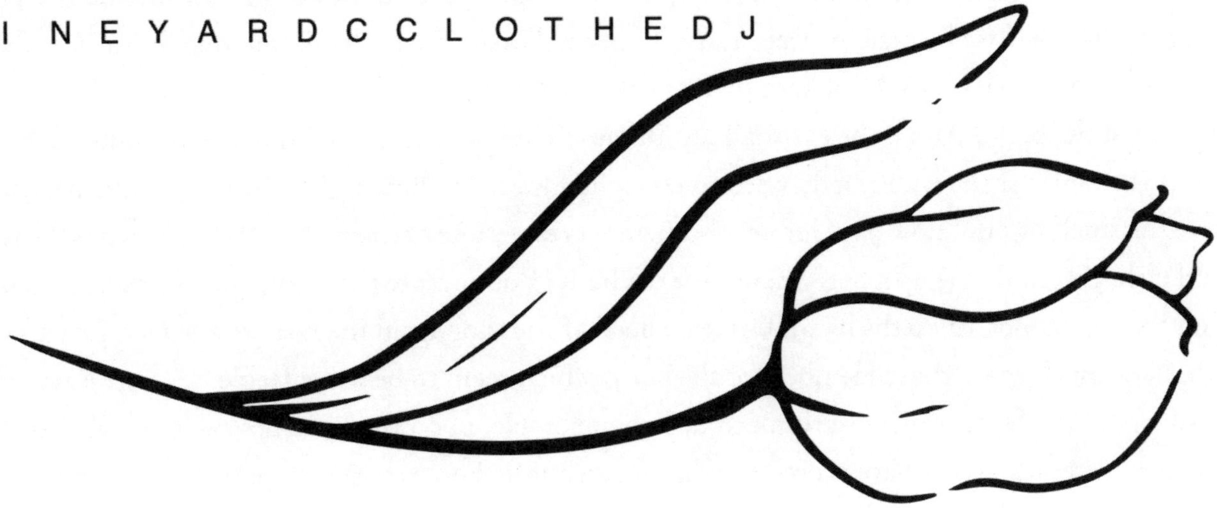

F W S Q S I L K I H O N O R L W L L
V E I I Y D Z K D Y Z O M Z O T B A
F I A S B N D P E X Y B X E Q O G W
U J R R D B H F L K T P I A M N X O
E C Q T S O Z D E N T U N K E G D F
V X T X O T M I S O N R T J R U A K
B G C T P U H K S W I P H N C E G I
L X J E T F S E E N Z L E J H L E N
E G F I L J L L L B L E G L A D I D
S P R A I S E S Y O K G A G N E W N
S A P R A I S E D E R G T E T R O E
E O R E J O I C E O K D E U C S Y S
D U T X F X G I R D L E S X D X S S
X U F G W V F I N E L I N E N T Q Z

SILK	PURPLE
KNOWN	IN THE GATES
ELDERS	FINE LINEN
GIRDLES	MERCHANT
HONOR	REJOICE
WISDOM	TONGUE
LAW OF KINDNESS	IDELESS
BLESSED	PRAISES
VIRTOUSLY	EXCEL
PRAISED	FEARS THE LORD

126. AND 127. SPIRITUAL GIFTS AND THE BODY OF CHRIST: 1 CORINTHIANS 12:1–27

Now concerning spiritual gifts, brethren, I would not have you ignorant....Now there are diversities of gifts, but the same Spirit. And there are differences of administrations, but the same Lord. And there are diversities of operations, but it is the same God which works all in all. But the manifestation of the Spirit is given to every man to profit withal. For to one is given by the Spirit the word of wisdom; to another the word of knowledge by the same Spirit; to another faith by the same Spirit; to another the gifts of healing by the same Spirit; to another the working of miracles; to another prophecy; to another discerning of spirits; to another divers kinds of tongues; to another the interpretation of tongues: but all these works that one and the selfsame Spirit, dividing to every man severally as He will.

For as the body is one, and has many members, and all the members of that one body, being many, are one body: so also is Christ. For by one Spirit are we all baptized into one body, whether we be Jews or Gentiles, whether we be bond or free; and have been all made lie to drink into one Spirit. For the body is not one member, but many. If the foot shall say, Because I am not the hand, I am not of the body; is it therefore not of the body? And if the ear shall say, Because I am not the eye, I am not of the body; is it therefore not of the body? If the whole body were an eye, where were the hearing? If the whole were hearing, where were the smelling? But now has God set the members every one of them in the body, as it has pleased Him. And if they were all one member, where were the body? But now are they many members, yet but one body. And the eye cannot say to the hand, I have no need of you: nor again the head to the feet, I have no need of you. Nay, much more those members of the body, which seem to be more feeble, are necessary: and those members of the body, which we think to be less honorable, upon these we bestow more abundant honor; and our uncomely parts have more abundant comeliness. For our comely parts have no need: but God has tempered the body together, having given more abundant honor to that part which lacked: that there should be no schism in the body; but that the members should have the same care one for another. And whether one member suffer, all the members suffer with it; or one member be honored, all the members rejoice with it. Now you are the body of Christ, and members in particular.

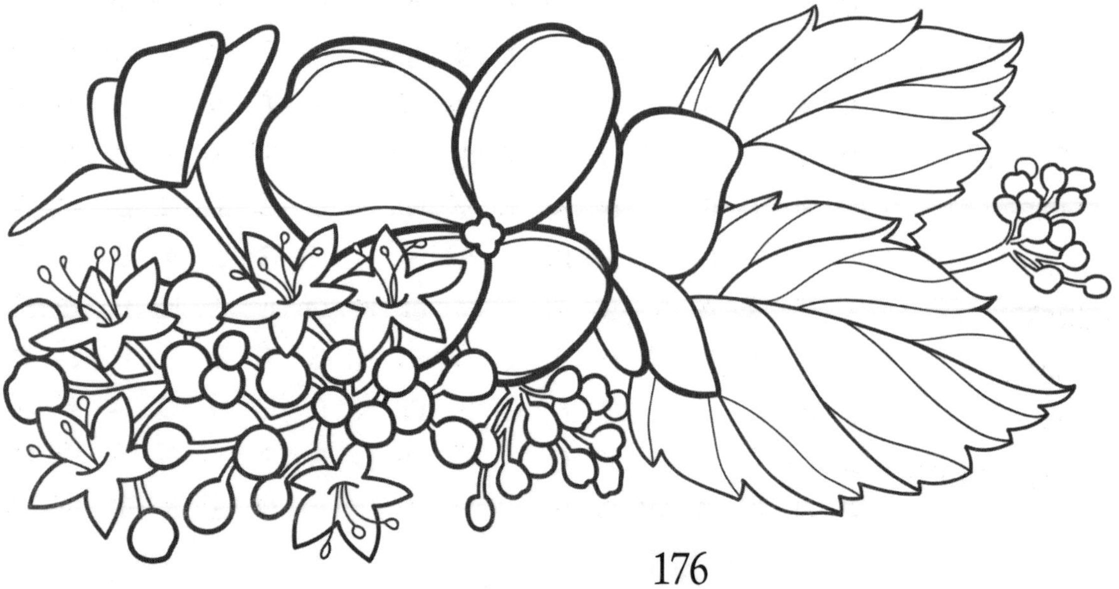

O	D	F	R	J	B	D	H	W	C	D	T	X	Z	C	X	K	I
P	B	I	P	H	G	N	S	B	A	H	E	F	S	H	V	N	N
E	P	G	S	R	I	S	P	O	R	C	V	R	N	R	W	O	T
R	R	S	D	C	O	D	P	C	E	E	T	W	K	I	I	W	E
A	O	E	P	I	E	F	E	I	H	Y	T	I	U	S	S	L	R
T	P	L	I	O	V	R	I	D	R	E	S	H	U	T	D	E	P
I	H	F	K	G	N	E	N	T	U	I	A	M	R	D	O	D	R
O	E	S	L	M	N	E	R	I	W	M	T	L	H	E	M	G	E
N	C	A	F	E	E	O	B	S	N	I	B	O	I	I	N	E	T
S	Y	M	A	Z	Z	M	R	O	I	G	T	I	F	N	A	O	A
R	D	E	S	I	Z	M	B	A	D	T	L	H	D	G	G	X	T
C	C	G	M	O	Q	H	B	E	N	Y	I	W	A	O	O	S	I
R	X	J	I	E	D	K	U	N	R	T	F	E	P	L	L	D	O
M	I	R	A	C	L	E	S	N	K	S	H	U	S	E	N	S	N
E	O	C	S	P	I	R	I	T	U	A	L	G	I	F	T	S	B

SPIRITUAL GIFTS
PROFIT WITHAL
SPIRIT OF GOD
OPERATIONS
WISDOM
HEALING
PROPHECY
TONGUES
SELFSAME
MEMBERS
BRETHREN
DUMB IDOLS
DIVERSITIES
IGNORANT
KNOWLEDGE
MIRACLES
DISCERNING
INTERPRETATION
ONE BODY
CHRIST

R	E	Q	T	D	R	I	N	K	D	W	G	W	D	M	A	L	S
Z	E	L	E	M	P	X	A	S	F	J	B	J	I	O	B	J	I
X	S	J	F	H	T	B	W	Y	C	R	O	L	Z	V	U	I	R
X	J	M	O	C	O	T	Q	F	J	H	E	Y	G	F	N	I	I
Y	B	D	E	I	V	N	G	B	L	W	I	E	M	E	D	Y	Z
K	Y	V	F	L	C	K	O	W	A	A	B	S	X	E	A	C	T
C	D	H	Y	J	L	E	Q	R	Q	P	C	P	M	B	N	H	O
X	B	O	N	D	Q	I	X	G	A	O	T	K	N	L	T	E	G
J	Y	I	P	F	E	W	N	X	T	B	W	I	E	E	U	A	E
E	W	X	G	E	T	Q	H	G	M	V	L	J	Z	D	G	R	T
W	I	L	Q	O	U	D	P	L	E	A	S	E	D	E	U	I	H
K	C	T	E	M	P	E	R	E	D	C	T	F	W	G	D	N	E
O	C	O	M	E	L	I	N	E	S	S	U	F	F	E	R	G	R
Z	S	O	U	V	X	N	E	C	E	S	S	A	R	Y	L	Y	F
P	T	W	G	E	N	T	I	L	E	L	M	E	P	C	L	W	X

BAPTIZED
GENTILE
FREE
HEARING
PLEASED
NECESSARY
ABUNDANT
TEMPERED
LACKED
SUFFER
JEW
BOND
DRINK
SMELLING
FEEBLE
HONORABLE
COMELINESS
TOGETHER
SCHIS
REJOICE

128., 129., 130. THE GREATEST OF THESE: CHARITY (LOVE): 1 CORINTHIANS 13:1–13

Though I speak with the tongues of men and of angels, and have not charity [love], I am become as sounding brass, or a tinkling cymbal. And though I have the gift of prophecy, and understand all mysteries, and all knowledge; and though I have all faith, so that I could remove mountains, and have not charity, I am nothing. And though I bestow all my goods to feed the poor, and though I give my body to be burned, and have not charity, it profits me nothing. Charity suffers long, and is kind; charity envies not; charity vaunts not itself, is not puffed up, does not behave itself unseemly, seeks not her own, is not easily provoked, thinks no evil; rejoices not in iniquity, but rejoices in the truth; bears all things, believes all things, hopes all things, endures all things. Charity never fails: but whether there be prophecies, they shall fail; whether there be tongues, they shall cease; whether there be knowledge, it shall vanish away. For we know in part, and we prophesy in part. But when that which is perfect is come, then that which is in part shall be done away. When I was a child, I spoke as a child, I understood as a child, I thought as a child: but when I became a man, I put away childish things. For now we see through a glass, darkly; but then face to face: now I know in part; but then shall I know even as also I am known. And now abides faith, hope, charity, these three; but the greatest of these is charity.

R	P	D	N	R	C	C	N	B	T	E	X	N	N	T	G	Q	F
E	U	R	C	H	H	W	U	D	O	P	A	S	Z	I	Q	X	E
M	P	K	V	T	A	Y	G	B	D	R	N	O	K	N	L	A	E
O	T	N	D	B	R	N	C	R	W	O	G	U	L	K	W	W	D
V	L	O	V	E	I	U	X	A	M	P	E	N	V	L	Y	M	T
E	A	W	I	T	T	A	W	S	I	H	L	D	J	I	R	O	H
M	S	L	I	U	Y	I	S	S	K	E	S	I	C	N	V	U	E
B	D	E	H	J	X	E	C	V	X	C	J	N	G	G	O	N	P
E	F	D	S	P	E	A	K	I	V	Y	P	G	N	P	M	T	O
S	M	G	S	X	N	N	L	N	O	T	H	I	N	G	E	A	O
T	D	E	Y	G	O	O	D	S	S	P	B	E	X	M	N	I	R
O	C	Y	M	B	A	L	M	Y	S	T	E	R	I	E	S	N	N
W	V	U	N	L	T	O	L	I	L	F	A	I	T	H	W	S	L
S	N	S	S	U	N	D	E	R	S	T	A	N	D	T	T	R	U

MEN
CHARITY
SOUNDING
TINKLING
PROPHECY
MYSTERIES
FAITH
MOUNTAINS
BESTOW
FEED THE POOR
SPEAK
ANGELS
LOVE
BRASS
CYMBAL
UNDERSTAND
KNOWLEDGE
REMOVE
NOTHING
GOODS

I	E	E	N	V	I	E	S	N	O	T	B	B	B	I	W	W	B
F	S	V	T	S	P	L	O	X	N	X	E	E	E	N	P	W	U
P	Y	A	R	U	E	R	R	I	O	R	N	A	L	I	R	T	R
E	T	P	U	E	J	E	O	U	W	X	O	R	I	Q	O	H	N
N	H	B	T	C	N	D	K	V	N	X	Q	S	E	U	F	I	E
E	Y	K	H	X	P	D	C	S	O	S	R	C	V	I	I	N	D
V	Y	W	X	C	H	N	U	V	H	K	E	T	E	T	T	K	Y
E	Z	H	T	R	G	W	O	R	I	E	E	E	S	Y	S	S	Z
R	G	I	M	O	W	A	C	R	E	C	R	D	M	J	G	N	Y
F	H	Q	C	P	V	A	U	N	T	S	N	O	T	L	T	O	N
A	J	P	U	F	F	E	D	U	P	J	A	T	W	L	Y	E	R
I	Q	B	A	L	L	T	H	I	N	G	S	Z	L	N	Z	V	H
L	H	B	S	U	F	F	E	R	S	O	E	R	Q	O	Y	I	J
S	J	G	I	V	E	M	Y	B	O	D	Y	E	D	O	F	L	Z
I	B	R	E	J	O	I	C	E	S	F	Y	H	O	P	E	S	I

GIVE MY BODY
PROFITS
ENVIES NOT
PUFFED UP
SEEKS HER OWN
THINKS NO EVIL
INIQUITY
BEARS
HOPES
ALL THINGS

BURNED
SUFFERS
VAUNTS NOT
UNSEEMLY
PROVOKED
REJOICES
TRUTH
BELIEVES
ENDURES
NEVER FAILS

PROPHECIES
KNOWLEDGE
VANISH
IN PART
IS COME
CHILD
UNDERSTOOD
BECAME A MAN
GLASS DARKLY
KNOWN

TONGUES
CEASE
PROPHESY
PERFECT
DONE AWAY
SPOKE
THOUGHT
CHILDISH THINGS
FACE TO FACE
GREATEST

P	B	E	C	A	M	E	A	M	A	N	P	L	O	C	H	F	C
R	P	J	C	R	G	N	H	R	P	K	B	C	T	H	T	K	R
O	O	G	I	L	G	J	L	K	E	Y	K	S	U	I	G	U	D
P	M	V	L	H	J	R	N	S	R	O	N	P	M	L	B	N	L
H	J	P	A	A	J	W	Q	P	F	K	O	C	Y	D	F	D	Y
E	T	R	T	N	S	L	F	O	E	Y	W	K	E	I	A	E	X
C	A	O	J	T	I	S	Y	K	C	L	L	I	G	S	C	R	H
I	X	P	N	B	H	S	D	E	T	T	E	N	I	H	E	S	Z
E	V	H	T	G	L	O	H	A	Q	J	D	P	I	T	T	T	C
S	Q	E	W	L	U	D	U	T	R	M	G	A	P	H	O	O	H
J	I	S	C	O	M	E	F	G	D	K	E	R	I	I	F	O	I
O	G	Y	U	S	W	F	S	P	H	X	L	T	H	N	A	D	L
Y	E	N	C	K	N	O	W	N	W	T	D	Y	N	G	C	U	D
Q	B	O	R	E	D	G	R	E	A	T	E	S	T	S	E	Z	V
C	E	A	S	E	K	B	D	O	N	E	A	W	A	Y	V	E	W

131 AND 132. THE ELECT OF GOD: COLOSSIANS 3:12–17

Put on therefore, as the elect of God, holy and beloved, bowels of mercies, kindness, humbleness of mind, meekness, long-suffering; forbearing one another, and forgiving one another, if any man have a quarrel against any: even as Christ forgave you, so also do you. And above all these things put on charity, which is the bond of perfectness. And let the peace of God rule in your hearts, to the which also you are called in one body; and be you thankful. Let the word of Christ dwell in you richly in all wisdom; teaching and admonishing one another in psalms and hymns and spiritual songs, singing with grace in your hearts to the Lord. And whatsoever you do in word or deed, do all in the name of the Lord Jesus, giving thanks to God and the Father by Him.

- PUT ON
- ELECT
- HOLY
- BELOVED
- BOWELS
- MERCY
- KINDNESS
- HUMBLENESS
- MEEKNESS
- LONG-SUFFERING
- FORBEARING
- ONE ANOTHER
- FORGIVING
- QUARREL
- FORGAVE
- CHARITY
- BOND
- PERFECTNESS
- PEACE OF GOD
- RULE

Z	V	L	J	J	G	R	P	P	E	A	C	E	O	F	G	O	D	C	I
Q	T	H	O	B	B	H	U	F	E	R	M	E	S	R	G	X	M	Q	R
E	O	E	H	N	N	O	U	L	C	F	F	S	Q	G	T	B	P	N	X
U	L	F	Z	O	G	T	W	M	E	I	O	H	B	N	Z	F	F	Z	M
L	D	E	Y	U	L	S	H	E	B	D	K	R	L	D	K	B	O	Q	C
P	Q	N	C	N	F	Y	U	N	L	L	C	Z	G	Z	E	C	R	T	L
E	M	F	R	T	N	F	F	F	Q	S	E	D	W	A	Z	X	B	G	B
R	J	C	M	V	E	A	E	R	F	I	A	N	S	P	V	A	E	O	E
F	G	S	C	Z	C	M	L	O	V	E	K	K	E	T	L	E	A	N	L
E	F	Q	Z	Z	U	L	R	T	D	C	R	G	E	S	C	Z	R	E	O
C	W	C	H	A	R	I	T	Y	C	J	K	I	X	Y	S	O	I	A	V
T	P	A	U	Q	M	X	J	C	Y	M	C	K	N	U	A	N	N	N	E
N	F	N	V	L	V	P	S	E	G	P	I	U	Y	G	B	O	G	O	D
E	Q	B	V	D	F	L	L	R	E	L	I	Z	Q	F	U	F	K	T	Z
S	U	I	O	N	X	J	M	P	U	T	O	N	M	Y	M	X	X	H	V
S	O	G	O	N	B	W	S	R	M	E	E	K	N	E	S	S	R	E	U
P	I	H	U	G	D	R	O	J	G	L	C	O	E	X	A	T	I	R	C
J	M	E	R	C	Y	F	H	Q	U	A	R	R	E	L	H	M	H	G	M
C	S	J	W	M	H	Z	B	I	F	K	I	N	D	N	E	S	S	T	E
O	I	V	V	Z	U	P	U	N	D	F	O	R	G	I	V	I	N	G	B

Q	T	E	A	C	H	I	N	G	W	K	A	C	O	B	W	H	Z	N	W
E	G	L	H	K	U	F	T	L	P	D	Q	A	S	M	D	I	Y	A	T
G	Z	B	D	G	K	T	U	F	V	P	Q	L	P	T	V	Q	I	M	T
R	L	B	E	M	C	P	L	F	R	W	R	L	I	R	R	R	T	E	H
A	O	F	G	E	G	A	Z	O	Y	O	I	E	R	D	W	G	A	O	E
C	R	I	C	H	L	Y	E	A	C	Z	F	D	I	W	O	W	C	F	F
E	G	F	S	I	N	G	I	N	G	Y	F	L	T	E	R	I	L	J	A
B	N	S	J	J	K	I	T	H	A	N	K	S	U	L	D	S	R	E	T
M	F	N	N	Q	M	M	W	N	G	P	B	J	A	L	O	D	A	S	H
W	O	R	D	O	R	D	E	E	D	Q	J	D	L	H	F	O	T	U	E
D	R	O	D	V	O	C	H	E	A	R	T	S	S	Y	C	M	I	S	R
R	C	C	J	Y	E	J	I	K	D	O	T	V	O	M	H	I	H	H	V
V	Z	F	B	V	G	K	D	V	L	O	V	V	N	N	R	A	A	Z	C
E	O	R	F	B	O	U	C	F	U	C	N	O	G	S	I	I	Q	S	W
K	E	R	E	J	A	B	Y	H	I	M	G	E	S	W	S	W	E	B	H
R	X	P	U	L	V	V	K	L	M	V	P	M	B	L	T	R	X	Q	Q
S	T	H	A	N	K	F	U	L	Y	Q	N	N	L	O	Z	N	M	T	N
I	X	N	N	L	O	U	G	X	T	J	D	N	A	S	D	M	X	I	K
X	H	A	D	M	O	N	I	S	H	I	N	G	X	G	B	Y	W		
Z	P	J	Z	Z	B	N	K	Q	P	S	A	L	M	S	D	F	F		

HEARTS
ONE BODY
WORD OF CHRIST
RICHLY
THANKS
GRACE
HYMNS
TEACHING
CALLED
THANKFUL
DWELL
WISDOM
THE FATHER
WORD OR DEED
SPIRITUAL SONGS
ADMONISHING
BY HIM
NAME OF JESUS
SINGING
PSALMS

133, 134. THE CHRISTIAN HOME AND GRACES:
COLOSSIANS 3:18–4:6

Wives, submit yourselves to your own husbands, as it is fit in the Lord. Husbands, love your wives, and be not bitter against them. Children, obey your parents in all things: for this is well pleasing to the Lord. Fathers, provoke not your children to anger, lest they be discouraged. Servants, obey in all things your masters according to the flesh; not with eye-service, as men-pleasers; but in singleness of heart, fearing God; and whatsoever you do, do it heartily, as to the Lord, and not to men; knowing that of the Lord you shall receive the reward of the inheritance: for you serve the Lord Christ. But he that does wrong shall receive for the wrong which he has done: and there is no respect of persons. Masters, give to your servants that which is just and equal; knowing that you also have a Master in heaven. Continue in prayer, and watch in the same with thanksgiving; meanwhile praying also for us, that God would open to us a door of utterance, to speak the mystery of Christ, for which I am also in bonds: that I may make it manifest, as I ought to speak. Walk in wisdom toward them that are without, redeeming the time. Let your speech be always with grace, seasoned with salt, that you may know how you ought to answer every man.

WIVES
HUSBANDS
LOVE
CHILDREN
PLEASING
PROVOKE NOT
DISCOURAGED
MASTERS
EYE-SERVICE
SINGLENESS
SUBMIT
FIT IN THE LORD
BITTER
OBEY
FATHERS
ANGER
SERVANTS
FLESH
MEN-PLEASERS
FEARING

Q	R	B	M	Y	P	D	R	C	H	I	L	D	R	E	N	S	F
I	I	P	I	E	E	R	I	G	Q	L	Z	K	L	G	P	I	A
Q	H	O	R	T	N	X	B	S	O	F	C	C	N	Z	A	N	T
Q	M	U	B	O	T	P	J	S	C	Z	L	Y	F	D	N	G	H
R	A	U	S	E	V	E	L	U	E	O	Y	M	O	E	G	L	E
F	S	D	D	B	Y	O	R	E	V	R	U	O	G	K	E	E	R
E	T	U	Q	C	A	U	K	R	A	J	V	R	Y	N	R	N	S
A	E	A	D	H	O	N	P	E	A	S	P	A	A	N	B	E	W
R	R	Q	R	N	A	R	D	O	N	P	E	L	N	G	U	S	I
I	S	I	R	V	U	N	I	S	F	O	C	R	M	T	E	S	V
N	P	L	E	A	S	I	N	G	N	M	T	R	S	T	S	D	E
G	F	I	T	I	N	T	H	E	L	O	R	D	Q	O	F	X	S
L	O	V	E	E	Y	E	S	E	R	V	I	C	E	J	A	S	U
R	I	T	S	U	B	M	I	T	S	L	C	F	L	E	S	H	O
D	C	A	U	N	O	L	X	K	K	Y	C	X	Y	Y	K	Z	P

R	P	A	J	U	S	T	G	L	R	L	F	D	M	K	K	U	B
V	H	E	K	S	P	E	E	C	H	Y	Q	M	Y	N	C	Y	H
D	N	Z	R	T	O	T	H	E	L	O	R	D	S	D	Z	P	E
P	O	R	J	S	H	I	X	E	I	K	G	O	T	M	B	R	Z
R	N	E	E	S	O	F	B	I	F	N	S	T	E	O	I	A	B
B	E	D	S	C	T	N	Q	X	C	O	H	H	R	N	R	Y	N
X	Z	S	J	W	E	P	S	P	S	T	M	E	Y	H	E	E	M
A	I	Q	P	A	R	I	S	J	E	T	D	A	M	T	D	R	A
R	C	H	G	E	A	O	V	K		O	E		R	H	E	A	N
E	I	K	D	F	C	L	N	E	V	M	Z	E	E	E	E	G	I
O	O	P	C	L	H	T	H	G	E	E	Z	N	W	Q	M	N	F
U	T	T	E	R	A	N	C	E	S	N	E	A	A	U	I	S	E
J	F	I	N	H	E	R	I	T	A	N	C	E	R	A	N	I	S
D	K	R	X	C	H	E	A	R	T	I	L	Y	D	L	G	J	T
V	L	D	Q	T	H	A	N	K	S	G	I	V	I	N	G	R	B

HEARTILY
TO THE LORD
NOT TO MEN
RECEIVE
REWARD
INHERITANCE
SERVE
DOES WRONG
RESPECT
PERSONS
JUST
EQUAL
HEAVEN
PRAYER
THANKSGIVING
UTTERANCE
MYSTERY
MANIFEST
REDEEMING
SPEECH

135. WISDOM CRIES OUT: PROVERBS 1:20–33

The book of Wisdom is included in the canons of some churches, but others consider it part of the Apocrypha. That book and several Proverbs personify wisdom as a woman.

Wisdom cries without; she utters her voice in the streets: she cries in the chief place of concourse, in the openings of the gates: in the city she utters her words, saying, How long, you simple ones, will you love simplicity? and the scorners delight in their scorning, and fools hate knowledge? Turn you at my reproof: behold, I will pour out my spirit to you, I will make known my words to you. Because I have called, and you refused; I have stretched out my hand, and no man regarded; but you have set at nothing all my counsel, and would none of my reproof: I also will laugh at your calamity; I will mock when your fear comes; when your fear comes as desolation, and your destruction comes as a whirlwind; when distress and anguish comes upon you. Then shall they call upon me, but I will not answer; they shall seek me early, but they shall not find me: for that they hated knowledge, and did not choose the fear of the Lord: they would none of my counsel: they despised all my reproof.... But whoso hearkens to me shall dwell safely, and shall be quiet from fear of evil.

WISDOM
CHIEF PLACE
OPENINGS
SIMPLICITY
SCORNING
KNOWLEDGE
MAKE KNOWN
REFUSED
DEVICES
CALAMITY
UTTERS
CONCOURSE
SIMPLE ONES
SCORNERS
FOOLS
REPROOF
CALLED
COUNSEL
LAUGH
WHIRLWIND

R	V	S	I	M	P	L	E	O	N	E	S	D	Q	R	M	J	L
C	E	C	K	I	H	W	U	I	K	M	P	E	O	L	W	S	A
A	G	P	H	K	E	H	I	F	O	V	J	V	P	A	H	I	J
L	S	Y	R	I	S	M	I	S	O	N	W	I	E	U	I	M	S
A	W	U	S	O	E	C	A	Z	D	O	A	C	N	G	R	P	C
M	F	G	T	Q	O	F	O	K	B	O	L	E	I	H	L	L	O
I	U	R	C	T	C	F	P	R	E	R	M	S	N	A	W	I	U
T	C	A	L	L	E	D	X	L	N	K	W	S	G	G	I	C	N
Y	O	P	A	Y	C	R	B	B	A	E	N	S	S	I	N	I	S
C	O	N	C	O	U	R	S	E	W	C	R	O	R	L	D	T	E
F	G	R	E	F	U	S	E	D	X	L	E	S	W	H	F	Y	L
O	L	G	U	S	O	S	K	S	C	O	R	N	I	N	G	T	H
Z	A	E	N	X	K	N	O	W	L	E	D	G	E	N	M	Z	I

136. THE VALUE OF WISDOM: PROVERBS 2:1–22

My son, if you will receive my words, and hide my commandments with you; so that you incline your ear to wisdom, and apply your heart to understanding; yea, if you cry after knowledge, and lift up your voice for understanding; if you seek her as silver, and search for her as for hidden treasures; then shall you understand the fear of the LORD, and find the knowledge of God. For the LORD gives wisdom: out of His mouth comes knowledge and understanding. He lays up sound wisdom for the righteous: He is a buckler to them that walk uprightly. He keeps the paths of judgment, and preserves the way of His saints. Then shall you understand righteousness, and judgment, and equity; yea, every good path. When wisdom enters into your heart, and knowledge is pleasant to your soul; discretion shall preserve you, understanding shall keep you: to deliver you from the way of the evil man,.... That you may walk in the way of good men, and keep the paths of the righteous. For the upright shall dwell in the land, and the perfect shall remain in it. But the wicked shall be cut off from the earth, and the transgressors shall be rooted out of it.

WORDS
INCLINE YOUR EAR
SILVER
TREASURES
BUCKLER
JUDGMENT
HIS SAINTS
EQUITY
EVIL MAN
DARKNESS
COMMANDMENTS
UNDERSTANDING
HIDDEN
RIGHTEOUS
UPRIGHTLY
PRESERVES
RIGHTEOUSNESS
PLEASANT
FROWARD
COVENANT

M	E	F	F	F	D	A	R	K	N	E	S	S	H	J	I	M	C
N	Q	O	R	B	M	M	I	S	J	P	I	O	I	H	N	R	O
E	U	G	O	U	L	Q	P	Y	R	G	E	P	D	Z	C	I	M
V	I	C	W	C	W	C	R	U	R	L	H	U	D	R	L	G	M
I	T	P	A	K	J	O	E	Q	B	M	I	P	E	I	I	H	A
L	Y	L	R	L	U	V	S	G	C	S	S	R	N	G	N	T	N
M	B	E	D	E	D	E	E	I	F	I	S	I	K	H	E	E	D
A	G	A	P	R	G	N	R	N	Y	L	A	G	C	T	Y	O	M
N	T	S	L	Y	M	A	V	K	S	V	I	H	T	E	O	U	E
W	L	A	I	Y	E	N	E	O	A	E	N	T	W	O	U	S	N
O	U	N	J	C	N	T	S	Z	E	R	T	L	E	U	R	N	T
R	J	T	M	X	T	D	H	M	G	T	S	Y	V	S	E	E	S
D	U	N	D	E	R	S	T	A	N	D	I	N	G	L	A	S	I
S	P	J	T	R	E	A	S	U	R	E	S	K	A	F	R	S	H
H	X	C	V	I	R	A	I	F	N	L	C	P	H	E	D	J	O

137. AND 138. THE EXCELLENCE OF WISDOM: PROVERBS 8:1–36

Does not wisdom cry? and understanding put forth her voice? She stands in the top of high places, by the way in the places of the paths. She cries at the gates, at the entry of the city, at the coming in at the doors....O you simple, understand wisdom: and, you fools, be you of an understanding heart....

Receive my instruction, and not silver; and knowledge rather than choice gold. For wisdom is better than rubies; and all the things that may be desired are not to be compared to it. I wisdom dwell with prudence, and find out knowledge of witty inventions. The fear of the LORD is to hate evil: pride, and arrogancy, and the evil way, and the froward mouth, do I hate. Counsel is mine, and sound wisdom: I am understanding; I have strength. By me kings reign, and princes decree justice. By me princes rule, and nobles, even all the judges of the earth.

I love them that love me; and those that seek me early shall find me. Riches and honor are with me; yea, durable riches and righteousness. My fruit is better than gold, yea, than fine gold; and my revenue than choice silver. I lead in the way of righteousness, in the midst of the paths of judgment: that I may cause those that love me inherit substance; and I will fill their treasures.

The LORD possessed me in the beginning of His way, before His works of old. I was set up from everlasting, from the beginning, or ever the earth was. When there were no depths, I was brought forth; when there were no fountains abounding with water. Before the mountains were settled, before the hills was I brought forth: while as yet He had not made the earth, nor the fields, nor the highest part of the dust of the world. When He prepared the heavens, I was there: when He set a compass upon the face of the depth: when He established the clouds above: when He strengthened the fountains of the deep: when He gave to the sea His decree, that the waters should not pass His commandment: when He appointed the foundations of the earth: then I was by Him, as one brought up with Him: and I was daily His delight, rejoicing always before Him; rejoicing in the habitable part of His earth; and my delights were with the sons of men.

Now therefore hearken to me, O you children: for blessed are they that keep my ways. Hear instruction, and be wise, and refuse it not. Blessed is the man that hears me, watching daily at my gates, waiting at the posts of my doors. For whoso finds me finds life, and shall obtain favor of the LORD.

PUT FORTH
COMING
YOU SIMPLE
UNDERSTANDING
EXCELLENT
SPEAK TRUTH
MY LIPS
MOUTH
RIGHTEOUSNESS
KNOWLEDGE
HIGH PLACES
SONS OF MAN
FOOLS
HEAR
RIGHT THINGS
WICKEDNESS
ABOMINATION
PERVERSE
PLAIN
RECEIVE

J	S	R	E	P	B	K	Y	S	J	N	R	O	H	E	G	R	F
L	D	Y	L	H	U	H	E	A	R	Q	E	X	E	H	R	I	U
Y	A	O	O	B	Q	T	F	H	H	G	C	R	X	I	I	G	N
W	W	V	A	U	B	S	F	X	C	E	E	V	C	G	G	H	D
S	K	I	H	B	S	W	P	O	P	R	I	Q	E	H	H	T	E
O	P	N	C	F	O	I	I	E	R	I	V	C	L	P	T	E	R
N	Q	L	O	K	O	M	M	L	A	T	E	C	L	L	T	O	S
S	B	F	W	W	E	O	I	P	M	K	H	M	E	A	H	U	T
O	P	A	N	R	L	D	L	N	L	Y	T	N	N	C	I	S	A
F	E	L	H	M	D	E	N	S	A	E	L	R	T	E	N	N	N
M	E	M	A	H	L	Q	D	E	L	T	I	I	U	S	G	E	D
A	V	R	Z	I	U	D	W	G	S	F	I	I	P	T	S	S	I
N	X	R	Q	M	N	B	A	B	E	S	D	O	G	S	H	S	N
T	M	O	U	T	H	Z	C	O	M	I	N	G	N	O	Q	O	G
Z	W	B	N	B	P	E	R	V	E	R	S	E	J	K	Z	W	X

INSTRUCTION
CHOICE GOLD
DWELL
WITTY
HATE EVIL
COUNSEL
NOBLES
RICHES
REVENUE
FOUNTAINS
SILVER
RUBIES
PRUDENCE
INVENTIONS
ARROGANCY
STRENGTH
JUDGES
HONOR
EVERLASTING
COMPASS

R	H	X	L	P	I	A	Q	S	T	R	E	N	G	T	H	N	M
X	E	O	J	W	Z	W	R	Y	P	A	N	E	B	I	L	O	I
R	L	V	N	T	E	A	I	R	E	L	E	M	S	L	U	B	N
I	U	D	E	O	J	B	H	T	O	S	Q	H	F	U	D	L	S
C	C	X	N	N	R	K	D	E	T	G	I	Y	K	O	P	E	T
H	H	J	H	V	U	X	H	A	S	Y	A	L	K	X	N	S	R
E	O	U	F	G	F	E	L	V	U	C	Q	N	V	J	V	W	U
S	I	D	I	N	V	E	N	T	I	O	N	S	C	E	X	F	C
U	C	G	A	Q	V	P	R	U	D	E	N	C	E	Y	R	A	T
R	E	E	V	Z	S	E	V	E	R	L	A	S	T	I	N	G	I
R	G	S	J	G	G	A	B	T	A	K	B	P	G	W	M	D	O
P	O	Y	B	I	U	Q	F	O	U	N	T	A	I	N	S	K	N
I	L	G	T	E	L	I	L	A	K	D	W	E	L	L	X	D	K
R	D	C	O	U	N	S	E	L	L	C	O	M	P	A	S	S	C
H	A	T	E	E	V	I	L	R	U	B	I	E	S	J	V	A	M

139. WISDOM BUILDS HER HOUSE: PROVERBS 9:1–12

Wisdom has built her house, she has hewn out her seven pillars: she has killed her beasts; she has mingled her wine; she has also furnished her table. She has sent forth her maidens: she cries upon the highest places of the city, Whoso is simple, let him turn in here: as for him that wants understanding, she says to him, Come, eat of my bread, and drink of the wine which I have mingled. Forsake the foolish, and live; and go in the way of understanding. He that reproves a scorner gets to himself shame: and he that rebukes a wicked man gets himself a blot. Reprove not a scorner, lest he hate you: rebuke a wise man, and he will love you. Give instruction to a wise man, and he will be yet wiser: teach a just man, and he will increase in learning. The fear of the Lord is the beginning of wisdom: and the knowledge of the holy is understanding. For by me your days shall be multiplied, and the years of your life shall be increased.

S	W	I	C	K	E	D	M	A	N	H	O	W	P	T	Y	V	D	M	C
R	U	N	D	H	P	J	L	G	Y	D	J	J	W	A	F	X	A	I	A
P	Q	R	M	A	E	B	M	O	O	P	O	X	F	B	U	G	F	N	T
P	I	M	E	P	A	R	E	B	C	H	H	X	T	L	R	K	O	G	F
S	Z	L	V	P	P	A	W	A	S	M	W	L	H	E	N	C	O	L	U
C	Y	I	L	R	R	U	L	I	S	C	H	S	A	U	I	C	L	E	D
U	M	Y	P	A	U	O	D	G	N	T	O	K	W	J	S	R	I	D	S
N	M	A	G	W	R	P	V	P	Y	E	S	R	Q	R	H	A	S	W	A
Q	V	U	I	S	L	S	P	E	C	V	C	L	N	H	E	A	H	H	J
S	F	C	A	D	P	L	H	J	S	C	G	E	W	E	D	P	J	T	K
I	Q	O	G	K	E	F	S	X	G	W	C	A	I	W	R	R	A	K	N
U	R	K	R	S	N	N	B	P	L	H	A	R	T	N	N	Z	V	S	O
O	K	P	L	S	N	D	S	I	J	O	T	N	J	O	Q	A	B	O	F
G	U	Z	U	J	A	O	T	E	W	S	V	I	R	U	H	S	J	E	D
X	Q	A	J	P	F	K	P	D	Y	O	Q	N	Z	T	R	H	F	H	O
L	G	A	K	O	V	D	E	C	O	E	J	G	P	U	J	A	W	O	D
S	J	T	X	X	J	J	A	C	I	Z	K	I	T	C	I	M	U	U	W
H	P	Z	D	Q	D	V	R	E	B	U	K	E	S	S	G	E	U	S	B
T	U	R	N	I	N	H	E	R	E	Z	D	T	C	K	B	S	Y	E	D
T	L	O	Q	S	E	N	T	F	O	R	T	H	C	S	X	S	J	V	T

HOUSE
HEWN OUT
PILLARS
BEASTS
MINGLED
HER WINE
FURNISHED
TABLE
SENT FORTH
MAIDENS
WHOSO
TURN IN HERE
FORSAKE
FOOLISH
REPROVES
SCORNER
SHAME
REBUKES
WICKED MAN
LEARNING

140. HUSBANDS AND WIVES: 1 PETER 3:1–7

Likewise, you wives, be in subjection to your own husbands; that, if any obey not the word, they also may without the word be won by the conversation of the wives; while they behold your chaste conversation coupled with fear. Whose adorning let it not be that outward adorning of plaiting the hair, and of wearing of gold, or of putting on of apparel; but let it be the hidden man of the heart, in that which is not corruptible, even the ornament of a meek and quiet spirit, which is in the sight of God of great price. For after this manner in the old time the holy women also, who trusted in God, adorned themselves, being in subjection to their own husbands: even as Sarah obeyed Abraham, calling him lord: whose daughters you are, as long as you do well, and are not afraid with any amazement. Likewise, you husbands, dwell with them according to knowledge, giving honor to the wife, as to the weaker vessel, and as being heirs together of the grace of life; that your prayers be not hindered

SUBJECTION
OBEY
THE WORD
WON OVER
CONVERSATION
CHASTE
ADORNING
PLAITING
GOLD
APPAREL
HIDDEN
CORRUPTIBLE
MEEK AND QUIET
GREAT PRICE
HOLY WOMEN
AMAZEMENT
KNOWLEDGE
HONOR
VESSEL
GRACE OF LIFE

U	G	C	O	N	V	E	R	S	A	T	I	O	N	I	U	K	O	I	Z
J	R	G	Y	F	N	S	G	T	R	K	D	A	J	Z	Z	N	Y	C	C
T	E	R	K	B	Q	U	H	T	H	E	W	O	R	D	L	O	F	Y	X
V	A	A	R	I	M	B	O	V	S	K	V	J	M	L	A	W	G	F	F
H	T	C	G	M	C	J	L	D	E	E	J	D	C	F	H	L	B	Q	A
B	P	E	N	E	K	E	Y	L	F	O	S	U	H	M	J	E	Q	C	M
R	R	O	M	E	O	C	W	K	B	W	A	I	Q	Q	T	D	U	O	A
X	I	F	G	K	S	T	O	M	C	I	O	G	O	G	C	G	L	R	Z
M	C	L	E	A	A	I	M	R	Y	U	S	N	U	L	O	E	A	R	E
X	E	I	D	N	T	O	E	Y	E	P	Y	A	O	T	M	R	W	U	M
A	G	F	S	D	N	N	N	M	M	Q	L	D	X	V	H	X	Y	P	E
L	G	E	W	Q	H	P	Q	J	E	Z	K	A	G	F	E	B	Z	T	N
B	R	O	Z	U	B	T	L	A	J	T	A	O	I	O	E	R	O	I	T
P	U	X	B	I	G	C	H	L	A	B	Y	T	U	T	L	C	O	B	D
F	U	S	N	E	B	M	C	H	A	S	T	E	Q	P	I	D	F	L	A
B	J	I	C	T	Y	U	O	H	W	W	V	R	I	H	T	N	B	E	U
C	W	O	R	V	Y	X	M	F	W	V	E	S	S	E	L	N	G	F	Y
I	R	M	H	I	D	D	E	N	Y	Z	I	W	S	A	R	H	Y	E	E
Q	Y	C	Z	A	D	O	R	N	I	N	G	P	H	O	N	O	R	H	S
H	E	T	N	J	P	L	G	E	W	L	X	A	P	P	A	R	E	L	I

141. TEACH THOSE YOUNGER: TITUS 2:1–8

But speak you the things which become sound doctrine: that the aged men be sober, grave, temperate, sound in faith, in charity, in patience. The aged women likewise, that they be in behavior as becomes holiness, not false accusers, not given to much wine, teachers of good things; that they may teach the young women to be sober, to love their husbands, to love their children, to be discreet, chaste, keepers at home, good, obedient to their own husbands, that the word of God be not blasphemed. Young men likewise exhort to be sober minded. In all things showing yourself a pattern of good works: in doctrine showing uncorruptness, gravity, sincerity, sound speech, that cannot be condemned; that he that is of the contrary part may be ashamed, having no evil thing to say of you.

Y	Q	K	E	E	P	E	R	S	D	M	H	O	L	I	N	E	S	S	B
L	E	K	G	R	A	V	I	T	Y	D	H	H	T	H	J	V	B	Z	X
T	P	C	H	A	R	I	T	Y	B	S	I	K	Z	V	D	Z	F	I	N
E	V	P	Z	I	L	D	O	S	N	G	Z	S	D	G	S	S	D	D	H
A	W	A	B	K	Y	U	R	U	R	A	G	L	C	N	B	H	V	G	E
C	H	T	B	L	A	S	P	H	E	M	E	D	U	R	G	I	Q	A	W
H	P	I	X	V	W	U	F	Z	C	L	H	O	W	W	E	Q	U	G	H
E	W	E	B	E	H	A	V	I	O	R	P	N	Q	L	A	E	U	E	T
R	T	N	U	M	F	L	J	C	P	R	A	E	S	J	A	Y	T	D	E
S	A	C	Y	R	V	E	X	P	O	L	W	X	O	D	J	S	Q	M	M
S	X	E	D	R	Y	G	N	E	A	O	V	J	B	O	Z	R	B	E	P
U	N	C	O	R	R	U	P	T	N	E	S	S	E	C	U	K	N	N	E
H	X	D	C	R	E	C	H	A	S	T	E	H	R	T	L	A	J	R	R
S	L	B	N	D	K	D	T	K	X	Q	R	L	D	R	K	J	Y	V	A
I	Y	B	S	O	U	N	D	S	P	E	E	C	H	I	T	J	A	X	T
Z	U	W	H	K	D	N	L	V	B	P	X	N	A	N	W	P	Y	B	E
T	X	Q	U	V	T	L	V	U	U	F	Q	S	I	E	I	Y	H	G	R
D	D	A	U	N	A	S	H	A	M	E	D	Y	U	O	V	L	W	U	X
H	R	K	D	J	W	O	B	E	D	I	E	N	T	G	R	A	V	E	P
X	J	H	S	V	L	J	A	G	S	I	N	C	E	R	I	T	Y	T	X

DOCTRINE
AGED MEN
SOBER
GRAVE
TEMPERATE
CHARITY
PATIENCE
BEHAVIOR
HOLINESS
TEACHERS
DISCREET
CHASTE
KEEPERS
OBEDIENT
BLASPHEMED
UNCORRUPTNESS
GRAVITY
SINCERITY
SOUND SPEECH
UNASHAMED

142., 143., 144. THE FAITH CHAPTER: HEBREWS 11:1–12:2

Now faith is the substance of things hoped for, the evidence of things not seen. For by it the elders obtained a good report. Through faith we understand that the worlds were framed by the word of God, so that things which are seen were not made of things which do appear.

By faith Abel offered to God a more excellent sacrifice than Cain, by which he obtained witness that he was righteous, God testifying of his gifts: and by it he being dead yet speaks. By faith Enoch was translated that he should not see death; and was not found, because God had translated him: for before his translation he had this testimony, that he pleased God. But without faith it is impossible to please Him: for he that comes to God must believe that He is, and that He is a rewarder of them that diligently seek Him.

By faith Noah, being warned of God of things not seen as yet, moved with fear, prepared an ark to the saving of his house; by the which he condemned the world, and became heir of the righteousness which is by faith.

By faith Abraham, when he was called to go out into a place which he should after receive for an inheritance, obeyed; and he went out, not knowing where he went. By faith he sojourned in the land of promise, as in a strange country, dwelling in tabernacles with Isaac and Jacob, the heirs with him of the same promise: for he looked for a city which has foundations, whose builder and maker is God. Through faith also Sarah herself received strength to conceive seed, and was delivered of a child when she was past age, because she judged Him faithful who had promised. Therefore sprang there even of one, and him as good as dead, so many as the stars of the sky in multitude, and as the sand which is by the sea shore innumerable.

These all died in faith, not having received the promises, but having seen them afar off, and were persuaded of them, and embraced them, and confessed that they were strangers and pilgrims on the earth. For they that say such things declare plainly that they seek a country. And truly, if they had been mindful of that country from where they came out, they might have had opportunity to have returned. But now they desire a better country, that is, a heavenly: wherefore God is not ashamed to be called their God: for He has prepared for them a city.

By faith Abraham, when he was tried, offered up Isaac: and he that had received the promises offered up his only begotten son, of whom it was said, That in Isaac shall your seed be called: accounting that God was able to raise him up, even from the dead; from where also he received him in a figure. By faith Isaac blessed Jacob and Esau concerning things to come. By faith Jacob, when he was a dying, blessed both the sons of Joseph; and worshipped, leaning upon the top of his staff. By faith Joseph, when he died, made mention of the departing of the children of Israel; and gave commandment concerning his bones.

By faith Moses, when he was born, was hidden three months of his parents, because they saw he was a proper child; and they were not afraid of the king's commandment. By faith Moses, when he was come to years, refused to be called the son of Pharaoh's daughter; choosing rather to suffer affliction with the people of God, than to enjoy the pleasures of sin for a season; esteeming the reproach of Christ greater riches than the treasures in Egypt: for he had respect to the recompence of the reward. By faith he forsook Egypt, not fearing the wrath of the king: for he endured, as seeing Him who is invisible. Through faith he kept the passover, and the sprinkling of blood, lest He that destroyed the firstborn should touch them. By faith they passed through the Red Sea as by dry land: which the Egyptians assaying to do were drowned. By faith the walls of Jericho fell down, after they were compassed about seven days. By faith the harlot Rahab perished not with them that believed not, when she had received the spies with peace.

And what shall I more say? for the time would fail me to tell of Gideon, and of Barak, and of Samson, and of Jephthae; of David also, and Samuel, and of the prophets: who through faith subdued kingdoms, wrought righteousness, obtained promises, stopped the mouths of lions, quenched the violence of fire, escaped the edge of the sword, out of weakness were made strong, waxed valiant in fight, turned to flight the armies of the aliens. Women received their dead raised to life again: and others were tortured, not accepting deliverance; that they might obtain a better resurrection: and others had trial of cruel mockings and scourgings, yea, moreover of bonds and imprisonment: they were stoned, they were sawn asunder, were tempted, were slain with the sword: they wandered about in sheepskins and goatskins; being destitute, afflicted, tormented; (of whom the world was not worthy:) they wandered in deserts, and in mountains, and in dens and caves of the earth. And these all, having obtained a good report through faith, received not the promise: God having provided some better thing for us, that they without us should not be made perfect.

A	K	R	F	E	M	E	C	H	H	Z	L	C	Y	G	P	B	M
M	A	Q	H	F	T	I	N	O	T	S	E	E	N	O	P	M	O
W	O	R	D	O	F	G	O	D	P	H	D	L	Q	O	F	C	R
V	R	H	K	M	Z	G	G	G	Y	O	S	P	K	D	R	A	E
L	S	K	P	W	H	F	R	D	W	P	Y	U	S	R	A	I	E
C	U	I	D	Y	W	B	F	A	B	E	L	F	U	E	M	N	X
E	W	J	L	A	P	P	E	A	R	D	D	A	B	P	E	J	C
N	R	I	G	H	T	E	O	U	S	F	T	I	S	O	D	H	E
O	S	A	C	R	I	F	I	C	E	O	H	T	T	R	Y	F	L
C	E	V	I	D	E	N	C	E	K	R	I	H	A	T	K	C	L
H	T	S	G	I	G	X	G	O	T	M	N	R	N	A	W	D	E
W	O	R	L	D	S	H	I	V	G	C	G	O	C	F	F	Y	N
G	O	U	N	S	E	E	N	M	E	N	S	H	E	K	D	J	T
B	M	B	V	T	R	A	N	S	L	A	T	E	D	Y	T	W	I
U	N	D	E	R	S	T	A	N	D	I	N	G	S	S	X	Q	U

SUBSTANCE
EVIDENCE
NOT SEEN
WORLDS
FRAMED
UNSEEN
ABEL
SACRIFICE
RIGHTEOUS
TRANSLATED
FAITH
HOPED FOR
THINGS
GOOD REPORT
UNDERSTANDING
WORD OF GOD
APPEAR
MORE EXCELLENT
CAIN
ENOCH

X	F	B	Y	B	U	I	L	D	E	R	S	A	B	M	T	R	S
K	S	R	E	W	A	R	D	E	R	C	K	R	K	A	M	X	T
X	U	F	L	L	S	E	E	K	H	I	M	K	O	F	T	O	R
I	N	H	E	R	I	T	A	N	C	E	Z	E	N	B	D	B	A
M	T	I	X	B	L	E	M	P	G	E	V	T	O	G	S	E	N
B	A	V	V	Q	B	E	V	L	R	W	X	S	A	P	A	Y	G
G	U	F	J	J	U	D	G	E	D	E	R	N	H	L	V	E	E
T	P	A	N	I	V	A	B	E	P	G	P	N	D	E	I	D	C
M	A	K	E	R	C	Y	H	S	W	P	X	A	T	A	N	C	O
Y	F	A	I	T	H	F	U	L	E	U	A	N	R	S	G	E	U
P	M	J	F	G	T	E	S	T	I	M	O	N	Y	I	O	O	N
T	B	M	S	O	J	O	U	R	N	E	D	I	S	N	N	C	T
Q	I	M	R	Y	H	Z	B	C	G	O	O	S	V	G	Z	G	R
C	O	N	D	E	M	N	E	D	X	B	F	J	V	X	N	T	Y
E	D	I	L	I	G	E	N	T	L	Y	A	C	H	E	I	R	H

TESTIMONY
BELIEVE
DILIGENTLY
NOAH
ARK
CONDEMNED
INHERITANCE
SOJOURNED
BUILDER
JUDGED
PLEASING
REWARDER
SEEK HIM
PREPARING
SAVING
HEIR
OBEYED
STRANGE COUNTRY
MAKER
FAITHFUL

V	M	M	J	O	E	L	O	P	A	S	S	O	V	E	R	C	F	T	Y
B	E	T	T	E	R	C	O	U	N	T	R	Y	I	B	S	N	A	W	L
U	O	Z	W	F	S	A	E	M	B	R	A	C	E	D	P	O	Z	S	L
V	C	X	V	H	C	A	F	M	Q	G	B	G	S	U	R	I	P	T	Y
Y	R	W	B	I	V	H	N	A	L	N	C	C	O	M	I	O	L	A	G
F	S	L	V	I	D	J	A	D	C	E	S	R	B	U	N	T	T	R	M
M	I	E	X	A	H	O	O	Z	V	F	U	E	T	L	K	K	N	S	X
F	W	G	A	W	L	N	U	Q	U	V	B	C	A	T	L	H	Y	O	V
C	H	E	U	S	T	D	H	A	G	I	D	O	I	I	I	D	L	F	V
U	B	F	A	R	H	N	V	G	P	C	U	M	N	T	N	D	M	T	N
A	A	T	G	U	E	O	R	H	K	L	E	P	E	U	G	F	A	H	T
I	K	J	N	L	O	U	R	Z	P	L	D	E	D	D	Y	H	F	E	Z
L	O	Z	X	L	W	J	V	E	Z	O	J	N	U	E	Z	K	A	S	Z
Y	I	N	N	U	M	E	R	A	B	L	E	C	V	Z	U	I	R	K	L
C	R	T	A	D	C	E	R	K	F	N	E	E	M	U	S	C	O	Y	A
V	I	M	O	U	T	H	S	O	F	L	I	O	N	S	T	D	F	O	M
G	P	J	I	G	P	I	L	G	R	I	M	S	C	O	A	Y	F	B	S
A	V	O	W	O	R	S	H	I	P	P	E	D	S	G	F	A	N	Y	Z
P	R	O	M	I	S	E	S	X	W	V	C	M	P	H	F	S	T	D	I
					H	I	R	A	F	F	L	I	C	T	I	O	N	V	Z

SAND	SEASHORE	INNUMERABLE
EMBRACED	PILGRIMS	BETTER COUNTRY
STAFF	AFFLICTION	RECOMPENCE
SUBDUED	OBTAINED	MOUTHS OF LIONS
MULTITUDE	WORSHIPPED	AFAR OFF
PROMISES	SPRINKLING	PASSOVER
	STARS OF THE SKY	FIGURE

145. GOD'S PERFECT KNOWLEDGE OF US: PSALM 139:1–24

O Lord, You have searched me, and known me. You know my downsitting and my uprising, You understand my thought afar off. You compass my path and my lying down, and are acquainted with all my ways. For there is not a word in my tongue, but, lo, O Lord, You know it altogether. You have beset me behind and before, and laid Your hand upon me. Such knowledge is too wonderful for me; it is high, I cannot attain to it. Where shall I go from Your Spirit? or where shall I flee from Your presence? If I ascend up into heaven, You are there: if I make my bed in hell, behold, You are there. If I take the wings of the morning, and dwell in the uttermost parts of the sea; even there shall your hand lead me, and Your right hand shall hold me. If I say, Surely the darkness shall cover me; even the night shall be light about me. Yea, the darkness hides not from You; but the night shines as the day: the darkness and the light are both alike to You....

I will praise You; for I am fearfully and wonderfully made: marvelous are Your works; and that my soul knows right well. My substance was not hidden from You, when I was made in secret, and curiously wrought in the lowest parts of the earth. Your eyes did see my substance, yet being imperfect; and in Your book all my members were written, which in continuance were fashioned, when as yet there was none of them. How precious also are Your thoughts to me, O God! how great is the sum of them! If I should count them, they are more in number than the sand.... Search me, O God, and know my heart: try me,... and lead me in the way everlasting.

A	C	S	W	I	N	G	S	A	U	C	Q	P	C	Z	D
K	O	H	R	D	H	Z	A	S	P	K	I	C	O	P	O
F	N	U	W	A	W	C	M	C	R	K	K	W	M	O	W
E	T	T	V	R	T	V	Y	E	I	I	D	O	P	S	N
A	I	T	W	K	O	T	R	N	S	M	O	M	A	S	S
R	N	E	O	N	N	Y	E	D	I	A	Y	B	S	E	I
F	U	R	N	E	G	O	I	D	N	F	I	E	S	S	T
U	A	M	D	S	U	U	N	C	G	A	A	S	M	S	T
L	N	O	E	S	E	R	S	I	Q	R	P	E	Y	E	I
L	C	S	R	H	I	H	A	J	B	O	Y	T	P	D	N
Y	E	T	F	M	J	A	Z	G	L	F	J	M	A	L	G
A	C	Q	U	A	I	N	T	E	D	F	O	E	T	N	M
T	Z	N	L	F	K	D	Q	R	N	L	I	G	H	T	Q
L	P	G	V	S	M	A	R	V	E	L	O	U	S	T	X

UPRISING
COMPASS MY PATH
TONGUE
YOUR HAND
ASCEND
WINGS
LIGHT
MY REINS
FEARFULLY
CONTINUANCE
DOWNSITTING
AFAR OFF
ACQUAINTED
BESET ME
WONDERFUL
UTTERMOST
DARKNESS
POSSESSED
WOMB
MARVELOUS

146. SEASONS: ECCLESIASTES 3:1–8

To every thing there is a season, and a time to every purpose under the heaven: a time to be born, and a time to die; a time to plant, and a time to pluck up that which is planted; a time to kill, and a time to heal; a time to break down, and a time to build up; a time to weep, and a time to laugh; a time to mourn, and a time to dance; a time to cast away stones, and a time to gather stones together; a time to embrace, and a time to refrain from embracing; a time to get, and a time to lose; a time to keep, and a time to cast away; a time to rend, and a time to sew; a time to keep silence, and a time to speak; a time to love, and a time to hate; a time of war, and a time of peace.

ECCLESIASTES 9:9

Live joyfully with the wife whom you love all the days of the life of your vanity, which he has given you under the sun, all the days of your vanity: for that is your portion in this life, and in your labor which you take under the sun.

EVERY THING
EVERY PURPOSE
PLANT
HEAL
BUILD UP
LAUGH
DANCE
CAST AWAY
LOVE
VANITY
SEASON
HEAVEN
PLUCK UP
BREAK DOWN
WEEP
MOURN
EMBRACING
SILENCE
HATE
PORTION

O	K	D	O	L	B	O	B	P	J	H	R	P	F	O	N	W	Z	U	A
E	S	P	A	V	S	I	L	E	N	C	E	V	O	E	W	D	N	H	Q
M	Z	T	X	N	S	X	I	L	A	U	G	H	Z	R	U	E	Q	E	G
B	F	N	O	M	C	Q	P	L	Z	Q	L	N	P	A	T	M	P	A	M
R	T	H	Q	M	J	E	I	P	O	F	M	W	R	K	D	I	C	L	O
A	D	T	A	L	Y	U	C	A	S	T	A	W	A	Y	P	B	O	T	U
C	V	J	V	R	O	A	U	N	D	S	Q	K	G	W	L	R	P	N	R
I	A	C	O	V	K	V	X	Y	W	V	T	A	O	Q	U	E	M	A	N
N	N	B	P	K	E	X	E	D	W	H	Z	H	R	P	C	A	N	N	H
G	I	B	L	J	D	Z	A	J	C	A	R	N	K	J	K	K	D	E	E
Z	T	Y	U	W	V	R	T	W	R	T	R	R	X	X	U	D	G	L	A
U	Y	X	A	I	B	U	J	E	L	E	E	K	C	P	P	O	M	G	V
X	C	X	T	N	L	F	S	E	T	N	U	U	F	U	T	W	Y	E	E
V	P	L	A	N	T	D	K	P	E	D	P	U	G	J	Q	N	I	G	N
I	M	Z	V	Z	O	R	U	D	A	P	K	F	B	M	B	I	I	U	D
W	I	B	X	U	P	Y	W	P	S	P	O	Y	Y	M	H	Q	M	C	P
E	V	E	R	Y	P	U	R	P	O	S	E	E	R	V	J	I	M	G	S
Q	D	B	K	C	Z	S	Y	H	F	L	W	D	J	H	F	H	J	H	J
H	L	V	R	H	P	Q	E	L	S	E	A	S	O	N	H	E	L	M	R
O	G	E	V	E	R	Y	T	H	I	N	G	Q	T	B	R	Q	A	P	V

147. THE SHULAMITE GIRL: THE SONG OF SOLOMON 1:1–7

Let him kiss me with the kisses of his mouth: for your love is better than wine. Because of the savor of your good ointments your name is as ointment poured forth, therefore do the virgins love you. Draw me, we will run after you: the king has brought me into his chambers: we will be glad and rejoice in you, we will remember your love more than wine: the upright love you. I am black, but comely, O you daughters of Jerusalem, as the tents of Kedar, as the curtains of Solomon. Look not upon me, because I am black, because the sun has looked upon me: my mother's children were angry with me; they made me the keeper of the vineyards; but my own vineyard have I not kept. Tell me, O you whom my soul loves, where you feed, where you make your flock to rest at noon: for why should I be as one that turns aside by the flocks of your companions?

SONG OF SONGS
SOLOMON
KISS ME
WINE
SAVOR
OINTMENTS
YOUR NAME
DRAW ME
CHAMBERS
BE GLAD
REJOICE
UPRIGHT
COMELY
TENTS
KEDAR
CURTAINS
KEEPER
VINEYARD
FLOCK
ASIDE

F	X	B	H	V	B	I	E	T	V	M	U	Z	A	S	U	T	K	E	X
W	Q	O	G	E	E	F	R	E	C	A	K	U	Z	A	O	Z	E	M	V
D	G	U	G	I	G	R	V	Z	Q	O	C	D	C	V	I	P	E	X	F
K	W	S	O	F	L	Q	R	K	O	F	M	C	E	O	N	B	P	E	L
X	I	I	O	Y	A	M	X	E	V	I	I	E	R	R	T	S	E	F	O
Z	N	T	B	N	D	U	L	D	G	I	O	Y	L	O	M	A	R	O	C
U	E	V	E	S	G	P	O	A	N	X	N	E	F	Y	E	G	C	W	K
Q	P	K	P	N	H	O	M	R	C	T	K	E	C	K	N	L	X	X	G
S	T	R	N	O	T	C	F	Z	E	J	D	K	Y	L	T	U	I	F	P
Z	J	I	I	A	Z	S	E	S	N	I	H	H	I	A	S	P	T	W	C
G	P	G	I	G	I	L	O	D	O	I	B	R	O	S	R	D	C	H	U
T	F	W	E	Q	H	S	J	S	F	N	W	S	I	W	S	D	U	Q	R
B	Y	H	F	F	O	T	T	C	Q	H	G	D	G	O	G	M	T	Y	T
G	D	S	T	D	Y	K	Z	O	V	R	J	S	J	O	W	I	E	K	A
M	F	R	I	Y	T	F	U	S	O	L	O	M	O	N	N	G	C	X	I
N	W	D	A	E	W	K	O	U	G	K	W	G	J	M	F	L	D	N	N
G	N	U	I	W	Y	O	U	R	N	A	M	E	T	S	J	Z	M	E	S
L	Q	W	S	E	M	M	E	S	E	Q	X	A	S	I	D	E	R	Y	M
K	Q	S	T	C	C	E	C	H	C	H	A	M	B	E	R	S	H	K	D
R	U	R	E	J	O	I	C	E	N	J	P	U	F	P	M	L	S	G	X

148. THE BRIDEGROOM PRAISES THE BRIDE
THE SONG OF SOLOMON 4:1–15

Behold, you are fair, my love; behold, you are fair; you have doves' eyes within your locks: your hair is as a flock of goats.... Your teeth are like a flock of sheep that are even shorn, which came up from the washing; whereof every one bear twins, and none is barren among them. Your lips are like a thread of scarlet, and your speech is comely: your temples are like a piece of a pomegranate within your locks. Your neck is like the tower of David built for an armory, whereon there hang a thousand bucklers, all shields of mighty men. Your two breasts are like two young roes that are twins, which feed among the lilies. Until the day break, and the shadows flee away, I will get me to the mountain of myrrh, and to the hill of frankincense. You are all fair, my love; there is no spot in you.... You have ravished my heart with one of your eyes, with one chain of your neck. How fair is your love, my sister, my spouse! how much better is your love than wine! and the smell of your ointments than all spices! Your lips, O my spouse, drop as the honeycomb: honey and milk are under your tongue; and the smell of your garments is like the smell of Lebanon. A garden enclosed is my sister, my spouse; a spring shut up, a fountain sealed. Your plants are an orchard of pomegranates, with pleasant fruits; camphor, with spikenard, spikenard and saffron; calamus and cinnamon, with all trees of frankincense; myrrh and aloes, with all the chief spices: a fountain of gardens, a well of living waters, and streams from Lebanon.

BEHOLD
BEAR TWINS
POMEGRANATE
FRANKINCENSE
FLOCK OF GOATS
WASHING
COMELY
BUCKLERS
YOUNG ROES
LIONS' DENS
DOVES' EYES
BARREN
ARMORY
MYRRH
SHORN
SCARLET
TEMPLES
MIGHTY MEN
DAYBREAK
RAVISHED

P	K	E	E	T	V	R	B	I	T	E	M	P	L	E	S	Q
R	O	F	F	L	M	U	A	A	X	S	Z	J	U	W	N	P
M	B	M	L	R	D	I	B	V	R	R	K	V	M	A	G	P
I	E	M	E	O	A	O	G	U	I	R	N	T	Y	S	Y	D
O	A	H	L	G	C	N	V	H	C	S	E	V	R	H	O	H
A	R	B	K	I	R	K	K	E	T	K	H	N	R	I	U	D
R	T	Q	Q	X	O	A	O	I	S	Y	L	E	H	N	N	A
M	W	L	H	Z	J	N	N	F	N	E	M	E	D	G	G	Y
O	I	L	Z	K	Y	Q	S	A	G	C	Y	E	R	A	R	B
R	N	S	H	O	R	N	V	D	T	O	E	E	N	S	O	R
Y	S	P	J	T	F	F	A	W	E	E	A	N	S	D	E	E
C	N	S	C	A	R	L	E	T	N	N	I	T	S	Z	S	A
B	G	C	P	I	G	G	P	Z	N	O	S	U	S	E	Z	K
B	E	H	O	L	D	T	C	O	M	E	L	Y	Y	O	Y	Q

149. THE LORD WILL POUR OUT HIS SPIRIT: JOEL 2:28–32

It shall come to pass afterward, that I will pour out My Spirit upon all flesh; and your sons and your daughters shall prophesy, your old men shall dream dreams, your young men shall see visions: and also upon the servants and upon the handmaids in those days will I pour out My Spirit. And I will show wonders in the heavens and in the earth, blood, and fire, and pillars of smoke. The sun shall be turned into darkness, and the moon into blood, before the great and the terrible day of the Lord come. And it shall come to pass, that whosoever shall call on the name of the Lord shall be delivered: for in mount Zion and in Jerusalem shall be deliverance, as the Lord has said, and in the remnant whom the Lord shall call.

COME TO PASS
AFTERWARD
POUR OUT
SPIRIT
ALL FLESH
YOUR SONS
DAUGHTERS
PROPHESY
DREAMS
VISIONS
SERVANTS
HANDMAIDS
WONDERS
HEAVENS
EARTH
BLOOD
SMOKE
DARKNESS
MOON
REMNANT

A	C	V	A	R	N	D	H	E	A	V	E	N	S	H	M	L	J	Y	R
L	C	X	L	C	F	O	M	R	Q	E	Z	U	F	U	Y	X	M	O	D
O	J	F	G	N	O	F	G	V	E	K	V	G	R	M	M	J	H	U	A
M	S	N	P	G	T	M	P	U	I	M	I	L	L	E	M	Q	B	R	R
D	Y	E	K	S	F	A	E	L	I	S	N	R	I	X	G	C	C	S	K
A	S	D	R	Z	G	O	F	T	Z	J	I	A	G	C	Z	B	C	O	N
U	J	M	A	V	F	C	S	T	O	O	B	O	N	N	Z	G	G	N	E
G	E	M	O	B	A	Q	H	P	E	P	P	W	N	T	D	U	J	S	S
H	J	A	Y	K	H	N	F	C	I	R	A	U	Z	S	R	X	E	G	S
T	I	J	K	D	E	A	T	Y	P	R	W	S	I	O	E	L	V	A	M
E	X	O	V	I	Y	H	N	S	W	V	I	A	S	E	A	O	R	X	I
R	P	O	P	Q	R	T	R	D	F	E	D	T	R	H	M	Z	E	K	H
S	M	U	T	O	G	L	A	G	M	O	Z	B	O	D	S	K	R	P	W
Q	P	O	M	T	U	L	D	L	A	A	S	W	M	A	D	J	B	M	O
L	V	N	O	E	H	R	X	E	Y	I	I	D	G	J	G	A	W	Q	N
Q	D	G	K	N	S	V	O	B	L	O	O	D	X	J	Q	X	C	R	D
Y	S	W	Y	O	B	V	G	U	P	U	L	U	S	I	S	L	P	Y	E
V	A	Z	T	L	W	M	N	E	T	P	R	O	P	H	E	S	Y	H	R
N	U	W	A	M	H	S	S	Y	E	O	O	V	G	Z	U	D	G	Q	S
N	K	C	E	A	R	T	H	J	L	D	A	L	L	F	L	E	S	H	I

150. THE WOMAN PERSECUTED: REVELATION 12:13–17

When the dragon saw that he was cast to the earth, he persecuted the woman which brought forth the man child. And to the woman were given two wings of a great eagle, that she might fly into the wilderness, into her place, where she is nourished for a time, and times, and half a time, from the face of the serpent. And the serpent cast out of his mouth water as a flood after the woman, that he might cause her to be carried away of the flood. And the earth helped the woman, and the earth opened her mouth, and swallowed up the flood which the dragon cast out of his mouth. And the dragon was angry with the woman, and went to make war with the remnant of her seed, which keep the commandments of God, and have the testimony of Jesus Christ.

DRAGON
EARTH
PERSECUTED
MAN CHILD
TWO WINGS
GREAT EAGLE
WILDERNESS
HER PLACE
NOURISHED
HALF A TIME
SERPENT
CAST OUT
WATER
FLOOD
SWALLOWED
MOUTH
ANGRY
MAKE WAR
REMNANT
COMMANDMENTS

F	J	B	C	O	M	M	A	N	D	M	E	N	T	S	V	S	J	V	H
H	M	U	O	N	P	E	N	D	R	A	G	O	N	O	F	A	Z	N	A
B	F	U	D	I	F	S	A	T	T	U	R	U	S	Y	L	Q	H	Q	L
C	K	J	N	L	M	E	G	R	S	H	Y	C	P	E	O	W	T	I	F
V	I	K	T	R	A	R	A	F	N	W	H	T	I	K	O	S	O	P	A
W	P	B	A	Y	N	P	J	A	O	A	A	I	Q	R	D	C	M	Y	T
M	Q	B	L	K	G	E	M	O	U	D	Q	L	G	J	O	T	O	H	I
D	A	Z	L	C	R	N	I	X	R	T	S	I	L	T	B	I	U	X	M
D	H	K	Z	U	Y	T	S	K	I	T	N	G	J	O	Y	K	T	P	E
H	E	O	E	B	T	U	S	I	S	E	W	Z	M	Q	W	Z	H	J	V
S	R	J	W	W	R	I	D	G	H	C	J	L	H	V	D	E	K	Z	H
M	P	G	Q	U	A	J	N	R	E	J	W	E	Q	G	G	P	D	F	F
X	L	W	K	B	K	R	F	F	D	L	T	J	Z	Z	H	E	Y	A	D
S	A	A	W	R	L	W	I	L	D	E	R	N	E	S	S	N	E	P	A
S	C	T	U	C	R	S	O	D	Q	L	U	N	V	E	R	C	A	K	R
K	E	E	G	R	E	A	T	E	A	G	L	E	P	G	B	I	R	S	Q
U	N	R	R	Y	H	K	M	L	S	C	A	S	T	O	U	T	T	G	Y
O	Q	L	E	K	U	A	L	Q	T	W	O	W	I	N	G	S	H	J	Q
T	D	Y	U	N	Z	E	M	A	N	C	H	I	L	D	F	T	P	S	R
P	E	R	S	E	C	U	T	E	D	H	K	R	E	M	N	A	N	T	F

1

2

3

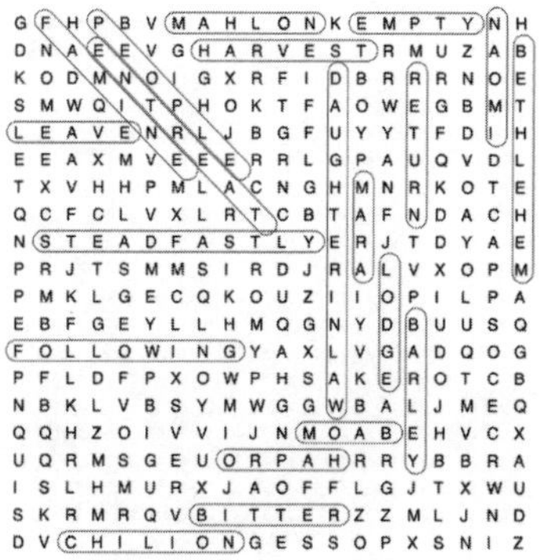

4

5

6

7

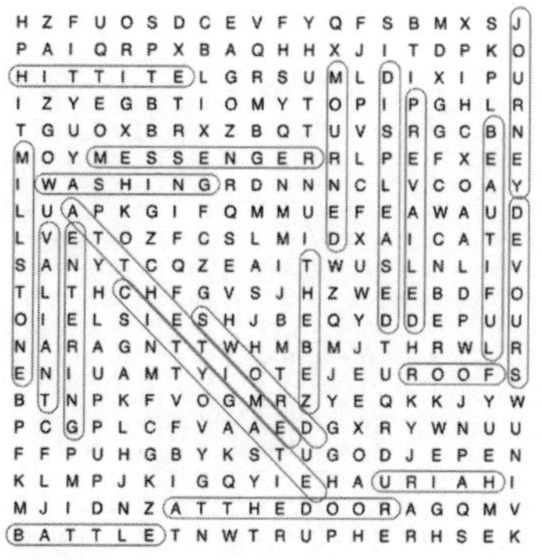

8

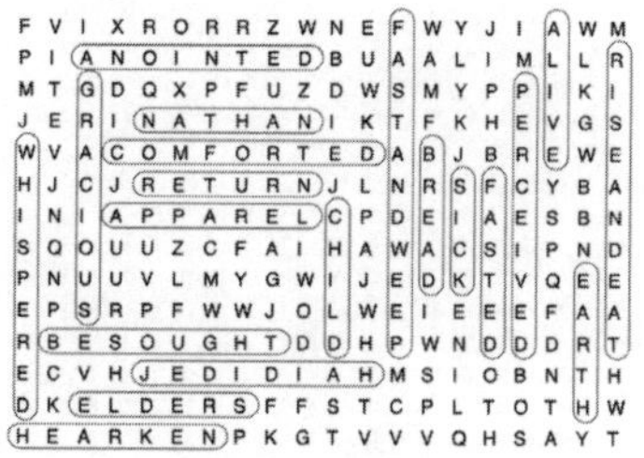

9

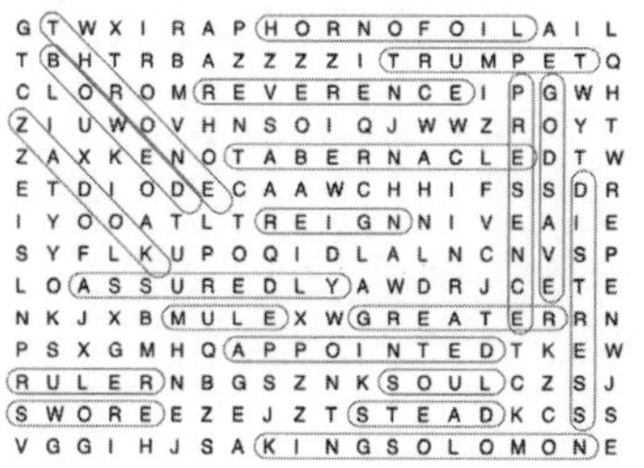

10

11

12

13

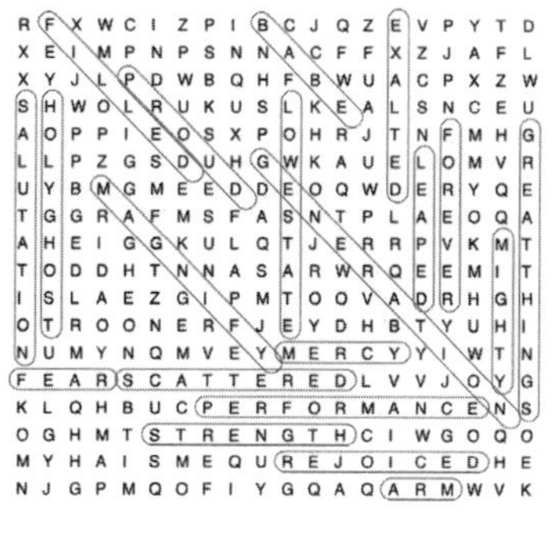

14

15

16

17

18

19

20

21

22

23

24

25

26

27

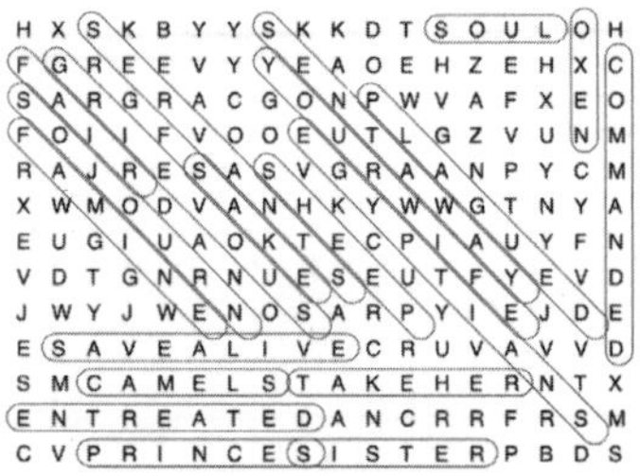

28

29

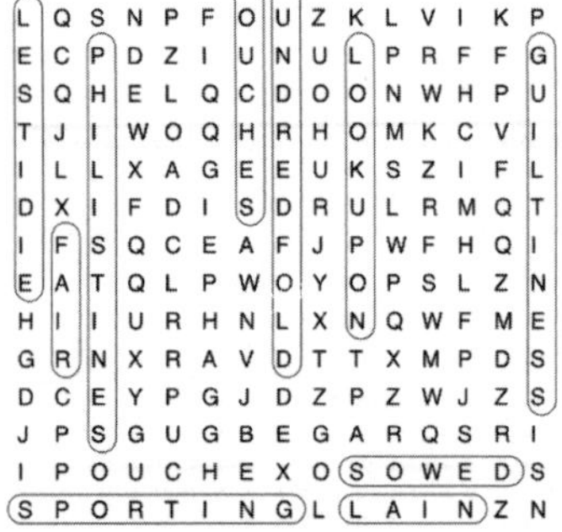

30

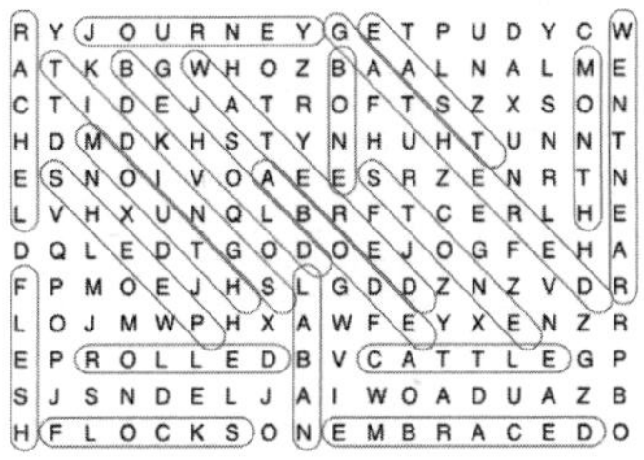

31

32

33

34

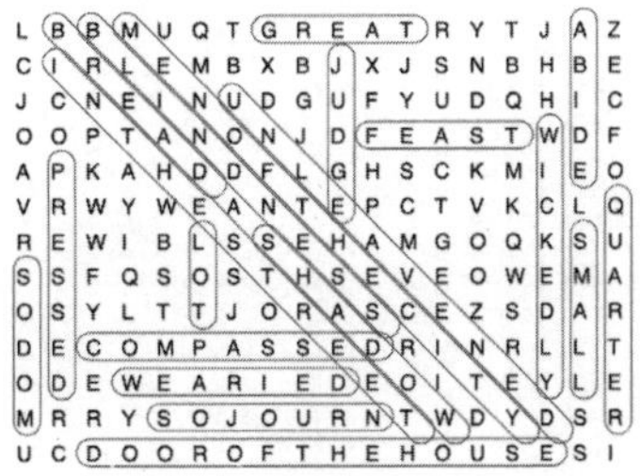

35

36

37

38

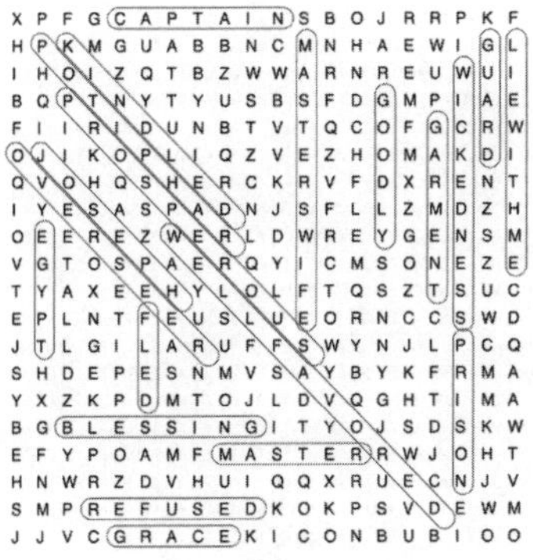

39

40

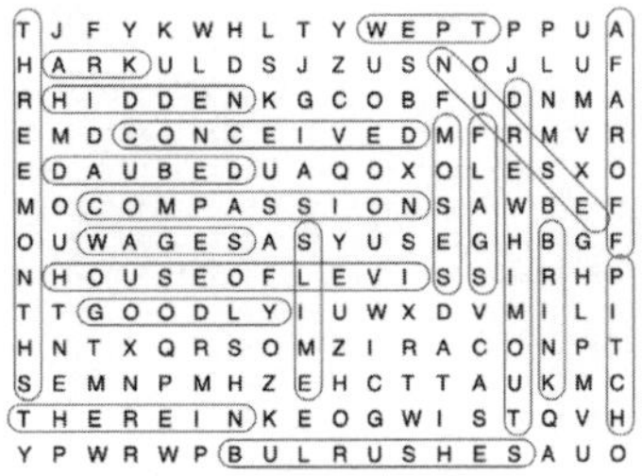

41

42

43

44

45

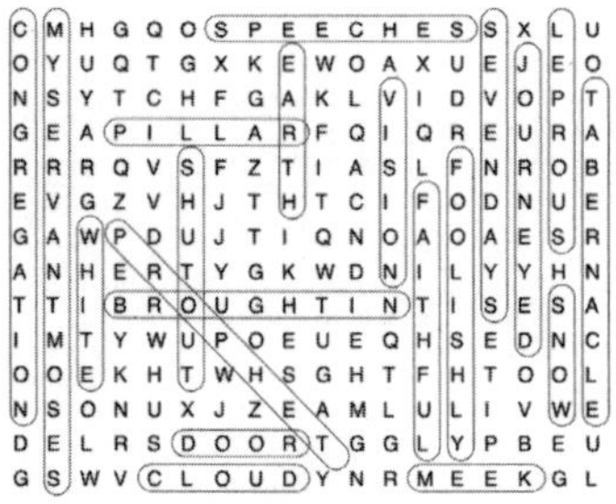

46

47

48

49

50

51

52

53

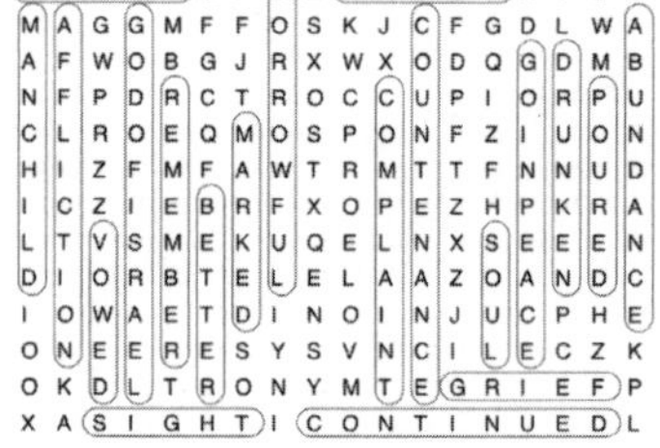

54

55

56

57

58

59

60

46 — SPEECHES, PILLAR, BROUGHT IN, TOOL, DOOR, CLOUDY, MEEK

47 — TRIBE, GILEAD, KORAH, TIRZAH, NOAH, ZELOPHEHAD, MAHLAH

48 — TENT NAIL, BEFORE YOU, OPPRESSED, GENTILES, DEBORAH, THIRSTY

49 — TRAVELLERS, DROPPED, AWAKE, HAMMER, RIGHTEOUS, NEEDLEWORK, REHEARSE

50 — VOWED A VOW, BEWAIL, AROERE, MIZPEH, OFFER IT UP, SMOTE, DANCES, SUBDUED, TIMBRELS, OPEN MY MOUTH

51 — LEVITE, LODGE, DIVIDED, DAMSEL, BE MERRY, BELIAL, STRAW, NO KING, JERUSALEM

52 — REPAIRED, DANCES, LACKING, ONE TRIBE, CUT OFF, CAUGHT, DESTROYED, ESCAPED

53 — JEROHAM, LOVED, YEARLY, WORTHY, LORD OF HOSTS, ELKANAH, PROVOKE, HANNAH, ADVERSARY, SHUT UP

54 — GRANT, RAZOR, SIGHT, CONTINUED, GRIEF

55 — HIS WORD, BOTTLE, ROSE, RETURNED, MORNING, FLOUR, TO THE LORD, LENT, APPEAR, CHILD

56 — ENLARGED, MINISTER, NONE, PROUDLY, SALVATION, EXCEEDING, BESIDE, PILLARS

57 — FAMILIAR SPIRITS, ASCENDING, RAIMENT, MORSEL, TREMBLED, SAMUEL, SAUL, PUNISHMENT, WIZARDS, UNLEAVENED, SNARE, DISGUISED, FAT CALF

58 — ADRIEL, LOVED HIM, EXPIRED, FORESKINS, MICHAL, SECRETLY, COMMUNE, LIGHT THING, SLEW

59 — ESCAPED, WATCH, WINDOW, CLOTH, MESSENGERS, SICK

60 — LINEN, OBEDEDOM, RETURN, ESPOUSED, SACRIFICED, DANCED, WEEPING

61

62

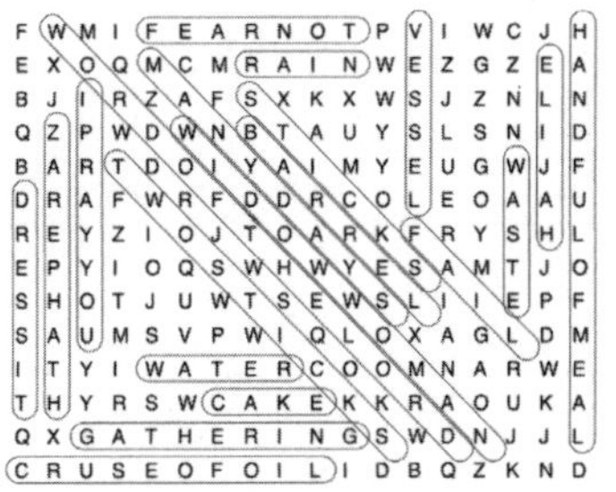
63

64

65

66

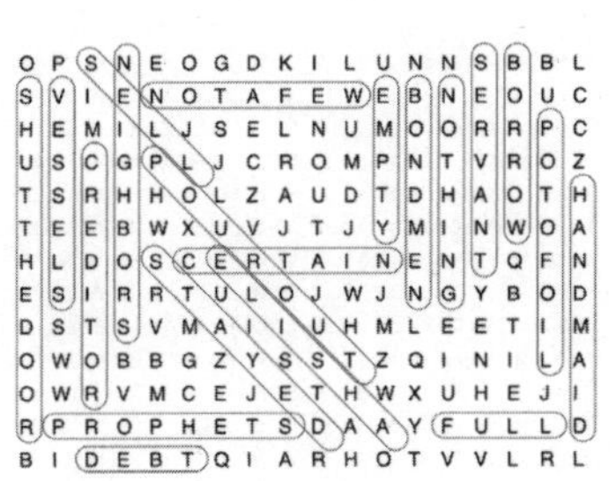
67

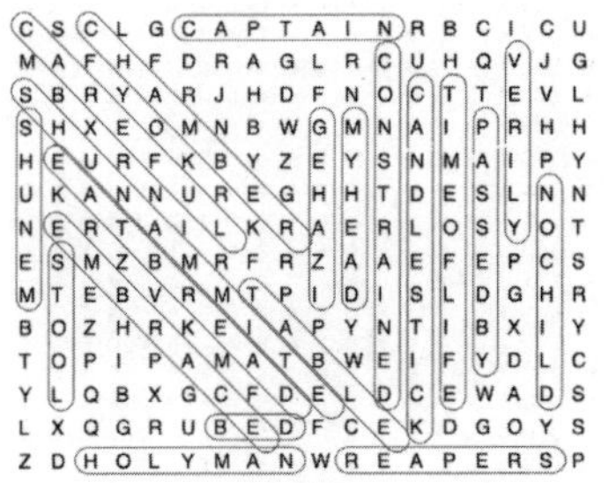
68

69

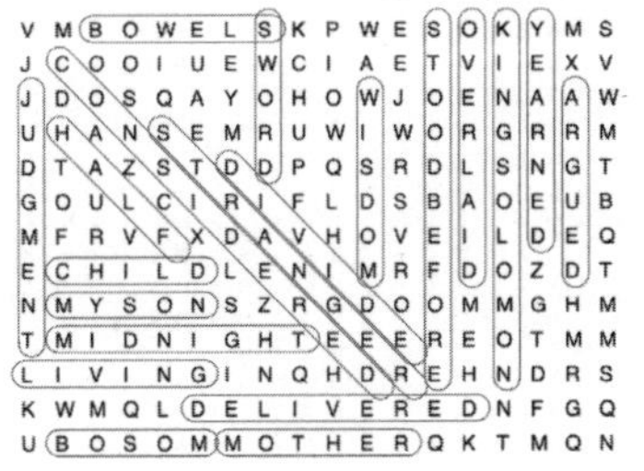
70

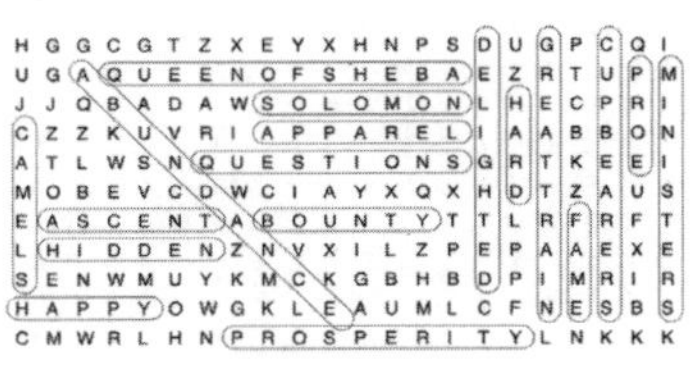
71

72

73

74

75

76

77

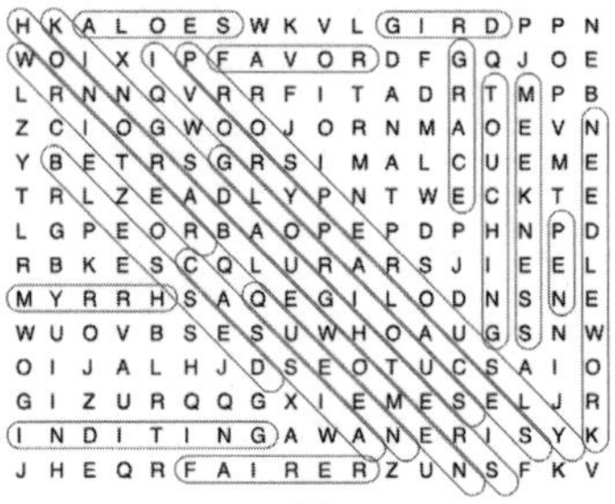

78

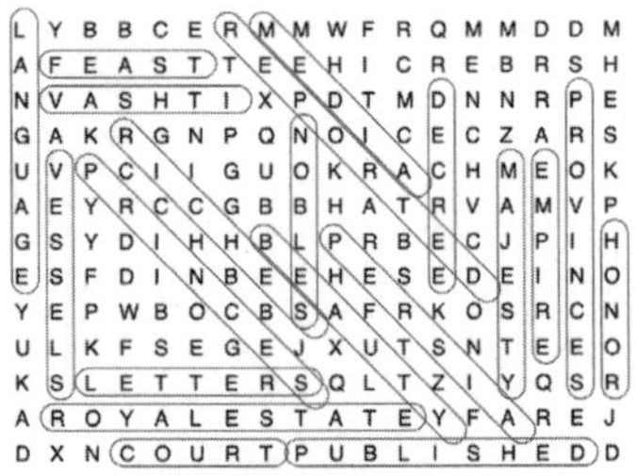

79

80

81

82

83

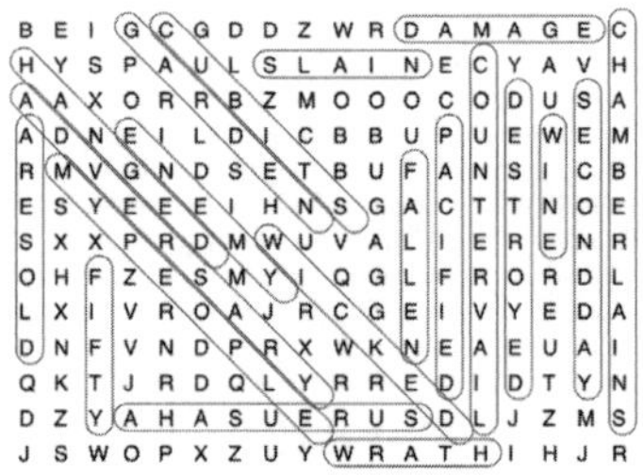

84

85

86

87

88

89

90

91

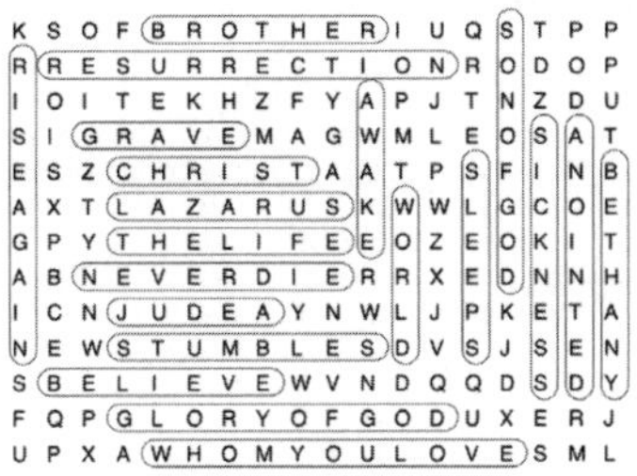

92

93

94

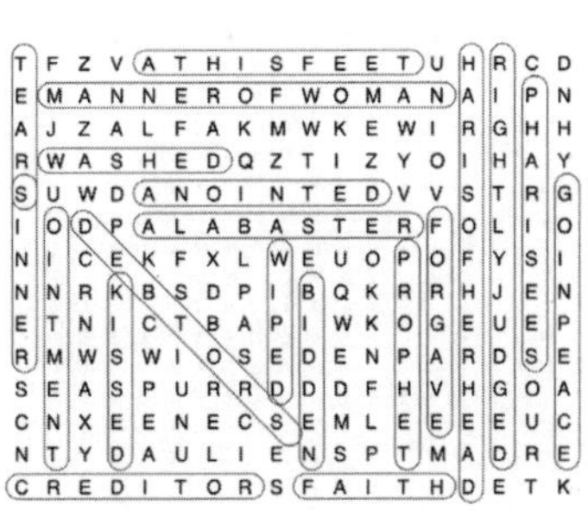

95

96

97

98

99

100

101

102

103

104

105

106

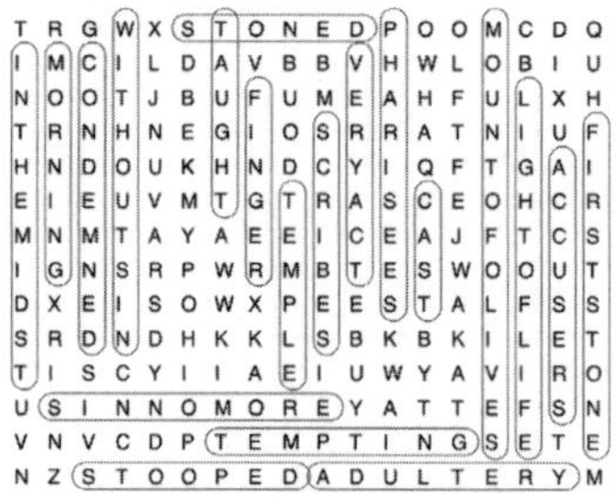

107

108

109

110

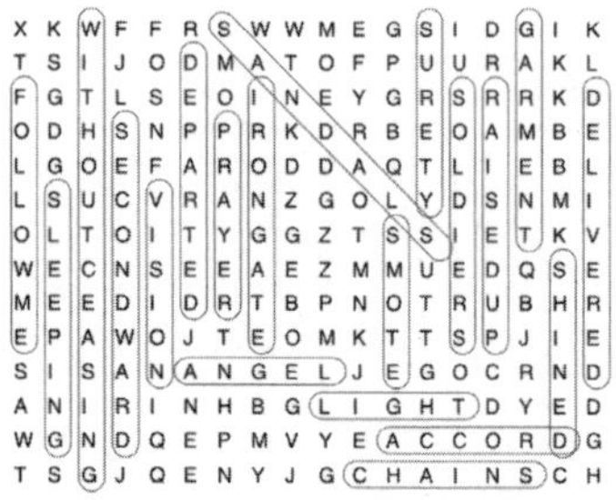

111

112

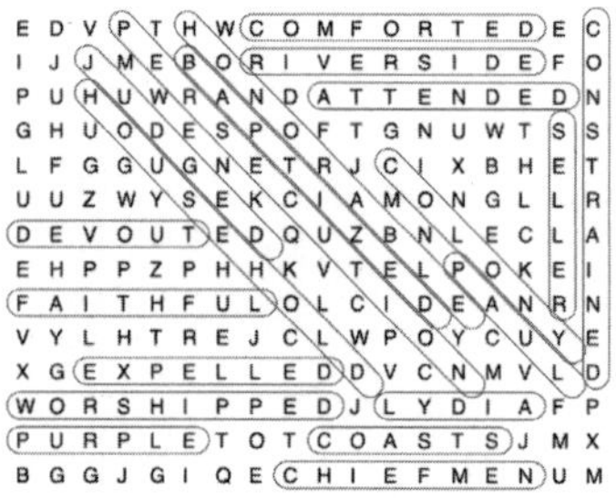

113

114

115

116

117

118

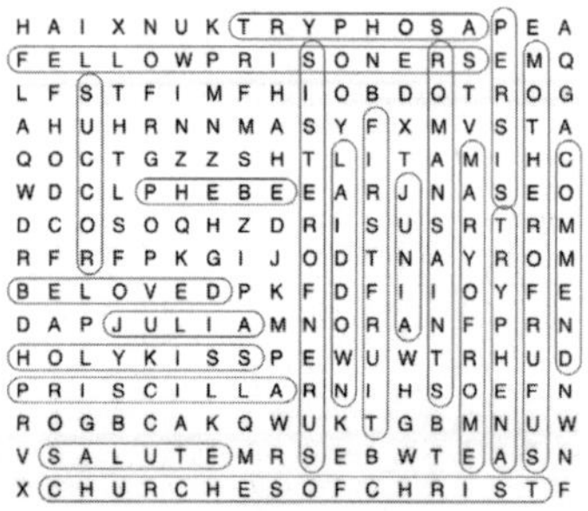

119

120

121

122

123

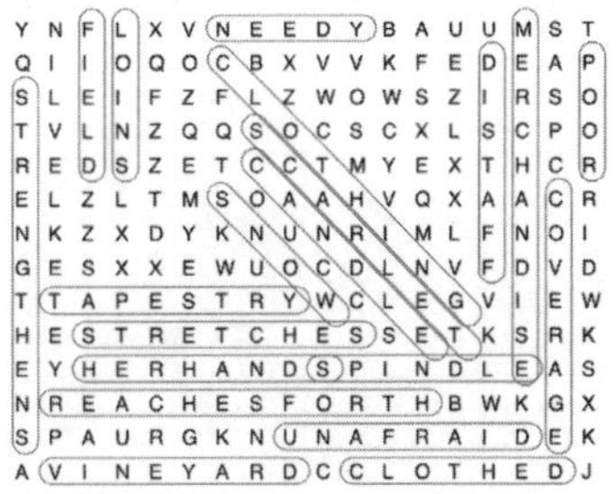
124

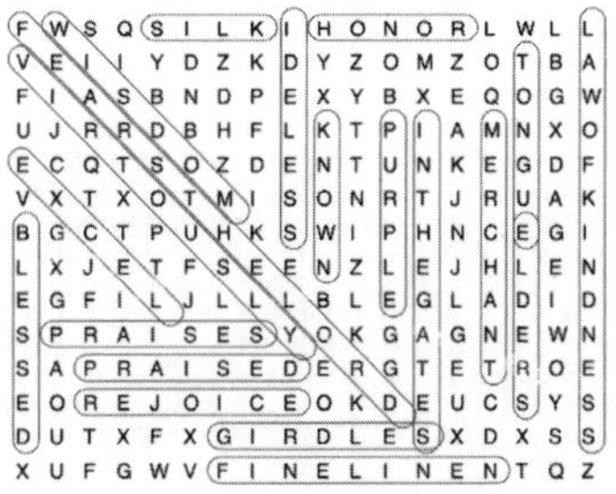
125

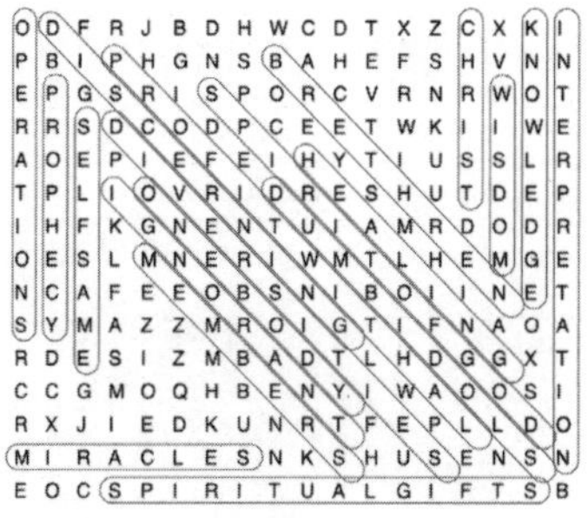
126

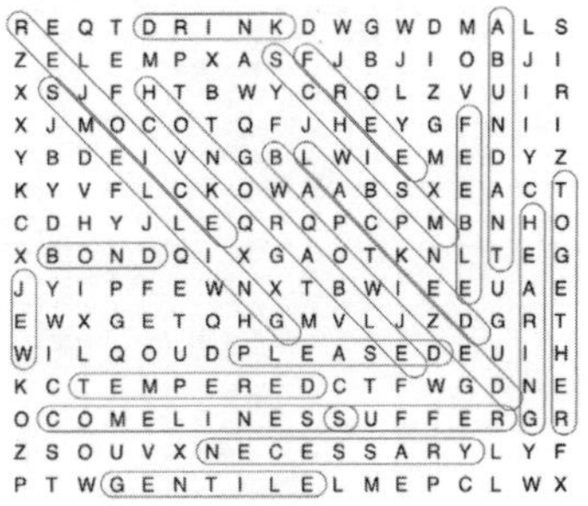
127

128

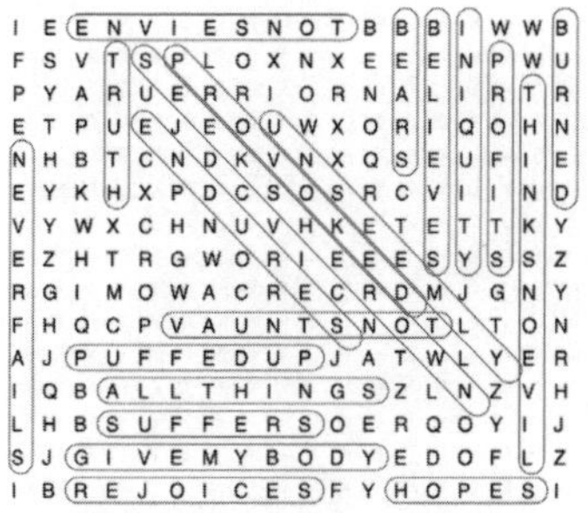
129

130

131

132

133

134

135

136

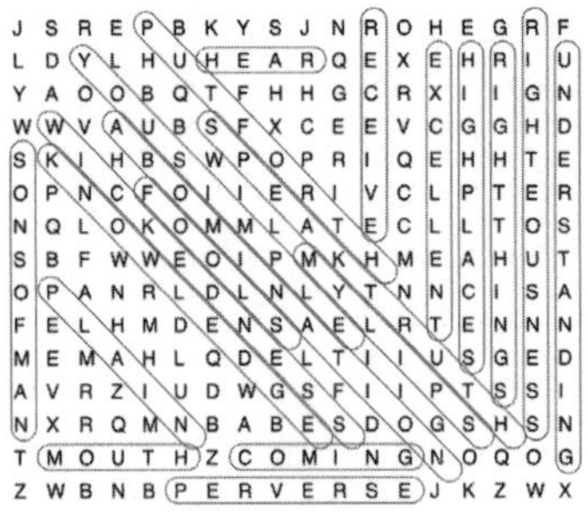
137

138

139

140

141

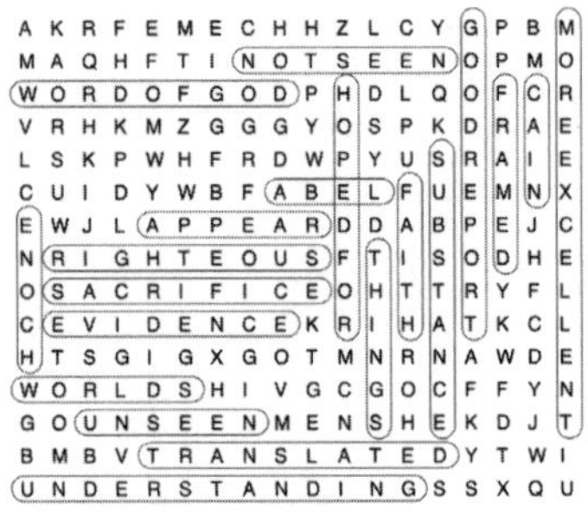
142

143

144

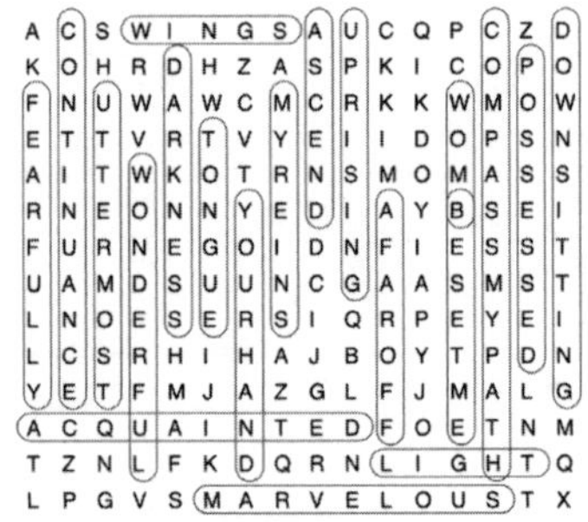
145

146

147

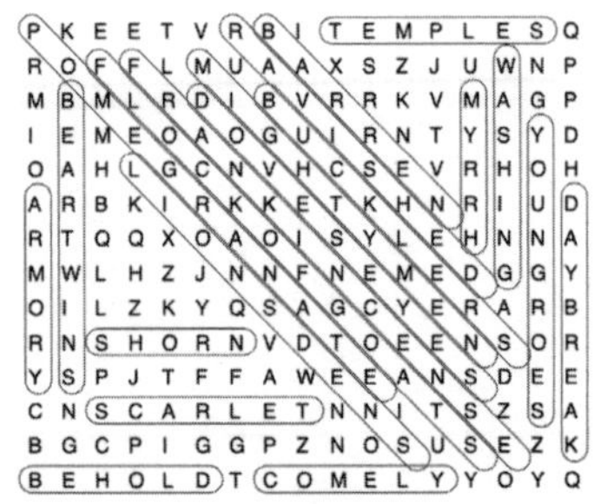
148

149

150